THIS WAS NORMALCY

By Karl Schriftgiesser

THE GENTLEMAN FROM MASSACHUSETTS:
HENRY CABOT LODGE

THIS WAS NORMALCY

THIS WAS NORMALCY

AN ACCOUNT OF PARTY POLITICS

DURING TWELVE REPUBLICAN YEARS:

1920–1932

by Karl Schriftgiesser

An Atlantic Monthly Press Book

Little, Brown and Company · Boston

1948

FIRST EDITION

Published April 1948

ATLANTIC—LITTLE, BROWN BOOKS
ARE PUBLISHED BY
LITTLE, BROWN AND COMPANY
IN ASSOCIATION WITH
THE ATLANTIC MONTHLY PRESS

*Published simultaneously
in Canada by McClelland and Stewart Limited*

PRINTED IN THE UNITED STATES OF AMERICA

FOR KARLA ELIZABETH SCHRIFTGIESSER

> . . . You had the wisdom and foresight
> to be born in the twentieth century.
> Go, go with love and health — your
> wonderful country never needed you
> more . . .
>
> — CLIFFORD ODETS

A Foreword

THIS BOOK does not pretend to complete objectivity — for no book that can be read ever achieves that end — but it is, I think, an accurate account of Republicanism triumphant and the effect of this triumph upon the American people from Warren Gamaliel Harding's nomination in 1920 through Herbert Clark Hoover's ruination in 1932. It was conceived and written for no ulterior purpose, political or otherwise. Its biases come from a reading of this history against a background of the definite and purposeful leadership of Franklin Delano Roosevelt, and from my having written a biographical study of the late Senator Henry Cabot Lodge, that gentleman from Massachusetts who was more responsible than any other individual for the American slaughter of the League of Nations. In starting this book it was my hope to discover what the party responsible for this greatest political tragedy in the history of the United States did with and to the America it thus isolated in the years that followed that dreadful example of partisan politics. I also hoped to discover why the Democratic Party abdicated its historic role as the party of the people for twelve chaotic years. If this dip into recent but not always distinctly remembered history has certain pertinence in the late 1940's, that is all to the good.

KARL SCHRIFTGIESSER

Londonderry, Vermont
September, 1947

Contents

THIS WAS NORMALCY

CHAPTER ONE

The Presidency Is Sold

NEVER in the political history of the United States had there
been such an obscene spectacle as that which took place in Chicago
in June 1920. The Presidency was for sale. The city of Chicago,
never averse to monetary indecencies, was jam-packed with frenzied bidders, their pockets bulging with money with which to buy
the prize. The Coliseum became a market place, crowded with
stock gamblers, oil promoters, mining magnates, munitions makers,
sports promoters, and soap makers, all drooling with anticipation
of success. The lobbies and rooms of the Loop hotels were in a
turmoil as the potential buyers of office scurried about lining up
their supporters, making their deals, issuing furtive orders, passing out secret funds.

Standing aloof from this scene, so like and yet so unlike many
others he had witnessed in the past, the dignified President of
Columbia University — whose own name was soon to be placed
on the auction block — was shocked.

Never, said Nicholas Murray Butler, who knew intimately many
of those well-dressed and well-fed millionaires who mingled with
and dominated the milling mob, had he witnessed such a mad
scramble to buy the Presidency of the United States. His stout
frame shuddered as he watched his beloved Republican Party
manifest its predatory hunger after eight starving years.

Prowling about with the millionaires and their satellites was a
moon-faced, red-haired man who looked like a happy bartender
but who was one of the smartest of the horde of top-ranking reporters on hand to record the Roman holiday. Like the president
of the great university, the editor of the *Emporia Gazette* loved
the Republican Party, even if twelve years before he had clung
to the coattails of Theodore Roosevelt as that angry huntsman
had wandered into the wilderness seeking revenge on William

3

Howard Taft. He, too, was shocked. A quarter of a century, or six and a half Presidential terms later, William Allen White wrote in retrospect:

> I have never seen a convention — and I have watched most of them since McKinley's first nomination — so completely dominated by sinister predatory economic forces as was this. It was controlled by a national committee representing plutocracy and United States Senators, the political representatives of what Theodore Roosevelt had called amalgamated wealth.

Sweating as profusely as any ordinary delegate under the almost unendurable Chicago sun were fifty or more men who, although but little known to the general public, exercised incredible power over the economic life of the American people. There was Samuel Vauclain, who ruled the vast Baldwin Locomotive monopoly; there were Harry Sinclair and E. L. Doheny, whose oily names were to take on sinister implications within the next four years; there was Ambrose Monell, the metals magnate; H. M. Byllesby, manipulator of public utilities; William Boyce Thompson, the copper king; Dan Hanna, a power in the great empire of steel; E. E. Smathers, first of the great sports promoters — to name but a few who were ready and willing to pay the price demanded. Rubbing elbows with them were scores of other agents of organized capital who had come to Chicago to protect the interests of organized agriculture, oil, railroads, telephones, steel, coal, and textiles.

Oozing through the crowd was the incredibly rich Republican Committeeman from Oklahoma, avid for power and dripping with oil. With that same fluid Jake Hamon was to anoint the heads of countless delegates until he was able to exert more influence than any other man in the convention. Peering at him through thick horn glasses was that renegade Democrat and minion of the House of Morgan, that great moralist who had raised the funds to defeat acceptance of the League of Nations, George B. Harvey. It was a motley crowd but each had with the others two things in common: access to wealth and access to power. And in the heart of each was one desire: to crush forever in the Chicago muck the name and ideals of Woodrow Wilson.

As Joseph R. Grundy, raiser-extraordinary of campaign funds

and indomitable lobbyist for the Pennsylvania industrialists, scurried about in the heat, and Harry M. Daugherty, a lawyer and lobbyist from Ohio, slapped the right backs and pumped the proper hands, the assembled journalists contented themselves with predictions. There were eight names, according to the *Literary Digest's* preconvention poll, from which the nominee would be chosen. Leading the list was General Leonard Wood. On Tuesday, June 8, when the convention was called to order, he was the favorite.

There were, however, many reasons why the more astute observers in the press seats expected the nomination to go to one of the other seven. In the order of polled popularity Hiram Johnson, the isolationist Senator from California, fresh from his bitter battle against Wilson's League, stood second. He was followed, in third place, by Herbert Hoover, the wartime Food Administrator who many people still thought was a Democrat, and in fourth place by Frank O. Lowden, the Governor of Illinois and champion of the large Midwestern landowners and grain growers. Following these stalwarts in order were Charles Evans Hughes, whom Woodrow Wilson had beaten in 1916; Warren Gamaliel Harding, an obscure, reactionary Senator from Ohio; Calvin Coolidge, Governor of Massachusetts, who claimed credit for having broken the Boston Police Strike; and William Howard Taft. Other favorite sons whose names had been mentioned from time to time did not matter, whatever the eventualities might be.

There were two main reasons why General Wood was discounted and both were senatorial. To the rank and file of Republicans General Wood, the Army Chief of Staff, was a man of heroic stature who had been robbed of his rightful position as head of the American Expeditionary Forces through the personal vindictiveness of Woodrow Wilson. He claimed to wear the mantle of Theodore Roosevelt. His most substantial support came from Wall Street. When Senator William E. Borah of Idaho heard of the tremendous expenditure of funds by his backers, as well as by the backers of Governor Lowden, he had arisen with righteous indignation in the Senate and charged, not without reason, that there was a plot afoot to "buy" the Presidency. Calling attention to the existence of a "saturnalia of corruption," he had forced a Senate investigation which revealed that the General's forces had collected and were spending $1,773,303 to clinch the nomination.

Colonel William Cooper Procter had contributed $710,000 of his Ivory Soap fortune to the fund.

When Harry Daugherty, who had his own candidate to offer for far less cash, heard this, he snorted, "There's not enough money in the world to buy the nomination for a man with epaulettes on his shoulders." It was a wise remark. Senator Henry Cabot Lodge, who was to preside over the convention, and his fellow comrades in the Senate soviet, which held the fate of the Republican Party in its hands, had no intention of allowing the nomination to go to Wood. From all economic and political standpoints the General was acceptable to Lodge's little group of legislative representatives of amalgamated wealth; but he was a soldier used to giving orders and they did not think he could be trusted with the power of the Presidency. They wanted a President whom the Senate could boss, for they were determined to keep the control of the government in the Senate where it had increasingly been lodged ever since the Civil War. They also knew that the revelation of the huge sums contributed by the oil, utilities, copper, and steel interests would be catastrophic fuel in the hands of any Democratic rival.

The Senate Committee on Elections and Privileges had done a good job. It dragged out proof that Governor Lowden, who had married into the Pullman family but who was an ardent defender of privilege even without that impetus, had received contributions totaling $414,000. Hiram Johnson acknowledged only $194,000; and the friends of Herbert Hoover thought his chances were worth but $173,000. The Ohio politicians who had listened sufficiently to the blandishments of Harry Daugherty had been grudging in their contributions to Warren G. Harding's campaign. Daugherty himself put up $50,000 ("Every cent that I had in the world"!) and Harding gave $1000. Harry Payne Whitney, the Wall Street financier and promoter, who was worth $72,-000,000 at his death in 1932, dropped $7500 into Daugherty's outstretched hand, as did Harry F. Sinclair, the oil man, to bring the acknowledged grand total up to $113,000, a small amount compared to what the others had to spend; but still not exactly "chicken feed."

The Republican National Convention thus came to order under a cloud of corruption, but nobody in Chicago gave it a thought. Blandly unconcerned with the unclean spectacle of bribed delegates, and of men of prestige and responsibility doing nothing to interfere, was the trim, scholarly chairman, Senator Henry Cabot Lodge. In one capacity or another he had been in official attendance at every Republican convention since 1884, the year which saw the spotted James G. Blaine nominated; but this was to be the year of his greatest triumph. He had been waiting for this occasion with increasing impatience since 1912. Nowhere was there a more implacable enemy of Woodrow Wilson than the slim, immaculate, bearded gentleman from Massachusetts, who was to deliver the keynote address and preside over open sessions (and one that was notoriously closed!) with his cultured snarl and cynical, blue-eyed stare. Nowhere was there one more determined to bring back into power the Republican Party and all it now stood for than the chairman of the Senate Foreign Relations Committee, who had made a party issue of the Peace. He bristled like a terrier with the importance of his dedicated task.

If Senator Lodge dominated the convention he also was a power behind the scenes. For months he and his fellow conspirators had been laying their subtle plans to keep the convention under their uncompromising control. The Senate oligarchy owned an almost exclusive authority over the Republican Party's affairs. Aligned with Lodge were such men as tough Reed Smoot of Utah, Frank Brandegee, the Connecticut Tory, cynical Jim Watson and patient Harry New of Indiana, wily Charles Curtis, the Kansas Indian, aristocratic James Wadsworth and pompous William Calder of New York. Although not all were delegates, each was present at Chicago, as also was Senator Philander Knox of Pennsylvania. Absent was paunchy Boies Penrose, the most powerful of them all, the great boss of industrial Pennsylvania, who was lying on his supposed deathbed at home. But close by that bed was a telegraph, a direct wire to Chicago, where his faithful henchmen, Senator Knox and lobbyist Joe Grundy, could be reached with a click of a key.

Suave Will Hays, the national chairman, who was soon to become arbiter of the nation's celluloid morals, opened the convention and turned the chair over to Senator Lodge. His broad, cultured voice rose to a scream more than once as he delivered the keynote address: a vitriolic diatribe, dripping with passion and scorn, against Woodrow Wilson and all that he stood for nationally and internationally. It was old stuff, but the sweating dele-

7

gates ate it up. A Boston correspondent wired, "Senator Lodge has made the issue of the coming campaign, and it can be summed up in one word — Wilson." But there was more to the speech than that. In one succinct paragraph the scholar in politics laid down the party line that was to endure for twenty years:

"We must be now and ever for Americanism and Nationalism, and against Internationalism. There is no safety for us, no hope that we can be of service to the world, if we do otherwise."

When Boies Penrose read those words his gross and ancient body rumbled with delight. Had he not, out of the wisdom of a life devoted to practical politics, predicted that the issue would be "Americanism"? When reporter Talcott Williams asked him to define the term, he replied, "Damned if I know, but you will find it is a damn good issue to get votes in an election."

It is an axiom of American politics that party platforms are written to be ignored; but every four years more blood and sweat, and perhaps even tears, are shed over the wording of these inflated documents than over any other partisan pronunciamento. At Chicago it took the Republican "brain trust" from Tuesday afternoon until late Thursday night to find the proper phrases with which to present the philosophy of Republicanism to the nation. The pages that were finally carried triumphant from the closely guarded chamber of the platform committee contained a masterpiece of reaction.

Chairman Hays had hoped that young Ogden Mills, a wealthy New York conservative, would superintend the writing of the platform, but the Senate soviet ruled otherwise and the task was assigned to Senator Jim Watson, whose reactionary mind could be depended upon to eliminate any semblance of progressive thought. He had the help of such enlightened gentlemen as Senator Lodge and Senator Medill McCormick of Chicago. Borah, too, was on hand to help guide the authors on foreign policy, as was William Allen White. The reporter-delegate was a thorn in the side of Watson and Lodge, but neither his nor Borah's mild progressivism could rescue the document from intellectual vacuity.

As these titans labored through long hours of desudation they were ever conscious of the fact that, as White later recalled, "every delegation . . . was loaded with one, two, or half a dozen representatives of national commodity interests — oil, railroads, steel, coal, and textiles." Since these interests were the flesh and blood of the party they had to be appeased in words of high purpose. This the committee proceeded to do. After blaming the Democratic Party for being unprepared for the war (still officially not yet ended) and unprepared for the peace, and taking some passing swipes at the abolition of civil liberties under Wilson's violent Attorney General, A. Mitchell Palmer, in the name of "constitutional government" (but at the same time, since the party was resolved to serve the open-shop system and the National Association of Manufacturers' so-called American Plan, making no strong resolution in behalf of these liberties), the platform makers went on to more important matters.

They favored cutting the public debt. They advocated lowering taxes on the wealthy through a reduction of the income levy and they promised to annul the excess profits tax and end the deflation of overexpanded credit. They denounced that devil's advocate, old High Cost of Living, in the very same breath in which they swore eternal allegiance to High Protection. They endorsed the Esch-Cummins act which would restore the railroads to private, competitive operation. They completely ignored all social legislation, the "burning issue" of Prohibition, and the dangerous issue of a soldiers' bonus. Elsewhere they wrote flowery phrases about welcoming Labor into "co-operation in a common task," and of course they hailed the farmers as "the backbone of the nation."

No one had expected a liberal philosophy from a party long dedicated to a return to what Senator Harding, in a forgotten speech in Boston in May, had in one full breath described as "not heroism but healing, not nostrums but normalcy, not revolution but restoration, not agitation but adjustment, not surgery but serenity, not the dramatic but the dispassionate, not experiment but the equipoise, not submergence in internationality but sustainment in triumphant nationality."

Having disposed of the domestic issues, the platform makers turned to the troubled international scene. Here they were on difficult grounds which called for some adroit maneuvering. Lodge, Brandegee, Watson, and other members of the Senate soviet would quite willingly have come out with a flat-footed declaration in favor of complete isolationism if they had thought they could "get away with it." The temper of the people was not yet entirely opposed to international co-operation through

9

the agency of the League of Nations. Within the Republican Party were many prominent and powerful persons anxious to salvage something from the wreck caused by Lodge and his cohorts in the Senate. Men like Nicholas Murray Butler, Elihu Root, former President Taft, President A. Lawrence Lowell of Harvard, and Thomas W. Lamont of the House of Morgan, had not turned their hearts and minds against the League. They were not yet ready to sabotage their ideals for the sake of partisanship.

That section of the platform dealing with the Republican Party's relationship to what undoubtedly was then the most pressing problem facing the entire world was a masterpiece of double talk.

"The Republican Party stands for agreement among nations to preserve the peace of the world" was its brave beginning. "We believe that such international association must be based on international justice, and must provide methods which shall maintain the rule of public right by the development of law and the decision of international courts, and which shall secure instant and general international conference whenever peace shall be threatened by political action, so that the nations pledged to do and insist upon what is just and fair may exercise their influence and power for the prevention of war." From this ambiguous endorsement of a mythical World Court the soothsayers went on: "We believe that all this can be done without the compromise of national independence, without depriving the people of the United States in advance of the right to determine for themselves what is just and fair, when the occasion arises, and without involving them as participants and not as peacemakers in a multitude of quarrels, the merits of which they are unable to judge."

Senator Lodge then got in his inevitable attack upon President Wilson, declaring that the "covenant signed at Paris failed signally to accomplish this purpose," that it "repudiated, to a degree wholly unnecessary and unjustifiable, the time-honored policy in favor of peace declared by Washington, Jefferson and Monroe." Furthermore, the splenetic Lodge added, "the unfortunate insistence of the President upon having his own way and without any regard to the opinion of the majority of the Senate, which shares with him the treaty-making powers," was wholly unwarranted. The Senators, he added piously, had performed their duty faithfully.

The platform makers again reverted to double talk when they pledged "the coming Republican Administration" quite meaninglessly to "such agreement with other nations as shall meet the full duty of America to civilization and humanity in accordance with American ideals and without surrendering the right of the American people to exercise its judgment and its power in favor of justice and peace." Upon this plank almost any candidate might teeter to his heart's content.

The platform was quickly adopted by the wilting delegates, who were anxious to get down to the vastly more exciting business of choosing a candidate. There was one jarring note. A member of the Wisconsin delegation, which was pledged to Robert M. La Follette, presented a minority report of one which called, among other things, for the government operation of the nation's stockyards. Boos and catcalls greeted this heretical suggestion. "Socialist, anarchist, Bolshevist!" screamed the affronted Republicans. "Throw him out! Eliminate him, Mr. Lodge!"

On Friday morning Senator Lodge's gavel rang loud and clear through the heavy air of the Coliseum, and the quadrennial outpourings of "A man who!" began. The first "man who" to be presented was General Wood and the honor of introducing him fell to Governor Henry J. Allen of Kansas. Mr. Allen was not happy with his task. A former progressive of liberal leanings, Allen had been chosen to offset Wood's dyed-in-the-wool conservatism. Wood's campaign managers were not very happy over the choice and they had compelled Allen to rewrite his encomium three times until it was a watered-down and wholly unconvincing speech. The Wood forces were desperately afraid that if Allen captured the convention with a brilliant address a move on the part of the progressive elements of the party to secure him the second place on the ticket would be enhanced. This they did not want and there was considerable pressure on the part of various powerful interests to keep him from getting the Vice-Presidential nomination. At a moment when it looked as if his chances in this direction were good he had been called to a room in an office building in the Loop where a group of men, representing Oil, had subjected him to a stiff cross-examination regarding his views on foreign policy, and about Mexico in particular. Allen's speech was resultantly dispirited and dull.

One by one the candidates — eleven all told, including Johnson,

Lowden, Hoover, Coolidge, Harding, Dr. Butler, Judge Peter C. Pritchard of California, Governor William Sproul of Pennsylvania, Miles Poindexter of Washington, and Howard Sutherland of West Virginia — were placed on the auction block. At the outset the aspirations of none but Wood and Lowden were taken seriously, although, after the first ballot, many present must have recalled Harry Daugherty's cynical prediction, published the previous February, that no candidate would be nominated on the first ballot, but that the victor would be named by a group of weary men sitting in a smoke-filled room "about eleven minutes after two o'clock on Friday morning."

The first ballot resulted in a deadlock — Wood, 287½; Lowden, 211½; Johnson, 133½ — with neither of the major contenders approaching the necessary majority. Governor Sproul led the also-rans, followed by Butler, Harding, and Hoover, in that order. The next five ballots showed no appreciable change. Chairman Lodge was seen to smile behind his whiskers and Senator Curtis chuckled to himself. As the afternoon wore heatedly on none of the lesser candidates yielded any ground. They were wise enough politicians to realize that if they stood firm they were in an advantageous position to trade; and the longer the deadlock the better their chances. Most of the delegates were ready to stay there all night if necessary and battle it out. The Wood forces and the Lowden forces were especially desirous of remaining until the proper deals could be made and one by one the delegations pledged to other candidates broke and came their way. And this was one eventuality that Senator Lodge was determined to prevent.

Ostensibly Senator Lodge was a supporter of General Wood, for whom he had voted on each of the ballots cast during the afternoon. (Earlier in the spring he had run out on his promise to support Governor Coolidge.) But long before the convention he and other members of the Senate soviet had agreed that if the chance presented itself they would do their utmost to promote the candidacy of one of their own members. This probably would be Senator Harding. Now, at seven o'clock, the chance came. After a whispered conference Senator Smoot moved for an adjournment, in spite of the fact that only a short time before the delegates had rejected such a motion by a vote of 701½ to 275½. Callously disregarding the obvious wishes of the delegates, whose

"Noes!" were overwhelming, Lodge adjourned the convention until the next morning. As Senator Smoot said, "*We* wanted the night to think it over."

Rooms 404–405–406 on the thirteenth floor of the old Blackstone Hotel, hot and stuffy like all the rooms anywhere in Chicago that torrid night, had been rented by Will Hays, the national chairman. But he was dining elsewhere that evening, leaving the suite free for the use of his friend and roommate, George Harvey, who was entertaining three important guests.

George Harvey, a native of Peacham, Vermont, was a political enigma. He had worked his way through newspaper offices in St. Johnsbury, Springfield, Massachusetts, and Chicago to the post of New Jersey editor of the old *New York World*. As a member of the New Jersey Governor's staff he had received the title of Colonel, which he proudly if somewhat incongruously bore. He had been an ardent supporter of Cleveland in 1892, as a result of which he had become an associate of President Cleveland's millionaire campaign manager, William Collins Whitney, promoter of public utilities. This association had brought him a small fortune and made him a minor figure in Wall Street. Some of this he had sunk in buying the *North American Review*. When J. P. Morgan and Company took over the financially embarrassed publishing firm of Harper and Brothers he was chosen by the banker to be its president. Later he edited *Harper's Weekly*. He was a vitriolic writer of hard-hitting editorials. He claimed personal credit for having been the first person publicly to endorse Woodrow Wilson (in 1906) for President of the United States and in 1910 had labored valiantly to make the president of Princeton the governor of New Jersey. The Morgan interests hated Wilson for his alleged radicalism and Wilson distrusted Harvey because of his close connection with the House of Morgan. The two quarreled, and, although Harvey supported Wilson's early New Freedom program, by 1916 the editor had turned completely upon the man he claimed to have "made" President. Thereafter he devoted his editorial talents, through the medium of *Harvey's Weekly*, to a continuous barrage of satire, ridicule, and barbed shafts against "Wilsonian officialdom" and the President's "Fourteen Commandments." It was Harvey who had persuaded Henry Clay Frick and Andrew W. Mellon to finance the campaign against the League of Nations.

13

On the night of June 9, 1920, when the vengeful and egocentric Harvey dined the three Senators, he was still out for blood. None of them — neither Lodge nor Brandegee nor Curtis — ever told exactly what went on in Will Hays's suite that night. In view of the results of that dinner it becomes clear why they were not inclined to boast. Presumably the first part of the evening was passed on a purely social level, but as soon as the coffee cups had been cleared away the four distinguished gentlemen got down to business. They understood each other very well. Frank Brandegee, who was to commit suicide a few years later in a moment of financial desperation, had helped Harvey in his quest for anti-League funds. Senator since 1905, when he had succeeded the late Orville H. Platt, he had an amazingly consistent record for voting against progressive legislation: the direct election of Senators, the Federal Reserve system, the income tax amendment, women's suffrage — even the extension of parcel post. Although only fifty-four he was, in spirit and practice, among the oldest of the Old Guard. As a member of the Foreign Relations Committee he had subjected Woodrow Wilson to a grueling cross-examination at the famous White House conference shortly after the President had presented the Versailles Treaty to the Senate. Senator Curtis, pink, pudgy and pompous, a far less able individual than the others, with a completely undistinguished record, was a competent errand boy for the Old Guard. He was a close friend of Sinclair and Doheny, the oil promoters, and a crony of Senator Albert B. Fall. In the Senate Curtis was the Republican whip and he had helped silence the vacationing Senators when word came from Paris that President Wilson, against his better judgment but upon the insistence of his Republican critics, had forced insertion of the Monroe Doctrine clause into the League Covenant, thus answering the most vital criticism the enemies of the League had invented up to that point.

As the after-dinner cigar smoke began to fill the room other Senators started drifting in until soon McCormick, Watson, Smoot, Wadsworth, and Calder were also present. The evening newspapers had reported that Boies Penrose was sunk in a coma in his Philadelphia home, but Joe Grundy was on hand. With the doors locked and guarded the permanent chairman, fastidious even in his shirt sleeves, took over the meeting. He explained that although he had come to Chicago in the interests of Leonard

Wood he was now convinced that the General's nomination, as well as that of Governor Lowden, would be ill-advised. He then referred to the terrific heat, to the weariness of the delegates, and to the expense of spending an unnecessary week end in Chicago. He did not think, he said, that he could control the convention over Sunday. In his opinion an effort should be made between then and the reconvening of the convention in the morning to agree upon a candidate. If any present resented this high-handed dictation they did not say so. Lodge was the party's leader; they were all members of the same gang. Nor were they surprised when he went on to declare that he had looked the picture over and was satisfied that the most available man was Senator Harding.[1]

The conference was not a cut-and-dried affair. It was more nearly a powwow. There was much coming and going. Nicholas Murray Butler was in and out during the evening. There was much telephoning. Penrose revived from his coma long enough to give Harding his blessing and have the word relayed early in the morning to the "smoke-filled room." Harding's name, however, was not accepted by the inner circle without considerable discussion. At the beginning Harvey had held out for Will Hays, but he was easily dissuaded. All the candidates whose names were in nomination were gone over, their vote-getting abilities and their party fidelity candidly discussed. At one time Lodge's own name was under discussion. But he and those others present knew that his age if nothing more was against him. By eleven o'clock the decision was reached to make Harding the candidate. From then on the little group was busy "reaching" the important state delegations and issuing the orders which made certain that they would "go along" when the balloting was resumed in the morning.

While all this was taking place Senator Harding, overcome by one of those seizures of despondency to which he was often subject, lay flushed and unshaven on a bed in the near-by Congress Hotel. He was discouraged. He had been drinking heavily. Perhaps his inamorata, Nan Britton, who was working as a clerk in the Republican National Headquarters, had been giving him a bad time. He was worried, too, over the possibility that his certificate

[1] This version, gathered from several sources, is probably more accurate than that given by Roxy Stinson, wife of H. M. Daugherty's close friend, Jesse Smith, before a Senate investigating committee, who insisted that Daugherty went to Harvey's room at 2 A.M. and made the deal which brought Harding the nomination.

of candidacy for the Senate, which he had entrusted to a friend, had not reached the State House at Columbus in time for the deadline. At the moment it looked very much as if he might as well be headed back to Marion, Ohio, and he wished he had never let his friend Daugherty talk him into flirting with the Presidential nomination.

At eleven o'clock he answered a knock at his door. There stood Myron Herrick, whose Lieutenant Governor Harding had been in 1903. His old chief now passed along the word that he had been chosen. The two of them left the hotel together on a mysterious errand and it was not until nearly 2 A.M. that Harding appeared at Will Hays's suite. All the plotters had retired except Brandegee and Harvey. The latter, more owlish-appearing than ever in the pre-dawn light of a hot June day, peered at him over his heavy horn-rimmed glasses and said: "Senator, we want to put a question to you. Is there in your life or background any element which might embarrass the Republican Party if we nominate you for President?" [2]

The shaky Senator stared for a moment at his questioner and then asked for time to think the matter over. He walked into one of the two adjoining bedrooms. Perhaps he knelt in prayer, for Harding possessed a simple religiosity to which he often turned in times of trouble. No one will ever know. Ten minutes later he presented himself before Harvey and Brandegee. There was, he said, no element, nothing in his past that would interfere. Harvey smiled, shook his hand, and called in the press. The late editions of the morning newspapers announced that the "leaders" of the party had settled on Harding and that he would be nominated that afternoon. The orders had gone out and, although the managers of the Wood and the Lowden camps announced

[2] Harvey was undoubtedly giving Harding a chance to inform his backers whether his affair with Nan Britton, the mother of his bastard child, was likely to leak out and become an embarrassing campaign issue. He also must have had in mind the vicious rumors that Harding was of part Negro ancestry, rumors already in pamphlet form and circulating in Chicago. Harvey, in telling the story, put an almost sepulchral interpretation upon it, as if Harding had been asked to consult his Maker upon his fitness to be President. There are two standard versions: Samuel Hopkins Adams, *Incredible Era*, p. 154; Mark Sullivan, *Our Times*, VI, pp. 63–64. Brandegee did not publish his version, nor did Harding. Harding's papers, which might have mentioned this dramatic event, were destroyed by Mrs. Harding after his death. The above quotation is from Adams's biography.

that they would fight it out on the floor until they won or were beaten, everyone knew that Warren Gamaliel Harding would be the Republican candidate.

True to their word the Wood and Lowden delegations put up the promised battle all next morning and throughout the early afternoon. On the sixth ballot Wood and Lowden were tied, and Harding had moved from fifth to third place. Chairman Lodge then called a long recess to allow time for some necessary off-the-floor trading. On the tenth ballot Harding was nominated, polling 692½ votes. The only delegation which failed to vote for Harding was that from Wisconsin, which went down the line to the bitter end for Fighting Bob La Follette. Ignoring their shouted objections, Chairman Lodge completed the Senate's victorious domination of the sordid scene by announcing that Warren Gamaliel Harding of Ohio had been unanimously elected.

There was nothing left for the cowed delegates, who had bowed their heads to the whim of their leaders, except to choose a Vice-Presidential candidate. In the excitement of railroading Harding's nomination through, the Old Guard had been forced to ignore the second place on the ticket. They met hurriedly under the rough wooden beams that supported the platform and quickly decided that this place should go to their colleague, Senator Irvine Lenroot of Wisconsin. Medill McCormick was chosen to present his name. His wordy and trite speech was received with apathy. So were the redundant seconding speeches. Everyone in the Coliseum knew that this was another dictation from the Senate soviet but no one was prepared to do anything about it.

No one, that is, except a delegate from Oregon. Throughout the voting, until the final ballot, he had with a foghorn voice cast his delegation's ballots for Leonard Wood. His name was Wallace McCamant. He now mounted a chair and shouted for attention. Senator Lodge had momentarily left the chair, which was occupied by Governor Frank B. Willis of Ohio. Not suspecting what was afoot Governor Willis recognized the gentleman from Oregon and settled down to listen, so he thought, to another paean of praise for Lenroot. He and the entire convention were startled out of their apathy when McCamant, with admirable brevity, nominated for "the exalted office of Vice-President" a man who "is sterling in his Americanism and stands for all that the Republican Party holds dear . . . Governor Calvin Coolidge of Massachusetts."

For the first time since the previous Tuesday a burst of spontaneous enthusiasm rocked the Coliseum. Six delegates arose in quick order to second the unexpected nomination. And for the first time in many years the Republican leaders found a convention out of control. As the cries of "We want Coolidge!" became a deafening chant, and the revolt against the Senate leadership spread, Medill McCormick rushed to the platform. Senator Lodge was resting at his hotel. But even if he could have got there in time he could have done nothing to swing the delegates back to Lenroot. It was not that they wanted Coolidge so much as it was that they were determined to demonstrate their belated independence. In many ways it was an exhilarating spectacle, the turmoil in the Coliseum; in another it was comic. To witness a hallful of hot and angry Republicans rising in revolt against their political masters and lining solidly up behind the silent, uninspiring Calvin Coolidge — the only time in his life that he caused anyone to deviate from normalcy — was something no one, an hour ago, would have believed possible.

But there it was: a mass easing of guilty consciences, a purging of souls. Only one ballot was necessary to carry the day for Calvin Coolidge. The vote was 674½ for Coolidge; 146 for Lenroot. And this time, when it was moved to make the vote unanimous, even Wisconsin went along.

And so the convention ended, with Warren Gamaliel Harding and John Calvin Coolidge the party's choice. Two men less qualified for the type of political leadership for which the country was in dire need in the year 1920 would have been difficult to find.

As the delegates were leaving the Coliseum, knee-deep in tattered banners, Frederick M. Davenport, who was covering the spectacle for the *Outlook*, buttonholed an "elder statesman." He said prophetically:

"Moral issues and idealism are going to wait awhile. The country has had its fill of them. Just now it doesn't care a rap about these things compared with its desire to get industry back on a sound basis and to have economic livelihood made more secure. And the country, including large numbers of conservative Democrats, is going to take to Harding and the Republican policies like a duck to water."

And very soon thereafter the *New Republic* said:

> Harding stands for a kind of candid and unpretentious reaction that everyone can respect, and that a great many people desire.

There were few to listen to the calm wise words of an obscure professor at Cornell:

> The time for national complacency is past. The sentimentalism that turns away from facts to feed on platitudes, the provincialism which fears ideas and plays at politics in the spirit of the gambler . . . will no longer serve. The time has come when the people of the United States must bring all their intelligence and all their idealism to the consideration of the subtler realities of human relationship, as they have to the much simpler realities of material existence: this at least they must do if America is to be in the future what it has been in the past — a fruitful experiment in democracy.[3]

In the obscene atmosphere of Chicago democracy had no chance.

[3] Carl Becker, *The United States, an Experiment in Democracy.* New York, Alfred A. Knopf, Inc., 1920, p. 333.

CHAPTER TWO

The Man from Ohio

WHO is Harding? What is his background? What has he said and done? How does he stand on the issues? These were the immediate and obvious questions which everyone asked when the news of his nomination went out from Chicago. Except in his native state of Ohio the answers required patient research, for in June 1920 Warren Gamaliel Harding was a nonentity.

The first results of this research must have been a shock to all who held the Republican Party in esteem. He was so little known and regarded in the East that his name had crept into the index of the *New York Times* less than forty times since 1909, in spite of the fact that he had been a United States Senator from the politically potent state of Ohio for nearly six vital years. His record in the Senate, when looked at from any point of view except that of party fidelity, was appalling. Prior to his elevation to the Senate his political history in Ohio was that of a party hack. His qualifications for president of one of the greatest nations in the world, struggling to recover from the greatest war in history, were entirely lacking. His choice as the Republican candidate was a fraud upon the people.

As a candidate Harding had one tremendous asset. He looked like a president. Tall, well built, with his handsome, ruddy face set off by a fine head of silvery-gray hair, he wore his conservative clothes with distinction, and he moved with grace. Women liked his looks and men recognized him as wholly masculine. He was easy to approach and yet he exuded a certain affable dignity befitting a holder of high office. Off the platform he spoke well; upon it, when at his best and familiar with his prepared speech, he was a more than compelling orator. But behind the magnificent façade was emptiness. His lazy mind was quite untrained to thinking and it worked in platitudes whenever it worked at all.

Senator Brandegee was even a little too generous when he said to Mark Sullivan shortly after the Republicans had made their choice: "There ain't any first-raters this year. This ain't 1880 or 1904 [1] . . . we've got a lot of second-raters and Warren Harding is the best of the second-raters."

Senator Harding was exactly fitted to play the role expected of him by the Senate oligarchy, the corruptionists, and Big Business. A product of the political school of Mark Hanna and Joseph Benson Foraker, and the protégé of that unscrupulous schemer, Harry Micajah Daugherty, he could be expected to act the part of President while others — and not only the oil thieves and the bootleggers — pulled the strings. He believed in the eternal virtues of property, and so would kick over no corporate apple cart. He hated democracy but he knew all the homely political tricks whereby he could fool an unwary people with a warm handclasp and a winning smile. If the "representatives of amalgamated wealth" had preferred a man with epaulettes, they nevertheless knew they had nothing to fear from Warren Harding. He was not rich, but like most small businessmen he worshiped wealth and the power and glory that accompanies it. He was a political descendant of the Federalists who had established the American System and whence stemmed the party to which, above all else, Warren Harding was faithful.

The trained seals of the Republican press — and then, as now, most of the important and successful newspapers were Republican in their leanings — quickly transformed Harding's tawdry career into a typical American success story. This called for journalistic magic, but plenty of magicians were on hand to take their lead from the ineffable Harvey and his satellite, Richard Washburn Child, who rushed to Harding's protection at the convention's end. Samuel G. Blythe, Joe Mitchell Chapple, Willis Fletcher Johnson, and many other journalistic bigwigs unloosed a flood of panegyrical prose which obscured the real Harding and created a new American myth. All that was missing in their tendentious accounts was the log cabin birthplace. Harding, unfortunately, was born in a small town in a frame house.

The small-town motif ran through Harding's life and it explained to an appreciable extent the limitations of his mind. His provincialism, his isolationism, and his moral hypocrisy were ab-

[1] 1880 — James A. Garfield; 1904 — Theodore Roosevelt.

sorbed from a lifetime of dwelling in small Middle Western communities whose horizons never extended beyond the county line. Residence in the state capital of Columbus and later in Washington, vacations in the Caribbean and in Europe, never made Warren Harding a man of the world. If he possessed many of the alleged virtues of a small-town upbringing, he also owned a full measure of its vices. At heart he was a joiner and culture to him was the playing of the home-town band.

At the time of his nomination Warren Harding was fifty-five years old. Until he had gone to Washington a few months after the war broke out in Europe, most of his life had been spent editing and publishing a small daily newspaper in an inconsequential Ohio city. This had been varied only by forays into the state political arena, where he had held various offices and had built up enough of a reputation to be elected United States Senator. He went to Washington with misgivings as to his fitness for the office, and in the next six years proved how right his qualms had been.

Warren Harding was the child of commonplace parents. His father was a veterinary turned homeopath who practiced his profession in a cluttered upstairs office in a Marion, Ohio, business block. In the surrounding countryside the old gentleman was better known as a horse trader than as a physician. His wife, the future President's mother, was an accomplished midwife. In the back villages where they had lived before moving to Marion it was whispered that the Hardings had Negro blood in their veins and because of this unprovable "stigma" they never became accepted by the town's socially elect; but neither were they entirely snubbed.

As a youngster Warren went through the motions of acquiring an education, but from the start he had the reputation of being a rather lazy fellow. He apparently had no outstanding ambition or any desire to revolt against the restricted environment of Marion's main street. He liked music and learned to play the alto horn well enough to join the Citizens' Cornet Band. He had a warm personality and a ready smile and was liked if not admired by the young people with whom he associated. At the Ohio Central College (long since disappeared, buildings, records, and all) in Iberia, Ohio, he learned enough to take a job as a country schoolteacher, but he lasted at this occupation for only one term. Then he read law in a Marion law office, but he found the intricacies of Blackstone too taxing and gave up very quickly any idea of being a lawyer. He then drifted into the insurance business, but once again, in spite of his affability, he found he was in the wrong field of endeavor.

There were, in the 1880's, two weeklies and one daily newspaper in Marion, a Republican stronghold and seat of a Democratic county. Both the weekly papers were political organs: the *Mirror* stanchly Democratic and the *Independent* just as stanchly Republican. The daily *Star*, caught in the middle, did not count. It was printed on presses held together by baling wire by an editor who was all but starving to death. It was on the *Mirror* that Harding got his first newspaper job.[2]

At that time he was not quite twenty years old. He spent much of his time hanging around the local poolroom, he played poker with the boys in the firehouse, he tooted the alto horn in the Cornet Band, and in the felicitous phrase of Samuel Hopkins Adams, he pursued "the casual lecheries of the unattached." A rather spineless but well-meaning lad, he often exasperated his hard-working but not very successful father, who one day burst out: "It's a good thing you wasn't born a girl. Because you'd be in a family way all the time. You can't say no."

In 1884, the year in which he acquired his first newspaper job, he also acquired his first hero. He was greatly stirred by the personality of the Man from Maine, the Plumed Knight, James G. Blaine. In that year Blaine was striving to hide his dishonesties behind a screen of red fire and to drown his opponent's damning attacks under the blare of a thousand brass bands. That was the year which saw thousands of Republicans desert their party for Grover Cleveland; the year in which young Henry Cabot Lodge swore undying fealty to the Republican Party. With the bravado of youth young Harding went his rounds as reporter for the Democratic *Mirror* wearing a Blaine-Logan campaign hat. The editor fired him.

Shortly after Blaine's defeat Harding and two other young men

[2] When Warren was in his early teens his father had become a part owner of an all but moribund weekly newspaper, acquired in one of his trading sprees. Warren had worked around the shop and liked it. It was then, as he later often said when in a nostalgic mood, that he got printer's ink in his blood.

23

bought the *Marion Star* for a few hundred dollars.[3] In the first issue under their sponsorship they announced that the *Star* would thereafter be an "independent" newspaper. Inasmuch as practically every small newspaper in Ohio in those days was dependent upon political patronage in the form of state or county advertising, a declaration of independence was a bold avowal. It did not last long: the *Star* soon started a small weekly edition that boldly proclaimed its Republican partisanship. "Republican for business only," sneered the rival weekly, the *Independent*.

In small-town journalism Warren Harding found his niche. His inability to say no served him well. His free-and-easy ways, that soft spot in his character which made him a joiner of such fraternities as the Elks and Odd Fellows, the Hoo Hoos, the Moose and the Red Men, helped him make a success of the *Star*. In later years he invented the word "inoffensivism" to describe the editorial policy which, with a few youthful exceptions, he followed throughout his career. In his early years, after he had bought out his partners and was the sole proprietor of the *Star*, he often indulged in crude personalities, and sometimes displayed an almost sadistic sense of humor, as when he once staged a fake raid on a roadhouse for the sole purpose of embarrassing a rival editor. This so enraged Harding's future father-in-law, a friend of the red-faced rival, that that estimable gentleman induced the affronted editor to print a full-page attack upon Harding, stating that the Hardings had always been considered Negroes when they lived in the town of Blooming Grove. There is no way of knowing what effect the charges of Negroism, both open and whispered, had upon Harding. He apparently did not go out of his way to answer them.[4]

Under the guidance of the handsome young editor the *Star* prospered moderately. He wheedled his share of patronage from

[3] Harding borrowed his share of the money from the Democratic editor who had fired him from the *Mirror*. (Adams, *op. cit.*, p. 4.)

[4] A full and fair discussion of these "charges" may be found in Adams, *Incredible Era*. They were, of course, revived during the 1920 campaign; but inasmuch as they were not exploited by the Democratic Party, they had little, if any, bearing upon the campaign. Nor do they appear to have had any appreciable effect upon Harding personally. Whether true or not they are hardly worth mentioning, except as an example of that native American intolerance and viciousness which comes to the fore, in one form or another, every four years.

the political leaders and was able to make a fair living. His acquaintances throughout the county grew, and if the *Star* was neither widely read nor greatly feared it was soon recognized as a going concern. Harding enjoyed most the writing of editorials. He acquired a florid, often bombastic style, which was never noted for its literary grace. He knew a good cliché when he saw one. Never a wide or avid reader — Harding would rather spend his evening playing poker than reading a good book — he did explore the conventional histories of his day. His political mentor became Alexander Hamilton and he developed an adolescent admiration for Napoleon, whom he always considered, as he once confessed, "a military marvel and a wonderful statesman." On the lighter side his favorite novelist was Edgar Saltus, whose *Imperial Purple* long remained his best-loved book.

Among the townsfolk of Marion Harding was regarded as a young fellow who was getting along all right in an unspectacular sort of way. In 1891, when he was twenty-seven years old, his fortunes changed for the better. In that year he married Florence Kling, the daughter of the town's richest man. Amos Kling was a hardware merchant who had made a fortune in nails during the Civil War and invested heavily in Marion real estate. A pompous, overbearing individual, Amos had no use for the easygoing young publisher. His daughter, however, considered herself quite lucky to have married him. Hers had been a somewhat tragic life. Her first marriage had ended when her drunken husband deserted her and left her with a small son.[5] After her divorce she had returned to live with her father. She was four years older than Warren, a rather harsh, overpolished, domineering woman whose obvious social and financial ambitions counteracted Warren's inherent laziness.

With Florence Harding taking over its business affairs, the *Star* prospered much more than it had under Warren. In spite of an affinity for professional fortunetellers and stargazers Mrs. Harding was a shrewd manager. Among their personal friends, who came often to their home to play poker, she was known as "the Duchess." Within a short time of their marriage it was apparent to all that she ruled the household, a situation which Harding accepted with amused tolerance. She was quite jealous of Warren and

[5] The son was adopted by Amos Kling. He died at the age of thirty-five. Warren and Florence Harding had no children.

inclined to nag him, but he went his easy way and there was no apparent friction in the childless Harding household.

A year after his marriage Harding lost his first political contest — the post of county auditor — and he did not again seek office until seven years later. During that time he and his wife had considerably increased the *Star's* circulation and revenue and had settled down to a quiet life in the better part of the town. Harding had come to know just about everybody there was to know, politically and financially, in the county, and the daily *Star* had long since lost whatever claim it ever had to "independence." On the wall of Harding's office were two significant pictures: one of James G. Blaine, the other of United States Senator Joseph B. Foraker. To the memory of one and to the deeds of the other Harding was ever faithful.

Joseph Benson Foraker was one of the state's three most powerful political bosses. Mark Hanna still reigned supreme over the state. In Cincinnati, however, even Hanna had to do business with Foraker, who, with the notorious George B. Cox, held that parish in the hollow of his capacious hand. A man like Harding was a good man for Foraker to cultivate, which he proceeded to do. For the newspaper which Harding ran was always and everywhere found on the side of the angels and against the man-eating shark,[6] an attribute which Foraker knew would be useful. Harding became Foraker's man in Marion.

In the late 1890's Marion was a growing town. Harding went after local advertising and got it and his bank account grew, aided no little by gifts of stock from a brewery and a farm implement manufacturer. The Hardings, who now owned their own home, were the first family in Marion to buy an automobile.

The *Star*, taking its cues from the violently imperialistic Foraker, supported the Spanish-American War and its attendant imperialism with jingoistic fervor; but for the most part it espoused the homely virtues and held aloof from mental strain. Its editor, who never wrote a word in its columns that was quoted beyond the borders of Ohio, confined his political activities to its platitudinous columns. In 1901, however, he was bitten by the political bug. In that year, although he failed to carry his home county, Warren Harding was elected State Senator. His career as statesman had begun.

[6] Adams, *op. cit.*, p. 47.

In the bars and back rooms of Columbus, Warren Harding was a prominent and popular figure for the next two years. He drank and played poker with the boys. He did not question the orders that were passed down to him from Foraker or Cox. He voted as he was supposed to vote. He was as popular with Hanna's crowd as with Foraker's and by his second term, when he was made floor leader, he was recognized as the official conciliator between the two gangs. Nicholas Longworth, Myron T. Herrick, and Atlee Pomerene, who served with him in the legislature, recognized his political ability. If he originated no legislation and seldom stirred the galleries with inspiring oratory, he served his purpose and deserved reward. This came in his nomination for lieutenant governor on the ticket with Hanna's hand-picked candidate for governor, Myron Herrick. Behind the slogan of "Herrick, Harding, and Harmony" he marched to victory in the election of 1903.

Warren Harding's single term as the presiding officer of the Ohio Senate (which is the main function of a lieutenant governor) was singularly lacking in interest. At its conclusion Harding, overcome by one of those spells of self-distrust and defeatism which marked his career from time to time until the end, returned to Marion to bask in the role of leading citizen, make friends at long last with his crusty old father-in-law, and resume the bathetic editing of the *Star*.

At Columbus Warren Harding became intimate with one man whose friendship was to play an overwhelming part in his subsequent career and in the history of the United States. Several years before Harding had first gone to the state capital, he and Harry Micajah Daugherty had met at a small-town political rally. At that time Daugherty was a sort of fringe politician who had failed to be elected attorney general of the state and had turned his legal talents to lucrative if less attractive uses. At that very first meeting Daugherty, as he afterwards often boasted, had been struck with the happy inspiration that Harding "looked like a president." Then and there he decided not to let this valuable asset go to waste.

Harry Daugherty was five years older than Harding and much wiser in the ways of politicians. Of Scotch-Irish ancestry, he had been born in Washington Courthouse in 1861. His father died when he was quite young and both he and his brother Mally had to go to work at an early age. Harry clerked in a grocery store and managed to get through high school. Although he lacked the usual college training he won his law degree from the University of Michigan in 1881 and settled down to practice in his home town. He became interested in local politics, was elected to the town council, and later became prosecuting attorney for Fayette County. For two terms he sat in the Ohio House of Representatives, the only time he held state office.

Upon leaving the legislature Daugherty resumed his law practice, which is a pleasant way of saying he became one of the most active lobbyists in Ohio. He represented, both in court and before the lawmakers, such powerful corporations as the American Tobacco Company, Armour and Company, Western Union, the Ohio State Telephone Company, and American Gas and Electric. "See Harry Daugherty" was axiomatic counsel for all favor-seeking public utilities. He knew his way around the State House, where he assiduously cultivated useful men like Warren Harding.

A vulgar, profane, loud-mouthed, and self-assured gentleman, Daugherty was never able to sell himself to the voting public, although he had a wide acquaintanceship throughout the state and many loyal friends. He not only had failed to be elected attorney general in 1895; but was also twice an unsuccessful candidate for Congress; and in 1916 when he ran against Myron Herrick for the senatorial nomination, he carried only three counties out of eighty-eight.[7]

Daugherty was a tinhorn gambler and a cheat. Early in his career as a lawyer he had been found guilty of unethical practices by the grievance committee of the Ohio Bar Association, but he was saved from disbarment by intervention of a friendly judge whose son later was associated with Daugherty in questionable activities around the Ohio State House. There Daugherty was known as "paymaster for the boys." In 1900 he solicited $1500 each from several insurance companies, telling them that the legislature was controlled in both houses by his friends and that it would pay them to have him around Columbus working in their interests. He engineered a number of what were then called "milker bills," a legal way of extorting money from interests threatened by legislation introduced for that purpose, such as the

[7] In 1920, as originator and manager of Harding's campaign, he did his best to be elected delegate-at-large to the Chicago convention, and failed. He had to attend as a private citizen.

"anti-cigarette bills" that used to fill the legislative hoppers. He was involved in the failure of a Columbus bank and only escaped prosecution because Governor James M. Cox was convinced that he could not be convicted and that prosecution might be perverted into charges of political persecution. While the Republicans controlled Ohio, Daugherty thrived. He had close connections with, if not membership in, the Ku Klux Klan, and these were of estimable value when Warren Harding ran for the United States Senate in 1914.

After his return from Columbus, Harding became increasingly intimate with Daugherty and his crowd, including the incredible, slightly foolish Jesse Smith. They drank and played cards together, they went off on fishing trips at a near-by "lodge" to which only their close political friends were invited. Harding found Daugherty an ideal companion and apparently saw in him good qualities which escaped others of a higher ethical nature. Daugherty became Harding's goad and, as the years passed, Harding became Daugherty's great purpose in life. Thwarted in his ambitions to hold high office Daugherty devoted his talents as tactician and manager to driving Harding, often against his will, onwards and upwards towards political fame.

Throughout Theodore Roosevelt's administration the *Star*, faithfully following the lead of Senator Foraker, supported the President, although its editorial page evidenced no tremendous enthusiasm for many of Roosevelt's more radical reforms. Foraker at one time had unsuccessfully tried to induce Harding to take over the editorship of a Columbus newspaper which he proposed buying for political purposes. He had supported Harding in his race for the lieutenant governorship in 1903, and when, a year later, Foraker had swung to Roosevelt's support, the *Star* had gone along. When Foraker, after his slippery, self-seeking fashion, broke with Roosevelt, this was reflected in Harding's newspaper. Especially was this true after Roosevelt hand-picked Ohio's William Howard Taft as his successor and Foraker announced his own candidacy for the nomination. But when it became apparent to Harding that Foraker stood no chance to win, the editor followed the path of expediency and quickly aligned himself with Taft. Foraker, as politically understanding a gentleman as ever came out of Ohio, did not hold this against his protégé. Nor was Taft to forget his debt.

In 1910 Foraker, although no longer Senator, was still a powerful figure in Ohio politics. His word was law in the Cincinnati region and his law was enforced by George B. Cox, a saloon-keeper who had amassed a fortune by keeping the slum dwellers of that city completely under his subjection. Boss Cox was the man whom Harding once described as "a great, big, manly, modest . . . grand marshal of an invincible division of the grand old Republican Party of Ohio" and to whom, he had added, "we yield . . . our deference and devotion." Foraker and Cox were this year to pit their invincible division against the forces commanded by Mark Hanna's descendants in Cleveland, who were trying to get the governorship for Teddy Roosevelt's son-in-law, Nicholas Longworth. Into the bitter party struggle Cox threw all his weight and won the first skirmish when Harding captured the Republican nomination.

The split in the party and the fact that the Democrats nominated a strong candidate in the person of Grover Cleveland's one-time Attorney General, Judson Harmon, militated against Harding's success. Harmon accused his opponent of being the tool of Boss Cox — which, of course, he was. The only answer Harding could make to his well-remembered pledge of "deference and devotion" was a whimper. Harmon won the election by 100,000 votes. Privately Harding blamed his defeat on the fact that Boss Cox had made him a scapegoat just to beat Nicholas Longworth, who at that time posed as a reformer, and to a friend he whined: "These things will happen as long as Tom, Dick, and Harry have the right to vote."

Warren Harding was not the only candidate to feel that year the ingratitude of Tom, Dick, and Harry. In this mid-term national election the Democrats obtained a majority of 50 in the House and stole 8 Senate seats from the Republicans. Senator Beveridge was tossed out by his fellow Indianans while Senator Stimson of New York was defeated by Governor Dix. And in New Jersey the Democratic president of Princeton University was elected governor in one of the most dramatic campaigns in the history of that state.

Crushed by his defeat for governor, Warren Harding decided to abjure politics forever. For the next two years he did manage to live in editorial obscurity. In 1912, however, President Taft, who had sent $5000 of his own resources to support Harding in his fight against Governor Harmon, called upon his friend for help. Taft liked Warren Harding. "A man of clean life, of great force as a public speaker, and attractive in many ways," was his description at that time. Taft was greatly pleased when Harding was chosen to place his name before the Republican National Convention that year. William Allen White once pictured him on that occasion — his first appearance before a national audience — as a "fine, statuesque figure, all tailored, pressed, the 'oiled and curled Assyrian bull'" who stood "with a red boutonniere in his lapel . . . and abused Theodore Roosevelt to the yipping delight" of the delegates.[8]

Two years later, in 1914, Harry Daugherty decided that his friend Warren was wasting both time and talents in the editorial sanctum of the *Star*. Daugherty was adamant in his belief that Harding could easily become a United States Senator. Disregarding Warren's soft pleas of unwillingness — for he knew that Harding "couldn't say no" — he directed his persuasive arguments to Mrs. Harding. That estimable lady turned the suggestion down with the compelling answer that, inasmuch as Warren was not a corporation lawyer, he would be unable to supplement his senatorial salary while living in the Capital. But Daugherty knew the Duchess, and his glittering picture of her potential place in gay Washington society won her around. Once she had made up her mind, Warren had no other choice than to become Senator.

Winning the race was not an easy assignment for Harding. The direct primary was in force for the first time and his nomination could neither be bought nor engineered in the state convention. Arrayed against him at the start was Senator T. E. Burton, who had gone to Washington under the Progressive banner and quickly allied himself with the most reactionary elements in the Congress. He was forced to quit the race on the grounds that he would endanger the entire party if he insisted upon seeking re-election. The bosses who talked him into surrender selected Warren Harding in his place. But with even this support Harding had to contend with former Senator Foraker, who was seeking rescue

[8] Harding continued to "abuse" Teddy during the campaign. In the *Star* he called Roosevelt "a blackguard, utterly without conscience and truth and the greatest faker of all time."

from the dark cloud of scandal which had overtaken him with the publication of the infamous Archbold letters that proved him in the pay of Standard Oil while still a Senator.

Foraker put up a formidable battle but prodded by Daugherty, although convinced that he had no chance of winning, Harding stumped the state and carried the day. His Democratic opponent, a crusading attorney general under Governor Harmon named Timothy Hogan, labored under the rural disadvantage of being a Roman Catholic and the urban disadvantage of having made many powerful enemies by his relentless prosecution of various election frauds of a kind that had always been accepted practice in Ohio. In his autobiography James M. Cox says definitely that it was "out of this Ku Klux revival that the political resurrection of Warren Harding came." Harding carried the state by a plurality of nearly 75,000 votes, and for the first time carried Democratic Marion County.

The *Cleveland Plain Dealer*, which was always fair in its opposition to Harding, painted a perfect picture of him at the time, using his own campaign speeches for pigments: "A speech by Mr. Harding knows neither time nor circumstance. It would have been as applicable at the time of Benjamin Harrison or James G. Blaine as to that of Theodore Roosevelt and Woodrow Wilson. It has not the slightest relation to current problems. . . . No one need doubt his sincerity, for he himself is a relic of the good old days which assuredly were good to the Republican beneficiaries. Time and conditions change, but not Harding."

Like water seeking its own level this relic of the good old days gravitated unerringly to the stagnant pools where floated such estimable progressives as Boies Penrose, Reed Smoot, and Henry Cabot Lodge. Not once during the six years he was a Senator did he do a thing or say a word that invalidated the *Plain Dealer's* description.

"I like the fraternity of this body," he once said of the Senate. He ignored its responsibility. Few Senators ever regarded the trust of office more casually. He was a frequent absentee from important sessions, and just as frequent a visitor to the race track and the ball park. No good game of senatorial or journalistic poker was complete without Harding sitting in. His critics called him "the ranking slacker," a phrase justified by the revelation that out of 245 roll calls he had responded to less than half. And when he did happen to be on hand he refrained from voting on 35 per cent of the motions.

From almost any point of view Harding's legislative record was a bad one. In all the time he was in the Senate he introduced 134 bills. One hundred and twenty-two of these were what the Senator calls "private" measures. Eighty-six were pension bills and 17 were bills for the relief of various Ohio financial and commercial institutions. The others, so-called "public" bills which bore his name, were measures of this nature: to encourage the teaching of Spanish, to authorize the loan of army tents to relieve the postwar housing shortage, to change the law protecting fur-bearing animals in Alaska, and to grant discarded rifles to the sons of veterans.

Harding's geniality and easygoing nature and the fact that his party regularity was unimpeachable — perhaps the latter more than anything else — brought him membership on several important Senate committees. Anyone glancing at the *Congressional Directory*, with nothing else as a guide, might have thought him one of the outstanding Senators. He was, in the course of his term, a member of these committees: Foreign Relations, Commerce, Naval Affairs, and Public Health. As heir to the seat of the jingo Foraker he was made chairman of the Committee on the Philippines. Each of these committees carried heavy responsibilities. The record shows that he successfully evaded them. His advancement to the powerful Foreign Relations Committee was purely political. Although he had been abroad twice on summer holidays he was totally ignorant of European affairs. He was selected for the post by the wily chairman, Henry Cabot Lodge, when that astute strategist packed his committee with men who could be trusted to aid in the sabotage of the League of Nations. His understanding of Philippine affairs can best be judged by his statement that "we ought to go on there with the same thought that impelled Him who brought a plan of salvation to the earth. . . . He gathered his disciples about Him and said, 'Go, ye, and preach the gospel to all the nations of the earth.' "

Senator Harding could always be counted upon to vote in behalf of Big Business and against Labor. He could be counted upon to address such gatherings as the Railway Business Association on such topics as "The Railways and Prosperity," but for all his reputation as a flamboyant orator he was not in great demand as a public speaker. When he did speak his words reflected his great worship of the power and rectitude of Big Business, his opposition to taxing the wealthy, to government operation of or interference with industry, even as a wartime measure. At the drop of a hat, he could be counted upon to defend, in jumbled rhetoric bespeaking his poorly trained mind, what he loved to call "the inherited institutions of the fathers." With facile ease he "drank wet and voted dry."

If William G. McAdoo is remembered for nothing else he deserves minor immortality for having said of Harding's speeches that they "leave the impression of an army of pompous phrases moving over the landscape in search of an idea; sometimes these meandering words would actually capture a straggling thought and bear it triumphantly, a prisoner in their midst, until it died of servitude and overwork." [9]

In 1916 Harry Daugherty, who never wavered in his belief that because Harding looked like a president he could be one, engineered his selection as temporary chairman of the Republican National Convention. A dreary, unenthusiastic convention listened in apathy to his platitudes and went on to nominate Charles Evans Hughes. Although the speech evoked little national applause, the convention allowed Harding to meet political leaders from all over the country, which he did with his affable smile. Daugherty asked little more. In 1919 old Boies Penrose spread the word around that Harding would be his choice for 1920, but after listening to a speech in Philadelphia which Harding made at his invitation, he growled: "Harding isn't as big a man as I thought he was. He should have talked more about the tariff and not so much about playing the cymbals in the Marion brass band."

Penrose may have talked about Harding, but it was Harry Daugherty who put him in the White House. In 1919 he appointed himself Harding's manager and began selling him on every possible occasion to the Senate leaders and to the members of the Republican National Committee. As usual Harding was reluctant to make any effort in his own behalf, but Daugherty kept after

[9] In 1920 Harding's philosophy of government was best expressed when he advocated "a New Freedom from too much government in business and not enough business in government." This was one of his straggling thoughts that he imprisoned in meandering words.

him, and late that year he announced his candidacy for the nomination.

Warren G. Harding was exactly what the *Nation* said he was: "A colorless and platitudinous, uninspired and uninspiring nobody," who was put forward by the Old Guard, "like a cigar store Indian to attract trade."

CHAPTER THREE

By the Golden Gate

WHILE the Republicans, still a little stunned by the turn of events, were mounting their dark horse for the first lap of what was to be a record-breaking ride to electoral victory, the Democrats floundered about in a quandary. They were deeply mired. Under normal circumstances the party of Jackson and Wilson should have welcomed a rival with a record as vulnerable as that of Warren Gamaliel Harding. But the times were not normal and the laws of politics are mutable. The hard times, the rising cost of living, the industrial turmoil, should have militated in behalf of Democracy, and might well have done so if it had been any year but 1920 and if the party had been led by anyone but Woodrow Wilson, or if the country had not been chained by the two-party system.

Although, within a brief quarter of a century, history was to recognize the essential greatness of Woodrow Wilson's vision and to place the twenty-eighth President of the United States among the immortals, in that year of transition he was a detriment to his party. He had become, in the words of Mark Sullivan, an unhappy victim, "the symbol of the exaltation that had turned sour, personification of the rapture that had now become gall, sacrificial whipping boy for the present bitterness." Such a simplification of the trend of the times does not explain everything, for it fails to cover certain important phenomena that must be taken into consideration if the reversal of Democracy is to be understood.

Most simplifiers of this postwar period tend to explain 1920 by reiterating that the people were tired of the war and its many governmental controls and restrictions and were craving a return to normalcy, to use the gauche word of Warren Harding's that became the destructive shibboleth by which the American public was led over the peak and down the hill to the valley of the Great Depression. To deny the existence of an almost abnormal desire to "settle down," on the part of the returning veterans as well as the civilian population, would be as silly as it would be to deny the existence of a strange restlessness among a people who had been wrenched from their usual way of life. But this does not go far enough. It does not explain how the war weariness, the craving for peace, and the restlessness were *used* by those imponderable forces then striving to gain supremacy over the people of the United States.

And they were "used," in the most disagreeable sense of that word. Senator Lodge, who may fairly be called the mouthpiece for all that was reactionary in American thought, stated with his usual bitterness the simple means by which the propertied interests of the country conspired, regardless of the resultant cost in human misery, to obtain a stranglehold on the national life. He announced the formula at Chicago, when he said: "Mr. Wilson and his dynasty, his heirs and assigns, anybody who with bent knee has served his purposes, must be driven from all control, from all influence upon the government of the United States." He was there referring not only to the Wilson of the League of Nations but also, and even more diabolically, to the Wilson of the New Freedom — the Wilson who, however inadequately, had struggled up to the very eve of war to bring about those national reforms which Theodore Roosevelt had talked about and which Franklin Delano Roosevelt was to turn into a program for national regeneration twelve years later.

Day by day, throughout the eight years of his administration, men like Lodge and Harvey had sneered at Wilson's penchant for political, economic, and moral reform. His Scotch stubbornness and his Presbyterian unbendingness, his seemingly cold personality, his suspicious and sometimes jealous nature, all helped make him the ideal whipping boy for those hungry politicians and profit-mad industrialists who rallied, in 1920, around the banner of Republicanism. They despised Wilson and all he stood for; and since they controlled the great avenues of public opinion, they were able to turn their hatred to good account. The wave of hatred for Wilson was inspired and fostered by the industrialists who recognized in Warren Harding a man who, as an average

American citizen worshiping at the shrine of success, would allow no harm to befall the gods of his little faith.

Under the direction of these interests it was not difficult to spread spite and hatred for the President they held responsible for America's entering the war and who, they now charged, was desperately trying to abandon national sovereignty for the mongrel flag of an alien League. With deliberation they stirred up what William Allen White has called "that witch's pot of mad malice" whence "rose the stench which produced Harding's election and became the Harding administration." Evil representatives of the great financial and industrial interests — the potential fascists of that day — did not need to creep through the night and meet in stealth to plan the theft of the nation from the people and turn Wilson into a scourge for this dreadful purpose: as individuals they rose simultaneously to protect their unregulated power and profits.

Woodrow Wilson had played into the hands of his enemies when he had asked for a "solemn referendum" on the issue of the League at the national election of 1920. It was the ill-advised but honorable gesture of a hard-driven leader who was willing to sacrifice his own life for the only means he knew for the preservation of peace. These enemies still felt and feared the integrity of the gray man who sat in his wheel chair in the White House recovering from the grim and wasting effects of his almost triumphant tour of the nation when he had brought his great plea for the League home to the people. Worn though he was and close to physical abdication of the Presidency though he may have come, Woodrow Wilson was not a figure to be taken lightly on the eve of the Democratic National Convention. His strength could not be counted, his hold upon the people could not be measured, in ordinary terms.

If Wilson's status was an enigma to the Republicans it was an equally unknown quantity to the Democrats themselves. Haunting the minds of the leaders of both parties was the specter of the gaunt President who, so they dreaded, might seek personal vindication at the polls. He was no respecter of precedent, as they well knew. Would he dare go to the people and ask them to return him a third time to the White House to finish the important business which, as he charged, a recalcitrant minority in the Senate had temporarily delayed?

This dangerous question had arisen for the first time early in the year and had caused much excited speculation. The *New York World*, which was rightfully regarded as President Wilson's semiofficial mouthpiece, had endeavored to minimize the rumors. In a strong editorial Frank Cobb, the *World's* great editor who had unchallenged access to the White House up to the time of Wilson's illness (when the doors were barred to even closer friends), declared: "All the new and pressing questions growing out of the War, which ought to be decided at the next election, would be submerged. No matter how the campaign began it would end as a conflict over the third term. . . . Wilson needs no third term nomination. He needs no vindication. . . . Let the record stand."

The editorial, of course, was written before the final Senate defeat of the Treaty of Paris which came in March. In the minds of many eager supporters of the League — and perhaps in his own mind — Wilson now needed vindication and, as many reasoned, this could only be achieved by a sweeping victory at the polls. Wilson had already placed himself on record as saying that the paramount issue would be the League. Indeed no other issue seemed to interest him at all. But he maintained a complete silence on the subject and the third-term threat was only a vague rumor as summer approached.

If the polls of the *Literary Digest* indicated any definite trend they showed a strong undercurrent in favor of returning Wilson to the White House. Early in June the magazine reported Wilson in second place. Leading the race at that time was Wilson's son-in-law, William Gibbs McAdoo, who had been Secretary of the Treasury until January 1919. The Treasury portfolio had given him great political power, his heading of the war bond drives had brought him wide contacts throughout the country, and the rank and file of the railroads, which he had managed during the war, were behind him. The lowest on the list was James M. Cox, Governor of Ohio, who up to this time had manifested little public interest in the League, although his progressive program in that pivotal state had attracted national attention.

The *Digest* published the results of its preconvention poll on June 12. The convention was scheduled to start on June 29. In between those two dates the favored *World* printed an exclusive interview with the President. What the President had to say to

Louis Seibold, the veteran political reporter, was of far less importance than Mr. Seibold's own word picture of the Chief Executive who, rumor had it, was a virtual prisoner in the White House. Seibold painted a glowing picture of the President's recovery from his protracted illness: he had gained twenty pounds in weight, his hand was so steady that he could sign documents "with the same copperplate signature" as of old, his humor was good, and he was working as hard as ever at his daily tasks.

To most observers of that day the interview was an open bid on Wilson's part for restoring public confidence in him. The friendly *New York Times*, whose publisher Adolph Ochs had pledged his paper to an undying espousal of the cause of international co-operation, asserted the day following the *World's* undoubtedly inspired interview that the President "had thrown his hat into the ring, not necessarily as a candidate but as the titular leader of the party." The interview and the *Times's* comment appeared eleven and ten days respectively before the Democrats were scheduled to convene in San Francisco, and in spite of the *Times's* cautious phrase regarding the possibility of a third term, they renewed the buzzing rumors that had not been stilled throughout the winter.

Further confusion was introduced into the ranks of the Democratic politicians by the announcement, on the afternoon which saw publication of the *World* article, that McAdoo would not seek the nomination. It was at once assumed that he had withdrawn in favor of his father-in-law, but this brought a quick denial from McAdoo. Wilson sat sternly silent. And the delegates began moving towards San Francisco, most of them in a strangely wondering state of mind.

Shortly before he departed for the Coast, Senator Carter Glass met Dr. Cary T. Grayson, the President's physician, and heard from the Admiral the alarming news that Wilson "seriously contemplates permitting himself to be named for a third term." The good doctor was disturbed. He realized that the exertion of campaigning would probably result in Wilson's death. Grayson begged Senator Glass to do everything in his power to restrain the convention from nominating Wilson. The President's faithful secretary, Joe Tumulty, also approached the Virginian with a similar warning. Postmaster General Burleson, too, had reason to believe that Wilson deeply desired the nomination.

Whether Wilson, huddled under his shawl in the stillness of the White House porch, actually hoped that the lightning would strike him for the third time or not, there was no doubt that he intended to remain the head of the party and that he expected *in absentia* to control the convention. He had made no statement and he had done nothing to squelch the rumors that he expected the convention to name him by acclamation. Such an action would be a complete vindication of his administration; it would show that he still had his grip on his party, and that the party was solidly behind the League. He could of course then decline the nomination and with a word dictate the choice of his successor.

But to whom would he give his blessing? Ten days before the convention opened he had told Senator Glass that his Red-baiting Attorney General, A. Mitchell Palmer, would make "a good president but a weak candidate." In the same conversation he had dismissed the candidacy of Ohio's favorite son, James Middleton Cox, then in his third term as governor, as a "joke." Even to as close a friend as Senator Glass he had kept quiet regarding his own son-in-law, McAdoo. At the last moment he had called several of the party leaders to the White House for conferences. For two hours he had gone over Homer Cummings's keynote address, suggesting many changes, until it expressed his own policies almost as well as if he had written it himself. At this session he expressed no preference for any of the avowed candidates and he let Cummings go without any impression that he himself sought the honor. With Senator Glass he discussed the proposed planks on foreign policy — the subject nearest his heart — and he prepared certain memoranda for the committee's guidance.

During these last hectic days Bainbridge Colby, his Secretary of State, was a frequent visitor. At Wilson's own suggestion Mr. Colby had broken with precedent and maneuvered his own selection as a delegate from the District of Columbia; and Wilson passed the word around that he would be very pleased if Mr. Colby were chosen permanent chairman of the convention. Bainbridge Colby was Wilson's agent, sent to the Coast to do his Chief's bidding. Through him the President expected to maintain control. No Senate oligarchy, no combination of bosses, was to direct the delegates, as they had the Republicans in Chicago. Whether Colby left with instructions to bring Wilson's name before the convention at the proper time, and in such a way that the delegates would be stampeded in his behalf, is a question that has never been answered.

On came the delegates to the Golden Gate — frock-coated Senators from the Deep South, their carpetbags bulging with forbidden bourbon; the big bosses from the North and East — Murphy of Tammany Hall, Brennan of Chicago, Taggart of Indiana; and the small fry, quivering with indignation at the Eighteenth Amendment and shivering with fear that their eight years' reign was over. What did such men care about such distant problems as the fate of Armenia? Why should these big fellows of Irish ancestry be loyal to Wilson, who had refused to "let" Ireland into the League? The New York delegation hated Wilson and was determined to vote to the end for Governor Al Smith, to the stirring tune of "The Sidewalks of New York." Senator David Ignatius Walsh, perennial bachelor and perennial junior Senator from Massachusetts, came with anger and orders to soften up the League plank as best he could.

In the summer of 1920 a disunited Democratic Party had considerably degenerated from the high ideals to which Woodrow Wilson, the father of the New Freedom and the great War Leader, had dedicated it. In the hectic days of 1912, it had, perhaps for the first time since the Age of Jackson, brought workers, intellectuals, the urban middle classes, and the Western farmers into a semblance of directed progress. Now these heterogeneous groups felt less than allegiance to the party. War weariness and chafing at controls were not exclusively Republican reactions. Liberals were disgusted with Palmer's Red scares and fascist raids. Radicals rebelled against Wilson's own harsh rejection of revolutionary Russia. Many a stanch Democrat, by no means isolationist in thought, wondered if Wilson were not too greatly absorbed with Europe and too little with the problems of the home front.

The Republicans had gone to Chicago seeking power; the Democrats now came to San Francisco hoping to preserve it. But there was no real leadership to guide them. Wilson was a ghost and there was no other great man available to lead the Democrats — or democracy. Bryan was politically dead; McAdoo had been called the Crown Prince too often; the rest were little men — almost as small as Harding. The reactionary leaders of the

Solid South, the Bryan "drys," and the anti-Wilsonites of the Northern machines, scrapping among themselves to dominate the party, added to the disunity that prevailed on the bright morning of the twenty-ninth of June.

Ten thousand persons filled the great hall in San Francisco when Homer Cummings of Connecticut brought the convention to order. The banging of his gavel was the signal for the unveiling of a huge, flag-decked, and illuminated portrait of Woodrow Wilson. At once the delegates and the visitors burst into a noisy demonstration that lasted for twenty minutes. But, as the paraders pushed their way through the aisles, the Tammanyites sat significantly silent, refusing to pay tribute to the man they had never liked. Suddenly one stocky, tall, handsome fellow jumped up, swinging his fists. He wrested a New York banner from its glowering guard and fought his way into the milling crowd. His name was Franklin Delano Roosevelt, Assistant Secretary of the Navy. But he was alone and hardly from the sidewalks of New York.

This early demonstration for Wilson convinced nobody but Bainbridge Colby that it had political significance. Colby, however, was sufficiently impressed to rush a message to the White House declaring that, unless he were expressly forbidden to do so, he would present Wilson's name for nomination "with the certainty that the convention would draft him to head the ticket." The President was moved. But some innate caution forbade him to act upon the suggestion at once. He sent word to his close advisers, at least two of whom were members of his cabinet, to discuss the proposal and forward him the results. The message from the White House shocked them. Colby had consulted with none of them before he made his plea. Behind the locked doors of a hotel room Josephus Daniels, Secretary of the Navy, Newton D. Baker, Secretary of War, Senator Joe Robinson, and Carter Glass faced the embarrassed Colby.

"I never saw more indignation and resentment in any small gathering," Daniels said. "We knew that Wilson's physical condition would not make his candidacy advisable, and moreover we were all agreed that Colby had misinterpreted the attitude of the delegates." The little group, all of whom were 100 per cent loyal to Wilson, knew that if the President were encouraged he would accept the nomination, even if it killed him. They sent the White

House a jointly signed message saying that they, who were on the spot and knew the situation, felt that Colby's suggestions should not be carried out. Wilson bowed to their judgment and the issue of the Third Term died, then and there.

As was to be expected the keynote address, delivered by Cummings, dealt mainly with the issue on which Wilson had asked a solemn referendum. He traced the Covenant's history and recalled how vigorously and successfully the President had met at Paris the criticism of the Republicans, rewriting important sections to please them. He denied the charge that Wilson was opposed to modification of the Covenant — it was "nullification" to which he objected. A militant speaker, Cummings dwelt at length on the theory that Wilson was a great martyr for a great cause; that, like Lincoln, Garfield, and McKinley, he had been "physically wounded" by his foes. He scored a forensic victory when he termed the Republican platform a "masterpiece of evasion" (which it was); but his greatest hit came when he called the roll of the twenty-nine nations that had already joined the League and asked if his listeners wished to hear the list of those who had held aloof.

"Yes! Yes! Tell us!" came in a roar from the floor.

"Revolutionary Mexico, Bolshevist Russia, unspeakable Turkey — and the United States!" [1]

Although there was no Senate cabal functioning in San Francisco after the fashion of Lodge's group at Chicago, Senator Robinson was able to muster enough support among his colleagues to defeat Bainbridge Colby for the post of permanent chairman. Carter Glass, President Wilson's other chosen emissary, was however picked to head the committee entrusted with the drafting of the platform. This was to prove a difficult and disheartening assignment. Many important questions were crying for a solution, questions that were traditionally up to the Democratic Party to answer: jobs, the high cost of living, the farm crisis, the railroads, social reform. But none was to be allowed to transcend the League of Nations. On the committee were some members who had no idea of allowing the distant Wilson to dictate to them. Against

[1] Revolutionary Mexico joined the League of Nations on September 8, 1931; unspeakable Turkey joined on July 18, 1932; and Bolshevik Russia on September 18, 1934. The United States of America, whose leadership at Paris in 1919, through Woodrow Wilson, made the League possible, never joined.

these Carter Glass was to wage valiant but far from successful battle.

The committee began their deliberations at seven-thirty in the evening. Throughout the night loud voices rose in anger from the locked rooms as the wordy and protracted struggle wore on. Most vehement was Senator Walsh of Massachusetts, who had aligned himself with the "near-irreconcilables" in the Senate fight against the League and who was now demanding a face-saving clause in the League plank. Others wrangled over the Irish question, over the party's stand on Prohibition. At three-thirty in the morning the committee turned the platform over to a committee of nine to put the League plank in final form. They finished it barely in time for the opening of the session that morning.

The result was by no means a victory for Woodrow Wilson. It praised him for his "courage and high conception of good faith"; and the words of its preamble were to have a poignant ring of truth twenty-five years later: "The Democratic Party favors the League as the surest, if not the only, practicable means of maintaining the permanent peace of the world and terminating the insufferable burden of great military and naval establishments. It was for this that America broke away from her traditional isolation and spent her blood and treasure to crush a colossal scheme of conquest." But the platform did not go all out in support of the League as President Wilson wanted it. "We advocate the immediate ratification of the Treaty without reservations which would impair its essential integrity, but" — and here was the voice of Senator Walsh, the Democratic colleague and partner of Henry Cabot Lodge — "we do not oppose the acceptance of any reservations making clearer or more specific any of the obligations of the United States to the League associates."

The rest of the platform was a distinct disappointment to those who had hoped the Democrats would show some brave signs of national leadership in contrast to the cowardly straddling indulged in by the Republicans. Obviously the party leaders, men like Joe Robinson, Glass, Cordell Hull (then a Representative), Vance McCormick of New York, Baker, Burleson, Cummings, or Colby — lacked the vision and courage to offer a domestic program designed to counteract the complacent falsity of Harding's "normalcy." Almost as darkly as at Chicago the shadow of Big Business fell over San Francisco. Neither labor nor the farmers were

45

offered anything beyond that dreamed up in Chicago. The praises of the administration were loudly sung in the document; the shades of Jefferson and Jackson were bowed to; the Republicans were called the root of all evil and the Democrats the fountainhead of all wisdom. In other words, the platform was a platitude, the suicide note of a great party about to do away with itself.

With a diplomatic forbearance he had not always shown in recent months, President Wilson hailed the platform, in spite of its shortcomings, as a declaration of conquering purpose which nothing could defeat. But he made no indication as to his choice of the man he hoped would carry this platform to the people. His innate sense of the proprieties kept him from speaking in behalf of his son-in-law, who had withdrawn his withdrawal and entered the convention the odds-on favorite.

After the usual nominating and seconding speeches, which brought twenty-two candidates into the open, the Democrats, hampered as always by the two-thirds voting rule, settled down to the dreary business of balloting. Besides McAdoo there were, at the start, three leading contenders. These were Attorney General Palmer, Cox of Ohio, and Governor Alfred E. Smith of New York. Although each had considerable strength, none could command enough delegates to indicate that he would be able to leap the two-thirds barrier earliest in the race.

In the meantime Edmond H. Moore, manager of Governor Cox's forces, had been developing his strategy with a political shrewdness worthy of a true son of Ohio. He was aware of the political unfriendliness that existed between those two ambitious men, McAdoo and Palmer, and knew that they would never join forces to break the inevitable deadlock. With this in mind he worked indefatigably to win delegates bound to go along in the early stages with one or the other of the two leaders, and he received many promises that, when the proper moment came, these men not only would themselves swing to Cox but would bring others with them. Moore's wide acquaintanceship and what Cox later called "his forthright method of dealing with men" stood him in good stead. The Ohio Democrats had come in force to the convention in a special train. The official delegation itself was packed with influential politicians like Judson Harmon and Senator Pomerene, and the swarm of nondelegates who had wide professional and business acquaintanceships which they put to good use.

The first ballot saw McAdoo and Palmer leading, with a difference of 10 votes between them. Cox, with 134 votes, was in third place. Smith, with 109, was in fourth, John W. Davis and Carter Glass, both of whom stood high in the betting as dark-horse contenders, received 32 and 26½ votes respectively. There was little material change until the tenth ballot. Then Cox moved ahead of Palmer, and on the twelfth ballot he stood ahead of both Palmer and McAdoo. The fifteenth ballot saw New York casting 73 votes for Cox and only 17 for McAdoo, and New Jersey casting her 28 for Cox. Things went along in an indecisive way until the thirtieth ballot, which saw McAdoo again swing into the lead, with 3 votes more than Cox corralled. The McAdoo drive was on. At the same time the anti-McAdoo forces burst into a derisive song — "Every Vote Is on the Payroll" — directed at McAdoo's "machine." This apparently had some effect, for McAdoo began to slide, losing votes on every ballot. When the thirty-ninth roll call was taken Cox had gained 82 votes over the preceding ballot, and again was in the lead with 468 votes. This was the turning point. Palmer slid downwards rapidly, but, as Moore had expected, practically none of his votes went to McAdoo. Cox picked up many; enough, in fact, so that on the forty-second ballot he was within four of a majority. The McAdoo forces vainly sought an adjournment, but the delegates, sensing that the end was near, voted the proposal down. Cox moved ahead. On the forty-fourth count, Cox won Colorado and Connecticut tried to swing to him, but before it could do so a delegate from Kansas got the floor and moved that Cox be declared the unanimous choice for the nomination.

There were obvious reasons, besides those of political commitments made on the convention floor and in the hotel lobbies, why the delegates settled on Cox to break the deadlock. Although as governor he had backed the administration of Woodrow Wilson, his name had never been closely identified with Washington. Although he had spoken in behalf of the League of Nations, he had avoided any real part in the bitter quarrels of 1919 and 1920. His stand on this question was less out in the open than Harding's. Harding, at least, as Senator had spoken and voted against the League at every turn with the bitter-enders. On the question of

Prohibition, already becoming a disturbing political issue, Cox's record as governor was such that he neither scared the "drys" nor worried the "wets." And his history as a "progressive" indicated that he could be counted upon to carry on in the White House his conception of what Irving Stone has called "the Democratic ideal of liberalism and government for the people." Because of these more or less intangible assets Governor Cox won the support of those many Democrats who, as Josephus Daniels blandly put it, "were anything but Wilsonian." And these included nearly all the political leaders and bosses from the big cities with their huge populations of diverse strains. Few if any of these hard-bitten politicians had any reason to suspect in June 1920 that James M. Cox would go "all out" for Mr. Wilson's League.

Governor Cox received the good news in Dayton shortly before five o'clock in the morning. He was about to retire (it was only 2 o'clock in San Francisco) when he received a telephone call from the exultant Moore, asking him his preference for Vice-President.

> I told him [Cox writes in his autobiography] I had given the matter some thought and that my choice would be Franklin D. Roosevelt of New York. Moore inquired, "Do you know him?" I did not. In fact, so far as I knew, I had never seen him, but I explained to Mr. Moore that he met the geographical requirement, that he was recognized as an Independent and that Roosevelt was a well-known name. I knew that his relations with the organization in his state were not friendly. With a small anti-Tammany group, he, as state senator, had voted against the Democratic caucus nominee for United States Senator, William F. Sheehan. This made it necessary for Mr. Moore to consult Charles F. Murphy, head of New York's organization, explaining to him what had moved me to this selection, but saying that if it were offensive, we would abandon the idea and go to Edward T. Meredith of Iowa. Murphy had gone to bed but Moore delivered the message. I can quote Murphy's exact words: "I don't like Roosevelt. He is not well known in the country, but Ed, this is the first time a Democratic nominee for the presidency has shown me courtesy. That's why I would vote for the devil himself if Cox wanted me to. Tell him we will nominate Roosevelt on the first ballot as soon as we assemble."

Mr. Roosevelt knew nothing of all this. The story of his nomination has been so badly bungled by biographers in the last few years that I think it appropriate to put in the record the exact facts.[2]

Although others — David R. Francis, Governor of Missouri, and J. Hamilton Lewis of Illinois — were also nominated for this post, the delegates listened to the plea of Joseph E. Davies, a delegate from Wisconsin and later the first United States Ambassador to the Soviet Union, who said: "Progressive Democracy believes that the battle is to be fought in the East and in the West; we believe that under such circumstances you must have a man equal in vision, equal in conservative capacity, equal in outstanding vision to the head of the ticket." The other candidates, seeing the trend, withdrew, and at Governor Francis's suggestion, Franklin Delano Roosevelt was nominated by acclamation.

The reaction of the public to the nomination of Cox was perhaps best expressed by Speaker Champ Clark, who said: "He was the best of the lot." Old Marse Henry Watterson, who had never really liked Wilson, was overjoyed, and urged the editors of his *Courier-Journal* in Louisville to "get on the bandwagon, boys." Like many another Democrat of the old school who mistrusted Wilson he felt the time had come for a change — within the party. McAdoo and Palmer were too close to the outgoing administration; Cox was not. He would be a good substitute for a man who, so Watterson and many others now felt, was "too much the doctrinaire, too much the humanitarian, too much the phrasemaker." Marse Henry at least saw in his fellow editor and publisher "a man of sense and judgment" who was a'yearning for "normalcy," and those not blinded by Wilson's greatness saw in Cox (whom Boss Joe Cannon had once said would make "a damned good Republican if he weren't a Democrat") a safe and sane liberal, a man of ordinary antecedents and beliefs, who could be trusted. As Ned McLean, Warren Harding's wealthy Republican friend, said, "The interests of this country will be safe in his hands." McLean's conception of the country's interests, it need hardly be pointed out, was not quite the same as that of the common man.

[2] James M. Cox, *Journey Through My Years*. New York, 1946, pp. 231–233.

In Republican circles a great deal was expected of Cox in the forthcoming campaign. The leaders of the party were not at all sure that Harding could defeat him.

As for the public reaction to Roosevelt: it was believed that his name was political magic and would far outshine that of Calvin Coolidge, the twangy Vermonter fresh from the golden dome of the Massachusetts State House.

CHAPTER FOUR

Democracy's Forgotten Man

SHORT, stocky James Middleton Cox, an energetic dynamo of a man, had just turned fifty years old when he was nominated for President of the United States on the forty-fourth ballot by the Democrats at San Francisco. At first glance, it would seem he was an ideal choice in this year of second-raters to meet on even ground the choice of the Republican Party. On the surface the two men had much in common. Not only were they both natives of the state of Ohio, which already had given six Republican Presidents to the nation, but in many respects their careers ran in parallel lines. Each had taught school, each had climbed the ladder to success in the newspaper business, and each had devoted several years to the "service of the public." But there the likeness ended.

If Governor Cox was scarcely better known outside his native state than Senator Harding, what little that was known about him, from almost every point of view, was far more favorable. Of the two men he was mentally and morally the superior. Unfortunately he did not "look like a president," although many persons, seeing his picture for the first time in the newspapers, had an uncomfortable feeling that they had seen him before. He had the build of Napoleon but photographically, with the sun on his spectacles, he looked vaguely like Theodore Roosevelt. Even this slight resemblance did not make him seem like a crusader or a man on a white horse. Behind his unprepossessing exterior, however, there were honesty of purpose and intellectual integrity, characteristics alien to Warren Harding.

At heart Cox was a mild liberal and a progressive, as those terms were measured in 1920. He had an understanding of the needs and aspirations of the common man and through the years he had acquired a political philosophy that might have served the country well had the fates decreed that he be President. But, in all honesty, he was still a second-rater whose character shone brightly only in comparison with a man like Harding. He was not brilliant. He was neither an original thinker nor a political innovator. To a great extent he was an individualist of the rugged type so common to his generation. He abhorred any hint of violent or purposeful change; and, a self-made millionaire, he detested "socialism" in any form. Although he was far more widely read than Harding and much more sophisticated than the editor from Marion, James Cox also had passed his life in a limited and provincial field.

James M. Cox best expressed his political beliefs when he said: "I sympathize with Jefferson's view that that is the best government that governs least — but in this age I consider that also the best government is the one that concerns itself most with the betterment of its people. Government must be a great living organism devoted to pushing the masses up the grade." A writer of punchy editorials and vivid news stories, Cox was no stylist; but seldom did he descend to the verbal gaucheries that the bombastic Harding delighted in. Developing his neo-Jeffersonianism further, Cox wrote for the *Forum:* "Government is merely a forum for mass action, and through government we can teach, inspire and set the example . . . no government is worth its salt that is not supremely concerned with the betterment of its people." He was convinced, also, that "the thought of the country is predominantly and decisively progressive." In November he was to be decidedly disillusioned on that score.

James Middleton Cox was a son of the Valley of Democracy which had gone all out for Andrew Jackson in that forgotten era long before Ohio became the birthplace of Republican Presidents. His grandfather, a New Jersey farmer, had trekked by covered wagon to the West and built with his own hands his meager house at Jacksonburg. Neither he nor his son became prosperous, nor did they hand down to the grandson a love of the soil. Jimmy's earliest ambition was to be a storekeeper. His mother was a devout Methodist who imparted her own strict ethical values to her son. She apparently played an important part in forming his character.

At school in Middletown, which he entered when he was fifteen, the boy was a good student. He lived at the home of a brother-in-law who published the local weekly newspaper. There he, as did Harding, early "got printer's ink in his veins." After two years of schooling he took a job as teacher in a rural school, and for a time helped out in a night school in the village. At the same time he aided his brother-in-law by gathering items for the paper and working around the shop. For two years he stuck to this routine and then he quit as teacher to devote his whole time to newspaper work. To add to his slim earnings he took on the chore of Middletown correspondence for the *Cincinnati Enquirer*.

The first of many journalistic legends of which he was the central figure started before he was twenty years old.[1] Late one night there was a bad train wreck on the main line near Middletown. The young reporter rushed to the scene. Sizing it up as a "big story" he sprinted back to the telegraph office. After rushing through a bulletin to the *Enquirer* he was seized with an inspiration. He knew that other correspondents would want the only line out of Middletown and that by the time he had gathered details of the wreck it would be choked with copy going to every paper but the one he worked for. He thereupon grabbed up an old newspaper and shoved it at the operator with orders to "keep sending" until he returned.

True to the pattern of such legends Cox was offered a job on the city staff of the *Enquirer*. There he lost no time in building up a reputation as one of the most dogged "legmen" the city had known. He seemed tireless in his digging for facts and he made it a point to beat all the other young reporters in town by always arriving first at a crime or fire. But nearly always someone else had to write his stories. He was of that fast-dying breed of newspapermen to whom the story itself meant more than the form in which it appeared in print.

In Middletown young Cox had become acquainted with a wealthy tobacco man named Paul John Sorg who was then serving on the board of education. When the millionaire went to Congress in 1894 as Democratic Representative he took Cox with him as his secretary.

The spring of 1894 was a good time for a young Democrat to go to Washington for the first time. The nation was in the grip of a

[1] This probably is apocryphal. Cox does not mention it in his auto-biographical *Journey Through My Years*. The same story, or a similar one, has been told about many other reporters. Probably it was an invention by his campaign press agents.

depression brought about primarily by the Sherman Silver Purchase Act, the McKinley tariff, and the extravagances of the "billion dollar Congress" that had high-lighted the administration of President Harrison. Grover Cleveland, whose "common sense, rugged integrity, courage, and intellectual honesty" greatly impressed the youthful secretary, would become President the next November. Ohio at that time was represented in the Senate by the immensely wealthy manipulator of the Nickel Plate road, Calvin S. Brice, the very antithesis of Cleveland. Young Cox was startled by the lavish displays of this red-bearded Democratic pirate. He was more taken by the quiet dignity of Richard Olney, who was to be Cleveland's Attorney General and secure the infamous injunction that broke the Pullman strike, and by the solid qualities of Congressman John G. Carlisle, whose common-sense attitude brought him the post of Secretary of the Treasury. But Cox's real hero of this period was then the young Hoke Smith, who brought great enthusiasm along with "traditional Southern liberalism" to the Department of the Interior. These Cox met in the course of his duties; he also could watch in action the giants of Congress — Mark Hanna, Morgan of Alabama, Platt of Connecticut, Aldrich of tariff fame, Hoar and young Lodge of Massachusetts. He did not fall under their spell. Instead he aligned himself, intellectually at least, with the fiery Populists and the Western radicals then making themselves heard. He became aware of the discontent, the demand for reform and the correction of social and economic abuses, that were in the Congressional air. One searches the record of Warren Harding in vain to discover that, even as a young man, he was ever aware of this trend.

Sorg, a Cleveland Democrat, was out of sympathy with the Bryanite elements which captured the Democratic Convention in 1896 and did not run for re-election. He tried to get Cox to continue with him, but the young man decided he would stick to newspaper work.

With $6000 borrowed from Sorg, a little of his own money, and the rest borrowed or raised by the sale of stock, Cox, at the age of twenty-eight, bought the *Evening News*, a rickety newspaper in Dayton, whose major asset was its Associated Press franchise. Housed in a narrow old building, with a twenty-year-old Bullock press, the paper claimed a circulation of 7500, but try as he would the new owner could find only 2600 subscribers. The backing of Sorg, who was a man of wide interests, gave the venture the prestige needed to insure the confidence of enough advertisers to keep it going.

Again true to the pattern of legends of this kind young Jim Cox made a success of the risky venture. He was tenacious and energetic and had grown tough fibers as a police reporter. Along the line he had developed definite ideas about how a newspaper could be successfully conducted. In the beginning he put the paper out with a staff of four reporters and a woman society editor. Often he had to borrow money to pay off the printers at the end of the week. But he loved the work and was determined to prove the worth of his idea. This was simple, and hardly original. Following the tradition of American journalism, he became a crusader.

With much more energy than style Cox pursued, one after another, the petty frauds and grafts of the growing industrial city of Dayton. He quickly attracted attention and as quickly made many enemies. These were just as often in the high places as in the underworld, and more than once they resorted to the invocation of the libel laws in vain efforts to put him out of business. Cox was a fiend for facts: none of the cases ever went to trial and he is said never to have paid a cent in tribute to call his antagonists off. Under such circumstances the *News* began to hold new readers — and with readers came the lifeblood of advertising.

One crusade did more than all others to establish Cox and the *News* as a power in the city of Dayton. In a series of news stories and flamboyant editorials the young editor (who by now could afford a meager staff to help him) revealed that the proposal of a group of Eastern financiers to consolidate Dayton's banks and take over its public utilities would be detrimental to the city's interests. A libel suit for $100,000 was filed against him. A rival newspaper was so certain that this time the upstart had been caught that it announced the forced suspension of the *News*. Cox, however, had made friends as well as enemies. He raised money for his bond and within a few minutes after the appearance of the rival's obituary announcement the *News* was on the street with an extra furnishing further details of the deal.

This victory really put the *News* on its financial feet, for Dayton businessmen began to realize its value to the community. Cox was able to hire the best reporters he could find in Ohio and to turn out a really worth-while product. Like his fellow editor in

Marion, Cox was not averse to accepting gifts of stock from local industries and within ten years he was able to expand and purchase another newspaper, the *Springfield Press-Republic* — which he promptly turned into a Democratic organ.

During this decade of hard-hitting effort James Cox found time to read widely. He was no admirer of either Alexander Hamilton or Edgar Saltus, but he did have a small man's fondness for books about Napoleon. Mostly he read American history and biographies of American political figures. Here again he liked facts; none of his reading seems to have ever given him a passion for the delicate or precise use of words. He was a restless, cocky individual who craved action and enjoyed the limelight his journalistic affrays brought to play upon him. He was a personable young man. His foes were many, but they were mostly political and few were personal.

Although a Democrat, James Cox admired the crusading qualities of Theodore Roosevelt, who led so many liberals astray in the early years of the century. He who had flayed a Wall Street "trust" in his own front yard recognized a political kinship with the man who carried a big stick. He did not, however, allow his admiration for Teddy to lure him from the folds of Democracy. In 1908 he decided to enter politics seriously. He ran for Congress, campaigning by automobile throughout the famous Ohio Third District of Butler, Montgomery, and Preble counties. That was still the era of brass bands and noisy processions. He had a fine time and rode into office with Judson Harmon, also a Democrat, who was elected governor, defeating his Republican and independent rivals by substantial margins.

In Congress his record was distinguished neither by his oratory nor by any legislation bearing his name. His first speech was against the tariff lobby and the Payne-Aldrich tariff bill. Cox came from a traditionally low-tariff region. The fact that industrial Ohio was an exporting district made it easier for him to believe that high duties, as he said, fostered monopolies and gave many corporations outrageous profits and worked hardship on farmers, workingmen, and the consumers. He enjoyed his first term and sought re-election. Because he had managed to slip a $250,000 appropriation into the appropriations bill for the Soldiers' Home near Dayton, he won it easily. His plurality of 10,000 against two opponents made him obvious gubernatorial material.

In 1912 Cox reasoned that Theodore Roosevelt's bolt from the Republican Party would split the vote in Ohio, thus offering an excellent chance for success to a Democrat who stood on a reasonably progressive program. He was right. He was nominated by acclamation at the state convention and on election day gathered nearly twice as many votes as either of his two opponents.

Two years before his election as governor both parties had called for a convention to revise Ohio's outworn constitution. This was ostensibly a nonpartisan affair, but when the convention was called the Democrats had a majority. They were able to put across a wide revision of the document, one which brought many reforms of the courts and gave the state far greater control over the sale of stocks and bonds, private banks, the liquor traffic, and other matters than it previously had enjoyed. Cox spoke widely throughout the state for the adoption of the new constitution, which had to be ratified by a referendum.

Cox based his campaign on the charter and promised legislative reforms to fit its new and liberal requirements. He told the crowds that his administration would stand beside the widely heralded La Follette administration in Wisconsin. A wave of enthusiasm for reform swept the state that year and Cox carried Ohio by 439,323 votes, which was nearly 14,500 more than Woodrow Wilson, who had spoken in his behalf, was able to gather. Once established at Columbus he and a willing legislature put across many of the reforms he had promised.

Perhaps the most important was the Ohio Workmen's Compensation law, which was drafted by William Green, later president of the American Federation of Labor, who was then a state senator from Coshocton. Other reforms were made in the school system, the highway system, the prisons, the laws controlling the sale of liquor, the registration of lobbyists, censorship of moving pictures, pensions for mothers, and the state budget. In 1913 disastrous floods swept the state but in their wake was created the Miami Valley Plan for flood control, which was a sort of forerunner of the New Deal's TVA.

In 1914 a combination of the Ku Klux Klan and Ohio Drys brought about Cox's defeat. This was the year which saw Harding elected U. S. Senator over Cox's attorney general, Timothy Hogan, mostly through the concerted efforts of the Klan, who were determined that no Roman Catholic should represent Ohio in the Senate. Governor Cox's opponent was Frank B. Willis, the political child of the Anti-Saloon League. There were other reasons for his defeat, among them a tax law passed with his approval, another being the Miami Valley Plan which scared the people north of Toledo for it threatened to flood wide areas of land. The liability insurance companies spent what Cox later said were "prodigious funds" because of his sponsorship of the state compensation law. Although labor was on his side he lost to Willis by 28,266 votes.

During these years Cox was a supporter of the policies of Woodrow Wilson. The downward revision of the tariff, the Clayton Act, and the Federal Reserve Acts were features of the New Freedom program which especially met his approval. In 1916 Cox was again nominated for governor. In that year Ohio was a doubtful state. Cox ran behind Wilson in the final returns. His second term saw no new major legislation, for, as the cautious Cox later explained, "Unrestrained reform would soon turn the thought of the state to reaction and the public estimate would be that we were controlled more by caprice than by constructive capacity." In 1918, mainly as a result of his nonpolitical record as war governor, he was elected for a third term, thus becoming the second Ohio governor ever to serve three terms. (The first was Rutherford B. Hayes.) Cox was the only Democrat elected on the state ticket for that year. Both the Congressional delegation and the state legislature went Republican.

Cox thus had a political record that far outshone the questionable history of his opponent. No to-the-last-ditch fighter for reform, he nevertheless had followed a consistently liberal course from the day he had entered politics. His journalistic career far outshone that of the editor of the *Marion Star*. In almost every way he was the superior of the two men striving for the Presidency in 1920.

CHAPTER FIVE

No Place to Go

THE independent voter, appalled at the obvious mediocrity of Warren G. Harding and disturbed by the generally unknown qualities of James M. Cox, was in a dilemma as the Presidential campaigns opened in the summer of 1920. Looking about he found he had no place to go and no one to whom he might turn to register his protest against the job done on him by the two great parties.

The Bull Moose fiasco of 1912 had turned the American public away from thoughts of salvation through a third party. Even now, as the clouds of depression gathered and unrest swept the ranks of workers and farmers alike, no tremors of independent political action were felt underground. Thousands of union workers, banded together under Samuel Gompers's leadership of the American Federation of Labor, had no incentive from on high to make effective use of their quiescent political potency. Neither the old Socialist nor the newly born Communist Party had anything tangible with which to lure the masses to electoral revolt.

For many years the Socialist Party had clung to its patient belief in evolution. Its few thousands of members had followed their quiet dream that someday and somehow capitalism would see the error of its ways and reform. But now its ranks were torn with dissension, the party was split into two warring groups, and its harried leaders were without drive or direction. One of these groups, known as the Militants, tried as best it could to face the realities of the situation confronting the postwar world. Wary of the traditional faith in the ultimate regeneration of the ruling classes, and certain of the inalienable association between capitalism and war, it urged continuously vigorous opposition to the *status quo* on the grounds that without it there was no hope of liberation from destructive exploitation.

Followers of this militant ideology, however, held little authority in the councils of the party. They had been shoved aside first in the crucial year of 1912 by the so-called Reformists, the right-wing element, who managed thereafter to hold a tight check on party affairs. This had resulted in a marked decline in membership — nearly one half — and the ranks had been further decimated in 1917 when schism over support of the United States in the World War had developed.

In spite of its eternal struggles an aura of respectability hung over the Socialist Party. Its leftward moves had never been recognized as a threat to capitalistic stability. The Socialists talked more than they acted. As a party they lacked vigor and had failed for many reasons to draw into their ranks the organized workers or the unorganized farmers, who might have given the party strength. Indeed, to many observers, it seemed in late years to have shunned both workers and farmers; and its followers consisted, to a great extent, of intellectuals and malcontents from the fringe of the two major parties.

The American Socialists more often than not were men and women of fairly recent arrival from the countries of Central Europe, many of whom brought with them the politics of their native lands, and failed to see the dawn of a new day in the Russian Revolution. In 1919, two years after the ten days that shook the world, the Socialist leader, Victor Berger, had denounced the revolution in terms as unequivocal as any uttered by Woodrow Wilson, and had forced a program of isolationism upon the party. Berger and Morris Hillquit joined in a demand that all good Socialists forget the so-called class struggle and concentrate on bringing about reforms in their own back yards. Municipality replaced internationalism as their arena. Indeed, on a national level, there were startlingly few differences between Socialism and the New Freedom which the Republican Party was preparing to bury under a landslide.

The intrigues that went on within the party kept it from functioning on any effective national scale as a minority party. Its polysyllabic debaters turned many a potential protestant away from its doors. So violent were its own disagreements that, in 1919, it was necessary to call an emergency convention in New York in the hope of bringing matters to a head. This meeting developed into a stormy row, and in the midst of the wrangling several dissenters walked out to hold their own convention. Out of this emerged overnight the new Communist Labor Party. To the aid of this splinter group crept all the believers in the use of force as a political weapon. Behind them crept the "Gestapo" of Attorney General Palmer, who had torn up the Bill of Rights at the first flash of red in the western sky.

With unprecedented brutality Palmer drove the radicals underground. So intense was his drive against Reds and Bolshevists, and many innocents who were neither, that the first convention of the new party had to be held in deepest secrecy "somewhere between the Atlantic and Pacific and the Gulf and the Great Lakes." At this the Communist Labor Party moved even further leftward, merging with the Communist Party. They called the child of this union the United Communist Party.

At the tumultuous convention of the Socialist Party the rightists fought determinedly to maintain a traditionally American isolation from all international affiliations. Against their position the leftists who had not broken away brought a powerful assault. In the end they carried their proposal for a rank-and-file referendum on the question of joining the Third International. The referendum resulted in victory for the left wing. The triumph, however, was short-lived. The Comintern rejected the membership of the American Socialists. This rejection pleased the right wing and the party proceeded to nominate its candidate for President. As it had done every four years since 1904, the choice fell on Eugene Debs.

The gentle but militant leader heard the news of his selection in his cell in the federal penitentiary at Leavenworth, Kansas, where he had been sent for violation of the wartime Espionage Act. This was the second time in the long and courageous career of the Indiana-born labor leader that he had been in prison. The first had come in 1894 when he had defied Attorney General Richard Olney's infamous injunction during the famous Pullman strike. At that time he had become converted to Socialism and four years later had formed the Social Democratic Party of America, which, after a series of mergers with other socialist groups, had become the party he now headed. An able propagandist, he had done more than any of his colleagues to keep the cause of Socialism an active, if minor, issue in American life. He now proceeded to conduct his campaign from his cell. Because of the unusual situation he did get his picture into the newspapers, and some few of them — on the theory that he had a "right to think wrong" — printed his statements; but on the whole the press of the country ignored him.

The press also ignored the platform of the Socialists, which was drawn up by the conservative elements of the party. It called the League of Nations a "mischievous organization" (the Socialist *New York Call* went further and said the League, as an issue, was "as vital as a dead cat in a gutter") but it urged immediate recognition of Russia, the signing of the peace treaties, and national opposition to militarism in any form. It castigated both Republican and Democratic parties as enemies of liberty. Domestically its most drastic plank called for the direct election and recall of the President and Vice-President, the selection of cabinet members by the Congress, and the recall of federal judges. Among other reforms which it advocated were the nationalization of all commercial business done on a national scale, a single tax on rental value of land, the payment of war debts by a progressive tax on war profits, and the establishment of a shorter working day by federal decree.

The Socialist candidates [1] garnered the largest number of votes in the history of the party at the November election. But the total — 914,980 of the nearly 26,500,000 votes cast — hardly signified any wide interest in the Socialist program as a means of protest against the conservative trend of the two major parties.

The Communist Party did not count. Not for several years was it to become an appreciable factor in American politics.

Elsewhere there were no leaders to tell the people of the dangers of the trap into which they were being led. The experience of Ray Stannard Baker, who had behind him in 1920 a quarter of a century of liberal thinking, was typical of those Americans who were looking for a place to go. "I attended . . . the convention in Chicago that organized the new labor party," the liberal reporter wrote to a friend. "But it was without constructive leadership. The recent joint convention . . . of the radical groups was a fizzle."

In both the major parties there were a small number of progressive men and women, inheritors of the tradition of the mugwumps who had deserted Blaine to follow Cleveland in 1884 and of the

[1] The Vice-Presidential candidate was Seymour Stedman of Chicago.

Bull Moosers who had gone with Theodore Roosevelt in 1912. They were, for the most part, members of the middle class. Realizing the need for political action a group of them, known as the Committee of Forty-eight, now sent forth appeals throughout the country to gather in Chicago in July.

The first organized group to respond was the Nonpartisan League, which had since 1915 been making noticeable political progress in the corn and wheat regions of the North Central states. In North Dakota the League claimed a membership of 200,000 among farmers. Its enemies, with some truth, described it as an "agrarian soviet"; but more charitable observers recognized it as representative of the more progressive groups which had not already been organized by the labor unions. The League was opposed to private monopoly, in the place of which it advocated public or state ownership, especially of the mills and warehouses to which the majority of its members shipped the sweat of their collective brow. The Governor of North Dakota and the majority of that state's legislature had been placed in office by the League; and in South Dakota, Minnesota, Idaho, and Nebraska it held many legislative seats. Like the Political Action Committee of later years it professed to be nonpartisan. It followed the philosophy of its leader, the aggressive Arthur C. Townley, in offering its support to candidates of either party whom it trusted to espouse its radical views.

Although the leftward fringe of agriculture, as represented by Townley and the Nonpartisan League, responded, labor, as represented by Samuel Gompers and the American Federation of Labor, did not. When the first call for co-operation had gone out the aging cigar maker had forbidden members of the Federation to attend. A few rank-and-file unionists, however, had defied his edict and gone on to the Chicago meetings, out of which deliberations had evolved the National Labor Party. Later it became the Farmer-Labor Party and as such it called a national convention to be held also in Chicago in June.

Filled with hope and a variety of ideas, a motley group of farmers, trades-unionists, small businessmen, and intellectuals flocked to the city determined to draw up a liberal platform and nominate a candidate for President. Most of the strength of this revolt against the two major parties lay among the independent Scandinavian-American farmers of Minnesota, and the agrarian rebels

63

— remnants of the old Populist and Granger movements — scattered through the North Central states. The representation from the East was slight. At the same time that these delegates were descending upon Chicago the Committee of Forty-eight (mainly made up of men and women mildly progressive in their political and economic views and on the whole sympathetic to labor and to the public ownership of utilities and resources) also gathered in Chicago.

The Committee of Forty-eight, dreamers, visionaries, and men of good will, made its appeal to those who were dissatisfied with reaction and resentful of unfulfilled promises, tired of political cure-alls, and yearning for an end to economic chaos, political tyranny, and the madness of competitive armaments — an appeal not too greatly different from that being made by the Republicans. They spoke bravely of the "abolition of privilege," which they defined as "the unjust economic advantage by possession of which a small group controls our national resources, transportation, industry and credit, stifles competition, prevents equal opportunity of development for all, and thus dictates the conditions under which we live."

The Forty-eighters, quite without funds of any effective quantity and lacking control of the organs of public opinion, were not, however, so naïve as to think themselves strong enough to launch a third-party movement alone. After listening to several hours of oratory, the majority of the delegates arose and marched in a body to the near-by hall where the Farmer-Laborites were in equally vociferous session. They were greeted uproariously and welcomed to the fold.

In the meantime the American Federation of Labor had turned a haughty shoulder to the Farmer-Labor convention; and the Nonpartisan League, following the dictates of Townley, its unbending leader, would have no part in the proceedings of protest. Nevertheless, the joint convention went bravely ahead, undeterred by the lack of leadership and the fact that it was, as a later historian said, a loose amalgamation of segments, a unification of disunity. But bravery was not enough.

At these strangely disorganized sessions there were present several who looked for political salvation to the leadership of Robert M. La Follette. They imagined that his national reputation as a fighting liberal and his proved capacities as an organizer might force wide attention to the program of protest they were about to offer. But La Follette would not go along. He wanted to write his own program, for one thing, because he regarded many of the Farmer-Labor proposals as far too radical. He won the opposition of many delegates because, at a time when the Ku Klux Klan was resurgent, he wanted to minimize the Negro question, whereas the delegates insisted upon coming out for complete Negro equality. The labor-minded also pointed out that La Follette, in spite of many prolabor acts in his record, had no deep interest in the cause of the workingman, nor did he countenance the radical demands made for an increasing share for labor in the management of industry. Radical though he seemed to certain Easterners, the renegade Wisconsin Republican skittered away from the Farmer-Labor stand on natural resources and public utilities.

On the whole the platform written at this confused convention turned out to be a singularly democratic document. It stressed the continuing need for the defense of civil liberties; it asked for the immediate recognition of Soviet Russia — and the Irish Free State; it repudiated American imperialism, especially in Mexico; it also urged that the Supreme Court be divested of its power to call acts of Congress unconstitutional; and it advocated public ownership of the railroads and proposed legislation designed to "check the evils of democracy."

With La Follette sulking, the delegates had considerable difficulty in finding someone to carry their banner. Finally they settled on the tall, striking figure of Parley P. Christensen, a genial lawyer from Utah and presiding officer of the convention. He was considered a genuine radical by some of the labor groups, having been counsel for the IWW, and he was acceptable to the Westerners because of his membership on the Committee of Forty-eight. His only opponent was Dudley Field Malone, the New York lawyer. Christensen won on the second ballot.

The Farmer-Labor Party, as the delegates to the joint convention called their organization, stood little chance. Definitely a minority party, it received little publicity in the newspapers, and being without funds it found the going hard when it came to holding meetings and rallies and getting out the independent vote. It was longer on economic lore than it was on political savvy. Its candidate, while a genial and wholehearted man, was a poor orator and writer, who really had no wide reputation in labor history. He managed, however, to poll approximately a quarter of a million votes, mainly in those scattered states where independent political action already had begun. But the Farmer-Labor Party created hardly a stir in the deep waters of political complacency in 1920. It promised no return to normalcy, as Warren Harding did.

CHAPTER SIX

It Was an Earthquake

THE aging and gouty Boies Penrose, who had only a few more months to give to the Republican Party, could always be counted upon to offer the right political advice at the right time. A confirmed cynic, he never minded what he said or whose feelings were hurt by saying it. Propping himself up in bed one day late in June he grumbled: "Keep Warren at home. Don't let him make any speeches. If he goes out on a tour somebody's sure to ask him questions, and Warren's just the sort of damned fool that will try to answer them."

The strategists of the Republican Party heeded the old sinner. Harding went home to Marion to sit on the front porch. There he was to remain throughout most of the campaign, although there were a few frightening occasions when it was deemed necessary for him to go out and let himself be seen. He was carefully nursed and tended by a coterie of great minds whose one purpose was to keep its cigar-store Indian from suddenly coming to life and scaring the daylights out of the people.

There were many good reasons why Warren Harding's best friends did not trust him. Albert Beveridge, who had reached that state of mind where he did not care who became President so long as the League perished, spoke with something of prophecy when he complained that unless Harding "were constantly surrounded by enemies of the League he might backslide from the position of the irreconcilables." Since this election was to be, by Governor Cox's open acquiescence to Woodrow Wilson's plea, a "solemn referendum" on the League, it was necessary to guard the man who "couldn't say no" from the blandishments of his party's progressives who were still attached to the theory of international co-operation. Hardly was the convention over when George Harvey, dreaming of the honors to come his way after

November, went to Marion. Accompanying him was Richard Washburn Child, the bright young man who soon was to escape the gaucheries of the democratic way of life to enjoy the privileges of Mussolini's new fascism. A member of the wealthy Washburn family of Worcester, Massachusetts, Child had been trained at Harvard, graduated into corporation law, and was now an editor of *Collier's Weekly* and a third-rate novelist. Like Harvey's, his assignment was to infuse Harding's statements and speeches with a semblance of meaning, and "so deftly did they employ language to conceal thought, that Harding himself was befogged at times."

The Republicans set up their publicity headquarters in Chicago. They placed Albert D. Lasker, an advertising magnate and expert in the ways of public persuasion, in charge. Child spent much time in the office. Acting as political censor was George Sutherland, British-born graduate of Brigham Young University, whose two terms in the Senate had ended in 1917. Between them they labored mightily to make the man who looked like a president speak and act like a man with the mental capacity for that high office.

The main problem of the Republicans was to keep Harding as quiet as possible, while being all things to all men on the League issue. Further than that all they had to do was to snipe at the ghost of Wilson, drone away at "normalcy," and not let the jibes of Governor Cox get under their skin. The Democrats were on the defensive if not, at the outset, on the run. It is not true, however, that a Republican victory was a foregone conclusion when the campaign got under way in the summer of 1920.

As was fitting, Senator Lodge set the keynote when he formally notified Senator Harding of his nomination. Between blasts of a half-dozen bands of the kind so dear to the heart of the old alto-horn player, and much to the annoyance of the plain folk gathered in and around the Chautauqua Building at Garfield Park in Marion, who only wanted to see and hear the home-town boy, the dapper gentleman from Massachusetts fulminated against the dreadful Wilson and the alien League. The crowd applauded him politely, but saved its cheers for Harding, resplendent in cutaway, striped trousers, and a purple tie, who stood for an hour and a half to deliver an acceptance speech which has gone down in history as a masterpiece of intellectual vacuity.

Mark Sullivan, who was present as a reporter, thought the ceremonies "exalted and moving," and the churchly atmosphere in which they were performed reminded him of something "to do with eternity."

While the nation's foremost political reporters made Marion their headquarters the Boston and New England press generally expended their best adjectival efforts in creating the myth of Calvin Coolidge. To the nation at large he appeared to be a cautious and inconsequential Yankee with a nasal twang who unexpectedly and in a firm voice had defied the Boston police-men's union when its members had gone on strike in a vain effort to obtain economic justice. He was not destined to play a very important or imposing part in the campaign. His dry voice, which uttered monosyllabic platitudes from a puckery mouth, and his chill Yankee manners, did not at once endear him to the populace. Senator Lodge detested him — although he had once supported him — and while Coolidge's stand on labor appealed to the prop-ertied class his mild acceptance of the principles of the League made him suspect to the rest of the Senate cabal.

After one or two abortive attempts to capture the public inter-est Coolidge was kept pretty much in obscurity. He had had a lengthy two-day conference with Harding, but the two men were not congenial. Coolidge's friend and mentor, the aging Murray Crane, Republican boss of Western Massachusetts, in spite of the discouragement of Chicago had not given up hope that the party would not utterly desert the League. He dis-trusted the head of the ticket. Coolidge had never shown any great passion for the League, but he had praised it in his un-enthusiastic way. He made no friends in Marion when, at the prompting of Murray Crane, he reassured those who feared the Republicans were "not proposing to continue our co-operation in Europe in attempting to solve the war problems in a way that would provide for a permanent peace of the world." His method of reassurance was to condemn the League Covenant as "subversive of the traditions and independence of America," and, in the vaguest of terms, to approve "the principle of agreement among nations to preserve peace." In other addresses he mildly defended the Covenant against the charges that it was intended to "create a super-government," and he even went so far as to say that the Republican Party could be depended upon to reject "what is bad" and adopt "what is good," so that the "power of this mighty nation" might be used "to minimize the chance of war and . . . insure, so far as possible, a durable peace." Thus he, like Harding, played both sides of the street.

Calvin Coolidge passed most of the summer posing for the photographers in the hayfields near his father's home at Plymouth, Vermont. He had little to say and the newspapermen enjoyed writing about his Yankee taciturnity. There the legend of Silent Cal was born. When he did speak it was to utter platitudes about individual rights, the national economy, obedience to law, and the sanctity of the home. Towards the end of the campaign he was called out of the hayfields to invade the Solid South with Governor Lowden and other party spellbinders. From the rear platform of the special train he warned the people of Kentucky, Tennessee, Virginia, West Virginia, and South Carolina against "the rising tide of radicalism" and urged them to combat it by voting the Republican ticket.

Meanwhile the "radical" leader of this rising tide, James Middleton Cox, was in a mild state of confusion at his home in Dayton. Now that he had so unexpectedly won the nomination he did not know exactly what to do. In his autobiographical *Journey Through My Years*, written more than a quarter of a century later, Cox takes great pains to show that from the start he had no qualms and intimates that, even if he had not visited President Wilson in the White House, he would have made acceptance of the League of Nations the paramount issue of the campaign. Several of his advisers were opposed to his aligning himself too closely with Wilson, a move they felt was politically unwise. Foremost in this school of thought was Cox's manager, Ed Moore, who stormed mightily when Cox announced his intentions of going to Washington to pay his respects to President Wilson. But Cox was adamant, and when Franklin Roosevelt stopped off at Columbus on his return from the Coast, Cox found the tall, handsome, youthful New Yorker enthusiastic about the plan. Together they went to Washington.

At the White House both were deeply affected by the utter weakness of the gray-faced and shawl-wrapped Wilson, who greeted them from his wheel chair on the portico facing the White House grounds. At the opportune moment Cox said:

"Mr. President, we are going to be a million per cent with you, and your administration, and that means the League of Nations." The President, in a voice scarcely audible, said, "I am very grateful." The two men then passed out through the White House. They paused long enough with Joseph Tumulty, Wilson's secretary, to write out in longhand a statement committing them to make the League the paramount issue in the campaign.

Over the years the impression has grown that Cox and Roosevelt campaigned almost exclusively on the League issue. While they did stress the League and pressed vigorously for its adoption in the event of their election, they did not neglect other matters. Cox particularly was highly articulate in calling attention to the vast sums of money the Republicans were spending. As he expressed it, the Republicans were raising "a campaign fund sufficient in size to stagger the sensibilities of the nation." Undoubtedly it was, for this year they were efficiently organized and they conducted their fund-raising activities with the well-geared practicality of a Red Cross or Community Chest drive. But for all the publicity Cox's speeches attracted, the sensibilities of the nation were not aroused, although in Eastern financial sections, New York particularly, Cox's animadversions on this theme stirred up some uneasiness. His assertions that the money the business interests advanced for Harding was "an investment to be paid back in the form of a license to establish such prices as they wished on their products, protected under a wall of high tariff," did not, however, arouse an apathetic populace.

A great many of Cox's Eastern friends were disturbed by his assaults. Thomas W. Lamont of the Morgan banking firm was not exactly pleased by his continual harping on this embarrassing theme, but to Lamont the League was paramount and he stuck with Cox. But Lamont was an exception. In a year which might well have seen an exodus of League Republicans from the party, there was instead a desertion of principle and thousands of intelligent Republicans, who could not have been fooled by the inadequate Harding, voted for him anyway. George Norris, the liberal-minded Senator, was disgusted with the choice made at Chicago, but on election he, too, placed his mark against Harding's name.

In his notification speech made at Dayton on August 7, Cox was unequivocal in stating where he stood on the League. "The first duty of the new administration will be the ratification of the treaty," he said. "The League of Nations is in operation. The question is whether we shall or shall not join. As the Democratic candidate I favor going in!" Harding already had made it obvious that he had no use for the League, although later he was to jump around so much that it was difficult for anyone to know exactly where he stood. Cox now threw the challenge at him. He accused the Senator of favoring a separate peace, which would disrupt Allied unity, a breach that could never be repaired by any vague "association of nations" such as Harding proposed to supplant the already existing and functioning League. As to the mooted matter of reservations, Cox supported the Wilsonian interpretation of the Democratic platform: "Our platform clearly lays no bar against any additions that will be helpful, but it speaks in a firm resolution against anything that disturbs the vital principle." Later he was to weaken a little on this point but not until it was obvious he was fighting a lost cause.

Thus Cox laid down the lines for what should have been, but was not, a campaign fought on a high level by two personalities on an issue of tremendous importance.

It has often been said that if Cox and Roosevelt had abandoned Wilson the results of 1920 would have been different. This was William Randolph Hearst's contention in the midst of the campaign. Through his chain of newspapers the flamboyant publisher advised Cox to drop the League of Nations and the "Wilson millstone" that was dragging him down to defeat. Similar advice came to him from other sources, particularly the party's leaders among the Irish, Germans, and other "foreign" elements. But for this advice Cox and Roosevelt had only contempt. They believed that in spite of the millstone their stand for progressive legislation, their liberal domestic policies, would successfully act as a counterbalance.

Their over-all intentions were summed up by Cox when he brilliantly generalized: "The house of civilization is to be put in order. The supreme issue of the century is before us, and the nation that halts and delays is playing with fire."

Neither Cox nor anyone else in the campaign put the great issue more clearly or more dramatically than Cox's running mate, who said to his neighbors at Hyde Park:

In our world problems we must either shut our eyes, sell our newly built merchant marine to more farseeing foreign powers, crush utterly by embargo and harassing legislation our foreign trade, close our ports, and build an impregnable wall of costly armaments and live, as the Orient used to live, a hermit nation, dreaming of the past; or we must open our eyes and see that modern civilization has become so complex and the lives of civilized men so interwoven with the lives of other men in other countries as to make it impossible to be in this world and not of it. We must see that it is impossible to avoid, except by monastic seclusion, those honorable and intimate foreign relations which the fearful-hearted shudderingly miscall by that devil's catchword "international complications."

Although many elements of the Democratic Party were not in accord with Governor Cox he was not in as difficult a spot as was Senator Harding. The befuddled Senator was completely dependent upon the orders of his advisers and without a vestige of leadership in his make-up. Thus there was a bitter struggle among his many advisers to get him to accept, if only for a day, their point of view. At one moment he would spout pure Lodge, at another he would sound more like Arthur Vandenberg, the Grand Rapids editor, and again he would whistle the tune of William Howard Taft and hum the words of Elihu Root.

Young, moon-faced Vandenberg, pounding out editorials for the *Grand Rapids Herald*, expressed the viewpoint of the Midwestern Republicans. In an editorial printed before the convention he had come out for a League Covenant so amended as to assure no interference with the protective tariff, the immigration laws, or the Monroe Doctrine. It was after a visit from Vandenberg that Harding made a speech in which he appeared to propose the rewriting of the Covenant so that the United States might join. "The League," he said in one of his most Hardingesque sentences, "can be amended or revised so that we may still have a remnant of world aspirations in 1918 builded into the world's highest conception of helpful co-operation in the ultimate realization" — a phrase which the more able of Harding's translators took to mean that he was not wholly opposed to the League. But hardly had he allowed this blather to evaporate when he blandly announced that the League was hopeless and had "passed beyond the powers of restoration."

It was not until just a month before election that he cleared away the doubts that bothered men of good will. He was forced to do this by the tactics of Cox, who had hammered away incessantly with demands that Harding make his ultimate position clear. Worried by the large and enthusiastic crowds that attended Cox upon his cross-country tour, Harding's advisers packed his bags and sent him off briefly from the isolation of his front porch. Late in August, on one of his jaunts, he had come forth with an idea for a new Association of Nations.

The Democrats were quick to demolish this with a few facts which should have been apparent to whoever had written Harding's speech. They showed it up for what it was, a ridiculous impossibility invented only to befuddle the people even more. There could, of course, be only one Association of Nations — the League. By virtue of Article XX the twenty-three nations had sworn to make no other compacts. Not even a Harding could honestly believe that these sovereign states would abandon the League, which they had accepted without reservations and which was already a going concern, for one dreamed up by an isolationist Senator in the midst of an American political campaign. A month later Harding had to admit that, while he still liked the idea, he was yet "without any specific program" for bringing into existence his Association of Nations.

But even to mention such an idea brought chills to men like Borah, Johnson, and Beveridge, and they went after the hapless candidate with relentless force. While they were firing at him he prepared a speech for delivery at Des Moines, Iowa. Apparently he failed to consult on this occasion with his chief ghost, George Harvey, for the speech was sent to Chicago for distribution. The speech had already gone out to the newspapers when publicist Lasker and manager Sutherland discovered that in it he nearly brought himself to the door of the League. A cry went out for Harvey and Senator Lodge, the speech was rewritten, and when Harding stood up to speak in Des Moines the venom of Lodge came forth. "The Paris League has been scrapped," he said, "by the hands of its chief architect. The stubborn insistence [of Woodrow Wilson] that it must be ratified without dotting an 'i' or crossing a 't,' the refusal to advise . . . with the Senate, in accordance with the mandate of the Constitution, is wholly responsible for that condition."

As to an Association of Nations, it would have to be one that would recognize America's "ultimate and unmortgaged freedom of action," that was certain. He would leave it to consultation with "the best minds" to find how that could be brought about! As to reservations, he said, and he might have been speaking of the entire Covenant: "It is not interpretation but rejection I am seeking."

Joy spread through the camp of Senators Johnson, Borah, Moses, and the rest. They took Harding to their bosom. Johnson went stumping the West, declaring there was nothing ambiguous about Harding, and Borah said he spoke for the entire country because he was "against any international league, association, combination, or alliance of any kind."

Whether wisely or not Cox now felt constrained to modify somewhat his strong Wilsonian stand. He agreed that there might be some honest objections to the League as it stood, and he agreed that there was no objection to certain reservations. But in spite of the criticism leveled at him by the more ardent proponents of the League, his apparent willingness to compromise suggested nothing that might be interpreted as countenancing any change which would annul United States responsibilities under the Covenant or weaken the League as an effective international organization. If President Wilson was disappointed he kept his thoughts to himself.

Harding's Des Moines speech was his most articulate and most forthright of the campaign. Although no one could be certain where this "whirling dervish" might turn next it brought no comfort to those few members of the Republican Party who still vainly clung to the forlorn hope that all chance for international co-operation was not lost. There were still some within its ranks who, like William Howard Taft, saw no reason why they could not have a Republican President and the League of Nations too.

During his Presidency Taft had shown himself to be an internationalist. He had long been an active leader of the League to Enforce Peace. But Taft was also an Ohio politician and a reactionary in almost every way. Like other leaders of his party he was not above playing partisan politics with the peace. He had known and for some reason liked Harding since he first knew him, and it was a foregone conclusion that Taft would support Harding, although it was difficult to reconcile Taft's and Harding's attitude towards the League. Taft, however, found it easy to convince himself that Harding, once in the White House, would support America's belated entrance. Thousands of other Republicans, all over the country, felt the same way. William Allen White received letters from countless progressive Republicans saying that they would vote the ticket in November and have their say later, when they would demand and get specific, progressive performance — or so they thought. Of course, none of these honest men and women knew of the commitments Harding, or Daugherty for him, had made. They did not know that "Bill" White, who had come to Harding's side after his white hope, Herbert Hoover, was eliminated, would be saying a few years later, "If ever there was a he-harlot it was this same Warren G. Harding." They were deluded, as were Elihu Root and other men of affairs who should have been able to read Harding's record more clearly, into believing that Harding would not go wholly isolationist as soon as he was elected. This attitude led Dr. Frank Crane to remark later that Harding was the first President to be "elected in the belief that he will not keep his promises."

Senator Harding, of course, had no scruples and perhaps he had — as Taft reported — promised to make Elihu Root his Secretary of State. With Senator Lodge in the chairmanship of the Foreign Relations Committee the Republicans would then secure ratification of the Versailles Treaty, with the League Covenant modified. The Republicans could thus take credit for bringing about what the hated Wilson and his party had failed to do. Root would then step out and Lodge, who had no hope left of ever securing his party's nomination for the Presidency, could spend his declining years across the street from the White House, directing the nation's foreign affairs.

Very few were the Republicans who, like Thomas Lamont, wept for the fate of "our old party" which had "turned its coat" and bowed down "completely to Borah, Johnson and Moses." Several college presidents, who had long supported the League, tried without success to lead a revolt of the party's intellectuals. Dr. Lowell of Harvard failed to find signers for a petition calling upon Harding to commit himself to a program of action. Dr. Irving Fisher of Yale went to Marion where Harding boldly told him that after election he planned to call a conference of League members and persuade them to agree upon the Lodge reservations as amendments to the Covenant. Dr. Fisher did not think Harding knew what he was talking about. George Wickersham, a leader of the American bar, said that all that was left to a man "who entertains the opinions I do upon international relations, and yet who so thoroughly despises the Democratic Party as I do, is merely to retire to private life and cultivate roses."

In the midst of all this befuddlement and confusion Herbert Hoover, who had at long last cast his lot with the Republican Party as befitted one whom the *New York Times* described as fearful equally of "radicalism, reaction, and the dominance of extremists in government," felt constrained to make his own position clear. Speaking in Indianapolis two days after Harding's Des Moines speech, he said:

"If there be persons supporting the Republican Party today on the belief or hope that this party is the avenue to destruction of this great principle, that the party will not with sincerity and statesmanship carry out their pledges to bring it into effect, then they are counting on the insincerity and infidelity of the Republican Party and its nominee. If by any chance it should fail, it will have made a deeper wound in the American people than the temporary delay in our adherence to the League of Nations. It will have destroyed the confidence of our people in party government, it will have projected us into the dangerous path of party realignment."

Mr. Hoover had much to learn about the nominee and the party of his choice.

Meanwhile Elihu Root became disturbed by the situation and undertook to find a way to salve the consciences of the pro-League Republicans. The author of the party's ambiguous foreign policy plank prepared a statement that, in the words of a later historian, was more worthy of a shyster than of Elihu Root. His only excuse for the remarkable document was political expediency. Its gist was that the Republican Party had long supported international co-operation, but when the party had tried to get the United States into the League (with the Lodge reservations) the way had been blocked by Woodrow Wilson! No matter what Harding had said, he had been for an amended League and would be for it when elected. Therefore a vote for Harding was a vote for the League.

Thirty-one prominent Republicans, including Herbert Hoover, signed the statement. It received wide publicity and undoubtedly had great effect in holding in line many Republicans who, thus deceived, were willing to play with the devil in order to get to heaven.

With commendable courage Governor Cox returned towards the end of the campaign to vigorous defense of the League. Before Irish and German audiences he examined and explained the dangerous Article X, which Woodrow Wilson had always insisted was the heart of the Covenant. But he might as well have been speaking to deaf men; and Republican orators made the most of the situation. The fact that Léon Bourgeois, a framer of the League and the Council's first president, chose this moment to discount the importance of Article X did not help his cause. And shortly before Election Day in Madison Square Garden, New York, Cox departed markedly from the Wilson line when he declared that the United States should assume no obligation to defend other League members "unless approved and authorized by Congress in each case."

In the White House the ailing President closely watched the progress of the campaign. For the most part Wilson kept silent, but shortly after Cox's wobble he issued a statement repudiating those who urged a policy of "defiant segregation" and, to a group of visiting Republican pro-Leaguers, he reiterated his belief in Article X. To the very end, in spite of reports from various sectors that Cox was losing the fight, Wilson believed, as he later told friends, "that a great program that sought to bring peace to the world would arouse American idealism and that the nation's support would be given to it.

"It is a very difficult thing," he explained patiently, "to lead a nation so variously constituted as ours quickly to accept such a program as the League of Nations. The enemies of this program cleverly aroused every racial passion and prejudice, and made it appear that the League would crush and destroy instead of save and bring peace. . . . Now the people will have to learn by bitter experience just what they have lost."

It was, however, not just the passions and prejudices aroused by the League that defeated Governor Cox. They did, however, play a large part. In such states as Massachusetts, Connecticut, Rhode Island, New York, New Jersey, Pennsylvania, Ohio, Indiana, Illinois, and Nebraska the racial line-up was against him. Irish Americans blamed Wilson, and through Wilson they blamed Cox, for refusing to intervene for the Irish Free State. The Italian Americans were not allowed to forget Fiume. The Germans could not forget the war. In the West the Ku Klux Klan fought him. Kansas was not alone in mistrusting him as a Wet. Women, voting for the first time in a Presidential election, associated him, a Democrat, with despicable Tammany Hall.

On the day after the election the *New York Times* explained:

> An irresistible combination of reasons, unreasons, and opponents bore him down. If he had been Jefferson plus Jackson he would have fared no better. Metaphysically speaking, it was not he who was defeated; it was a composite figure of many illusions, legends, errors, dissatisfactions, grudges; a Mumbo Jumbo who represented to some high prices and taxes, to others a certain fondness for slow delivery in Mr. Burleson's department, and so on *ad infinitum*.

In his attacks Cox had shown quickness, wit, and continuous and sharp attack. It is true he never got at the heart of what was wrong with the country, for he lacked the philosophical equipment. He was too old-fashioned a liberal to get deeply beneath the surface. Yet even had he gone deeper it is doubtful if he could have whipped a tired and disillusioned American people to a high pitch of moral indignation. As Irving Stone has pointed out the people were tired: tired from the war, tired from suffering and bloodshed, tired from being geared to the breaking point, tired from the vast expenditures of money, morale, and manpower, tired from eight years of idealism, tired from personal government, tired from internecine wars in Washington. For just a little while they wanted to be let alone, to sleep in the sun, to recoup their energies and enthusiasm.

"It wasn't a landslide," gasped Joseph Tumulty, Wilson's former secretary, when he saw the returns; "it was an earthquake." Warren Gamaliel Harding had carried 37 of the 48 states; 16,152,220 men and women had voted for him and Calvin Coolidge. Only 9,147,553 had cast their ballots for James M. Cox and Franklin D. Roosevelt. The Republican candidates had won 404 of the 531 electoral votes.

It remained for Calvin Coolidge to explain what had happened on November 2, 1920. In 1929 he wrote in his revealing *Autobiography*:

When the inauguration was over I realized that the same thing for which I had worked in Massachusetts had been accomplished in the nation. The radicalism which had tinged our whole political and economic life from soon after 1900 to the World War period had passed. There were still echoes of it and some of its votaries remained, but its power was gone.

It was not to return for twelve long years.

CHAPTER SEVEN

It's *Their* White House

ON THE night of the inaugural reception Mrs. Harding entered the room in the White House where it was to take place and found the servants drawing the shades. They said that this was to keep the crowds on the outside from staring in at the invited guests. With a wave of the hand Mrs. Harding ordered the windows left unshaded.

"Let them look if they want to," said the Duchess, who always insisted the Hardings were "just folks." "It's *their* White House."

Although honestly spoken Mrs. Harding's expression of the democratic spirit was an ironic jest. For it was during the Harding administration that the gates were closed against democracy by those agents of plutocracy and monopoly who had placed Warren G. Harding at the head of the state. In the presence of the Hardings the vulgarity of democracy was to replace the dignity of Democracy that had been esteemed and honored in that mansion during the last eight years.

Poker games played in shirt sleeves by men sipping highballs in defiance of the law of the land, filling the ancient rooms with cigar smoke and raucous laughter, became an almost nightly spectacle in the old house on Pennsylvania Avenue. The soft, paunchy, slouching Harding, his jaw packed with chewing tobacco, presided there over a motley crew. Any night might see him playing for high stakes with drunken Charley Forbes, reckless Senator Brandegee, simpering Jess Smith, thieving Secretary Fall, incompetent Ned McLean, to name but a few of those who were to bring disgrace to the administration.

Cry as the times might for moral and political leadership they were to get mighty little from Warren G. Harding and those whom he selected to help him in his tremendous task. In one of his few recorded criticisms of his successor, Woodrow Wilson came close to the truth when he asked:

"How can he lead when he does not know where he is going?"

If Harding did not know where *he* was going, those who surrounded him had a very clear idea where *they* wanted to go.

The millionaires who had poured $8,000,000 into the Republican trough knew where they wanted to go. The 200 giant corporations and 50 leading financial institutions which controlled America in 1921 knew where they wanted to go. They also knew that neither President Harding, nor Attorney General Daugherty, nor Secretary of the Treasury Mellon would raise an obstacle in their chosen path.

The press of the United States, controlled by these men and corporations, knew that with few exceptions its role was to point with pride and never view with alarm. Its motto was to be "All's right with the world." It was to convince the people that a Golden Era of peace and prosperity had arrived and that if they followed the mandates of Harding, Daugherty, Mellon, and Hoover they could share both.

Secretary Fall and the boys from Ohio — as unsavory a gang of psychopaths and thieves as ever invaded a national capital this side of the Balkans — knew where they wanted to go. And they knew, too, how much to charge others who wanted to go along for the ride. But Fall and Daugherty, Forbes and Jess Smith, and all the rest of the gangsters of this truly "incredible era," were in reality merely symbols of a greater corruption which overtook the country during the next twelve disastrous years. They cannot be ignored by the historians, but their thefts and violences and the sounds of their revelry, so often described in so many volumes, were only coincidental to the abdication of the democratic spirit that was the fundamental crime perpetrated upon the people in these years.

During the campaign Warren Harding had expressed his willingness to be guided by the advice of the "best minds." The phrase had captured the popular imagination. It was remembered when, in the interim between election and inauguration, the President-elect announced his cabinet. Here and there a few cynics were heard to remark that if these were the best minds the Republican Party could offer it had indeed a collectively low I.Q. But such voices were rare and, on the whole, Harding's selections were greeted with editorial praise.

Heading the list and lending it the dignity it sorely needed was Charles Evans Hughes. A tall, dignified, bewhiskered man, his face and fame were both well known to, and respected by, the people. He possessed prestige. He had risen to public prominence through his youthful investigation of the insurance companies of New York. As Governor of that state, as Associate Justice of the Supreme Court of the United States, as Presidential candidate against Woodrow Wilson in 1916, he had acquired the reputation of a statesman. Now, as Secretary of State, the highest office in the gift of the President, he was expected to lend luster to the new administration.

Few people knew it then, but Mr. Hughes was far from being Harding's own choice. If he had had his own way Harding would have given this post to his close friend and Senate associate, Albert Fall of New Mexico. Harding considered this oil-drenched rancher and sheepherder from the Alamo, whose inspired animosity to Mexico was notorious, one of "the ablest of international lawyers." Fortunately for Harding and for the country, Harding was dissuaded from making the appointment, partly by Fall himself, who saw richer fields ahead of him in the Department of the Interior. Harding's second choice was George Harvey. Always faithful to his friends, Harding felt constrained to offer a rich plum to the man who had been one of his closest advisers. But pressure was brought on Harding to give the post the deepest consideration and Harvey was crossed off the list. As consolation he was sent to England to be Ambassador at the Court of St. James's. There, in knee breeches and horn-rimmed glasses, this great diplomat who once stated that "the national American foreign policy is to have no foreign policy," afforded a certain amount of sadly comic relief.

For a time Harding toyed with the idea of living up to his vague half-promises of associating the United States with some kind of World Court. It was planned to make Elihu Root Secretary of State. This elder statesman would hold office long enough to accomplish this purpose. As chairman of the Foreign Relations Committee Senator Lodge would take charge of maneuvering the result through the Senate. Root would then retire and Lodge, who deserved well of his party, would be allowed to spend his declining years as Secretary of State. This scheme, which might eventually have led the United States into the League of Nations — but a League recast by Republican leadership and deodorized of all traces of Woodrow Wilson — came to naught. The conservative and trustworthy Hughes was given the post.

To most of the party's progressives, and even to some liberals without the party, the choice of Herbert Hoover as Secretary of Commerce seemed the happiest of all of Harding's selections. His inclusion in the cabinet, however, did not sit well with many of the party's regulars. Senator Lodge, for example, distrusted his recent conversion to Republicanism after having become world famous as Woodrow Wilson's Food Administrator. Senator James Reed of Missouri was to annoy him on the grounds that he was more British than American. Others recalled that he had expressed himself, even during the campaign, as favorable towards the League of Nations. His well-publicized activities in behalf of the relief of Belgium during the war, however, had endeared him to the vast majority of the people and it was confidently expected that he who had been so great a humanitarian would work towards the welfare of the common man in his new post. Elsewhere his reputation as a great engineer and an astutely successful business-man was welcomed by those who worshiped efficiency.

The least known of all of Harding's cabinet selections was Andrew Mellon, who, in a short time, was constantly to be referred to as the greatest Secretary of the Treasury since Alexander Hamilton. As in the case of Secretary Hughes, he, too, was not Harding's own choice. Indeed, although Mellon was one of the richest men in America, Harding had never heard of the shy, wispy, gray little man from Pittsburgh until he was rather force-fully called to his attention by certain of the party's most powerful figures. For years Mellon had been a heavy contributor to the Republican treasury and a tremendous power in the political-industrial setup of the Pennsylvania machine. He had managed to wrap a veil of silence about himself, his private and public life, and to live in self-imposed secrecy while amassing a fortune for himself and his family. He was head of the aluminum trust, the owner of oil wells, banks, coal mines, distilleries, steel mills, utility companies, and a vast number of allied corporations. If, at the time, America owned a Croesus, it was Mellon. He too deserved well of the Republican Party, if for no other reason than that it was Mellon's bank which had underwritten the party's $1,500,000 deficit.

To such a man even the powerful Boies Penrose bowed in deference and Senator Philander Knox skittered when he spoke. Having decided that he was not now averse to entering public service and helping Harding as one of the best minds, Mellon's men made their justifiable demands upon the President-elect. But since he was unknown to Harding the President mildly objected. Harry Daugherty, however, was convincing when he told Harding that "a man who can quietly make the millions this modest-looking man has gathered in is little short of a magician. If there is one thing he knows it is money." Furthermore, argued Daugherty, if you don't take Mellon you can't have Hoover. Harding was convinced. Later, when the poker cabinet was meeting in regular session, he learned the truth of Daugherty's assertion. Mellon, who had more money than all combined, invariably was the heavy winner.

There was, of course, some commotion when Mellon's name was announced and the extent of his vast holdings was made known. But objection ceased when he blandly offered to resign from his directorates in the vast corporate empire controlled by him. After all, he had nothing to lose in making this gesture towards integrity. His brother could sit in for him. And he did.

Of all the other cabinet selections — with the possible exception of Will Hays, to whom, as chairman of the Republican National Committee, went the traditional patronage post of Postmaster General — only one had real qualifications for his post. Honest, outspoken, and (in his way) a true liberal, Henry C. Wallace of Iowa was probably the most capable man in the Republican Party for the post of Secretary of Agriculture. As such he was not without his enemies both within and without the cabinet. Surrounded as he was by men of whose faults he was too well aware, his life in Washington was to be an unhappy one. But with the passing of the years he stands out, head and shoulders, above the rest of the "best minds."

Redheaded, muscular, gray-eyed Henry Cantwell Wallace was a true son of the Middle Border and a true son of the soil. As editor of *Wallaces' Farmer* and as secretary of the Corn Belt Meat Producers Association, he had long fought for better conditions for the farmers, particularly for fairer freight rates and against

85

packer domination. He was by no means a radical. Few of his projected reforms were directed in behalf of the share-cropper class; the majority were in behalf of the large operators of farm lands. He was a cautious man who hoped, as he said, that "someday we may perhaps find a way. . . ." He dreamed of equality of agriculture with industry and sought not to abolish tariffs, but to make the tariff "effective for agriculture."

Wallace had long distrusted Herbert Hoover and had fought certain of his actions as Food Administrator. He could not understand how Hoover's career as a mining engineer, stock promoter, and administrator of Belgian relief funds fitted him to take wartime control of the production and distribution of American foodstuffs. Wallace had attacked Hoover in the columns of his farm paper, charging him with trying to "bamboozle the farmers" and even, in the matter of hog prices, with "juggling the figures" with this end in view. In 1920 he had refrained from committing his paper to the support of any potential candidate until after the nomination, but he was outspoken in his condemnation of Hoover's "mental bias" against the wishes of the farmers, saying that Hoover was "a typical autocrat of big business . . . able, shrewd, resourceful, and ready to adopt almost any means to accomplish his ends. Farmers do not underestimate Mr. Hoover's ability, but they fear it."

During the campaign Wallace, who had helped draft the Republican farm plank, ghosted many of Harding's speeches touching on the desperate plight of American agriculture; but, evidently not trusting the candidate, he had helped form a group of farmer-politicians into a bloc which would bring pressure upon the administration to "do something" for agriculture after the election. It was mainly at his insistence that, just before he accepted the post of Secretary of Agriculture, a group met at a Detroit hotel to lay plans for 1921 and onward. At this meeting the so-called Farm Bloc, which was to wreak such havoc with the policies of Presidents Harding and Coolidge, had its origin. Wallace went reluctantly to Washington, for he had no great admiration for Harding's weak character. Like other trusting souls, however, he hoped that through experience the Senator from Ohio would grow up to the job of being President.

For Secretary of War Harding chose John W. Weeks, a genial, bluff, former Senator from Massachusetts, who had made a fortune

86

through the Boston brokerage firm of Hornblower and Weeks. A self-made Yankee from Lancaster, New Hampshire, who had been graduated from the U. S. Naval Academy in 1881, he had helped keep the Massachusetts coast inviolate from Spanish gunboats during the war with Spain and had come up in politics in the city of Newton, where he had been both alderman and mayor. He had served in Congress nearly ten years and had been named by the General Court to the Senate on the death of W. Murray Crane. Senator Lodge had nominated him for President in 1916, but two years later the people of his state had retired him in favor of a brash young Irishman named David Ignatius Walsh. An orthodox Republican, Weeks had followed the financial lead of Senator Aldrich; he had vigorously opposed independence for the Philippines, voted against women's suffrage, and become known as the "smiling statesman." As a $100,000 personal contributor to the 1920 War Chest and as one of the leading money-raisers in Wall Street and State Street, he deserved his reward.

As Secretary of the Interior, a post hitherto not regarded as one of the juicier plums, Harding named the man whom he held in highest esteem in the Senate, Albert B. Fall. It has never been proved that an outright deal was made in Chicago by the "oil interests" for Fall's appointment to this post, but likewise it has never been disproved to the satisfaction of impartial historians. During the Teapot Dome investigations Senator Thomas Walsh made every effort to ferret out conclusive evidence, but even if he failed in this particular aim, and even if no deal was actually made, Fall's selection was eminently satisfying to those predatory interests who were looking forward to free enterprise in the nation's oil reserves.

A slight investigation of Fall's past record would have shown his unfitness for the post. He had long been a bitter enemy of conservation, a major concern of the department he was now invited to head. He had defied the government by ranging his sheep in violation of the law over the range of the Alamo National Forest. He was a bad rancher and had gone broke trying to raise sheep. As a Senator his record was not imposing. He spent much of his time and energy trying to stir up trouble with Mexico. He was an old advocate of sending armed American forces across the border to "police" that country in the interests of American oil investors.

He was a jingo of the worst variety. For some reason the handsome Harding admired the ex-judge from New Mexico, who dressed and looked like an old prospector from the plains. Fall had his other friends, and when his name came up before the Senate the impeccable Lodge moved that his name be confirmed without the formality of referring it to a committee. If anyone objected his words were drowned in the applause that arose on both sides of the chamber.

In one of those frequent moments of mental aberration to which he was subject Harding had sought to name Charles M. Schwab, the steel magnate, as Secretary of Labor. He was quickly restrained from making a fool of himself and his party. In Schwab's place he nominated James J. Davis of Pennsylvania, who had once been a steelworker but whose main claim to fame was as Director General of the Loyal Order of Moose. Known as "Puddler Jim," Davis was a believer in "Gomperism," but he was known to be "safe," and since Labor raised no voice against him he was easily confirmed.

Others who added distinction to Harding's administration were Edwin N. Denby as Secretary of the Navy, Richard Washburn Child as Ambassador to Italy, Old Doc Sawyer, the Marion, Ohio, homeopath, as Brigadier General and physician to the White House, and Charles R. Forbes, a hard-drinking adventurer, as Director of the Veterans Bureau.

Surrounded by these men, and others of no greater character, Harding looked upon himself not as leader of party and people, but as chairman of a board of directors. It was his belief, as he took office in March 1921, amid appropriate pomp and ceremony, that government was a simple business that could be run as simply as a corporation. With this attitude he set out to govern a nation just emerging from a war and a depression, a nation to which a still chaotic world was looking for leadership.

At home a number of major problems awaited his attention. A partial list of these show how staggering indeed was the task he had undertaken. Awaiting government action were the problems of waning national finances, unemployment, taxation, immigration, the tariff, the agricultural debacle, the peace treaty, action on the League of Nations or a World Court, relations with Mexico, the Far East, Russia, the regeneration of Germany, the war debts, and the matter of reparations.

Warren G. Harding had no program with which to meet these problems. He turned now for support to the three men in his cabinet who seemed best suited for the heavy chores of government which irked him. To Secretary Hughes he gladly surrendered all leadership in foreign affairs. Abysmally ignorant about finances, he gave Secretary of the Treasury Mellon full reign. Unemployment and kindred matters he turned over to Secretary Hoover. He trusted these men as he trusted those he knew well — Fall, Attorney General Daugherty, Secretary of the Navy Denby, who were the ones to bring disgrace upon his name.

From March 4, 1921, Presidential leadership, in the best sense of that phrase, was unknown in Washington. Harding lacked the capacity to give it; Coolidge lacked the courage or the will; and Hoover lacked the opportunity, although, in a happier time, he might have done so.

The economic and political situation in the United States and throughout the rest of the world cried for positive action by the executive branch of the government in 1921. The agricultural situation alone was enough to distress anyone at all seriously concerned with the national economy. In industrial areas there was widespread unemployment. Business was depressed. Bankers were unhappy. In the very month of Harding's election had occurred one of the worst economic depressions since the 1890's.[1] Although it was to last less than a year, during its peak prices reached new

[1] The economic condition of the United States at the beginning of the Harding administration may be seen from the following facts and figures. The index of all commodities declined in 1921 from 227.9, the 1920 level, to 150.6 (1913 = 100). Farm products and raw materials fell even lower, while the drop in manufactured products was only slightly less. In these two years retail prices, which had not risen as high as wholesale prices, slumped between 12 and 13 per cent. Industrial production, which had reached its high point in the third quarter of 1919, when it was 19 per cent above the 1914 level, reached a low that was only 2 per cent higher than the 1914 figure in the second quarter of 1921. In 1914 price terms, the gross national product was reduced from $40.1 billion in 1920 to $37.6 billion in 1921. Before the depression ended late in 1921, an estimated 4,754,000 persons were unemployed; 100,000 bankruptcies had taken place; and 453,000 farmers had lost their farms. Corn that sold on the farm at $1.88 in August 1919 was bringing but 42 cents by the end of 1921; wheat had fallen from $2.50 a bushel to $1.00 or less. See Frederick C. Mills, *Prices in Recession and Recovery*, N. Y., 1936; Simon Kuznets, *National Product in Wartime*, N. Y., 1945; E. Jay Hovenstine, Jr., "Lessons of World War I," *Annals*, American Academy of Political and Social Science, March 1945; Federal Reserve *Bulletin*, October 1945; and *Yearbook of Agriculture, Washington*, 1928.

high levels and a wave of buyers' strikes swept the country. Prices fell as a result, but employers cut wages to offset the decline in prices, and between five and six million people found themselves jobless. This was the way things were when the smiling Harding entered the White House with the Duchess and Laddie, the dog.

CHAPTER EIGHT

The Willing Servant

THE last of the crowds had hardly dwindled away from peering through the windows of "their White House," and Calvin Coolidge was no more than unpacked in his rooms at the New Willard, when President Harding called the Sixty-seventh Congress into extra session. It was of this Congress that Calvin Coolidge, who presided over it, was to declare:

> It would be difficult to find two years of peacetime history in all the record of our republic that were marked with more important or far-reaching accomplishment.

The Sixty-seventh Congress immediately devoted its attention to the measures that had died by virtue of President Wilson's veto on the eve of his leaving office. One was the tariff; the other, immigration.

The American tariff law had not been revised since 1913, the year which saw the passage of the liberalized Underwood Act as an integral part of Woodrow Wilson's New Freedom. At that time the old standards that had existed since the Civil War had been abandoned and new methods of establishing competitive rates had been devised. Duties had been cut on finished products, a large number of raw materials (including sugar and wool) had been placed on the free list, and simple ad valorem schedules had replaced the old, restrictive specific duties. The Republican Party was pledged to a restoration of "high protection" and the lame-duck session of Congress had tried to beat the gun by passing a measure increasing duties of raw materials. President Wilson, fully aware that the measure would succeed in 1921, had promptly and sternly vetoed it with an incisive and prophetic message. With characteristic sternness Wilson had pointed out that the proposed new rates equaled or even exceeded those of the iniquitous Payne-

Aldrich tariff and that the relief the measure offered the farmers was illusory. With prophetic potency he stressed the fact that our new position as a creditor nation made a liberal policy necessary if our debtors were to use exports to help pay their debts. As Wilson saw it the bill was no "emergency measure," as it was called, but the cornerstone of a permanent and disastrous high-tariff policy, that would "stand in the way of the normal readjustment of business conditions throughout the world, which is as vital to the welfare of this country as to that of all the nations." His warning was ignored.

The special session, as if in defiance, passed another "emergency measure," raising duties on raw materials. Congress was prodded by the new Chemical Foundation of America, founded in 1920 on the confiscated remnants of the huge prewar German dye industry, among other powerful industrial lobbyists.

In the meantime the House Ways and Means Committee, under Representative Fordney's chairmanship, and the Senate Finance Committee, headed by Senator Porter J. McCumber, were recasting the tariff structure, schedule by schedule, and recasting it nearer their hearts' desire.

In the Senate there were few opponents of protection to be found. In neither house was the consumer adequately represented. In the White House was a man who, by his own admission, had little if any understanding of what was going on. Senator Norris, who had come (as he said) to Congress an ardent Republican filled with respect for the "tariff policy of my party," was appalled by the spectacle of "powerful, well intrenched interests" whose agents were enforcing "their demands on members of Congress." He spoke and voted against the measure, but he was almost alone.

Propaganda was spread far and wide through the press in an effort to raise what the fighting liberal from Nebraska called "the fearsome specter of an invasion of American markets by European industry and labor. Nationalism was becoming the most strident note in the world. Tariff walls were thrown up hastily in defense against other tariff walls. Trade was languishing." But the powerful lobbies were, as he said, "out in the open, unabashed and confident."

Under the pressure of these lobbies the threat of competition to the monopolies from abroad was removed with decisiveness. In the tariff act that was soon to replace the emergency legislation the highest rates in American history up to that time were established. These effectively shut out most foreign goods, the importation of which might have brought a domestic demand for reduced prices. Furthermore the American monopolists were quick to become a part of the network of international cartels then beginning to spread, thus bolting the back door of their "economic empire" against attack.

When the Fordney-McCumber tariff came from committee in April 1922, it was seen that the general tendency was to approximate the levels of 1909 and only a few minor items were cut below the level of 1913. In Congress there was but little genuine opposition. A few Western progressives raised their voices and some old-fashioned Southern Democrats grumbled in vain. President Harding signed the act with satisfaction. It was one of the first definite steps down the road to promised normalcy.

Two items of interest were connected with the passage of the Fordney-McCumber tariff. During the Senate discussions Senator Smoot of Utah, representing the beet sugar interests, sought to persuade Cuba to limit its sugar crop by 65 per cent of normal output in return for tariff reductions. "Ultimately the same result was obtained more simply," says a historian of Congress, "by a misleading announcement of the Department of Commerce, headed by Herbert Hoover, which implied that the shortage had already occurred, thereby enabling the sugar interests to raise prices to a point which netted them . . . a profit of $55,000,000 during the first three months." Another "deal" was the raising of the duty upon aluminum houseware for the purpose, so it was argued, of protecting an "infant industry." In America the infant industry, already a lusty one, was controlled by the American Aluminum Company, which in turn was owned by Secretary Mellon and his family. Immediately after the passage of the act it declared an additional heavy dividend. Of even greater significance to the general public was the fact that as soon as Congress had so obligingly raised the duty on aluminum from 2 to 5 cents a pound the Aluminum Company at once jumped the price of the element by 3 cents a pound. Thus the buyer of pots and pans now paid additional tribute into the pockets of their own servant who was already one of the richest men in the land. The Golden Era had surely begun.

As a conciliatory gesture to the public, the ultimate consumer, and perhaps to the consciences of the perpetrators of the act, the Fordney-McCumber Tariff Act established an Advisory Tariff Commission. This was supposed to be a step towards the scientific arrival at rates by trained and nonpolitical commissioners. Under its provisions the commission was empowered to recommend to the President the raising or lowering of rates by as much as 50 per cent. Strangely enough Presidents Harding, Coolidge, and Hoover seldom took advantage of this power — except to raise rates.[1]

Having set up (through the Emergency Tariff Act) the first barriers of isolationism, the special session of Mr. Coolidge's greatest Congress turned its attention to the erection of further barricades against the outside world. The same arguments of the fearsome specter of European invasion as were used in behalf of the tariff were now used in behalf of the restrictive Immigration Act, which Woodrow Wilson had vetoed in his last weeks of office.

Supported by organized labor, which trembled at the thought of cheap labor from Southern Europe, by the American Legion, and by such organizations of 100 per cent Americanism as the Ku Klux Klan, the act met with little opposition. There were plenty of "economists" to warn against the dangers of an influx of starving Europeans. Exponents of "Nordic superiority" were loud in their explanations of the impending threat to the American race. With few exceptions the American press was filled with tales of the terror of Red Russia. Secretaries Hughes and Hoover spoke often against the Red Menace and Attorney General Daugherty was as excited and as active as A. Mitchell Palmer, his predecessor, had been. On this score no party lines were drawn.

It was at first proposed in the House to suspend all immigration to the United States indefinitely, but cooler heads in the Senate forced a compromise measure. The act, as finally agreed upon, limited the number of immigrants from each foreign country each

[1] Presidents Harding and Coolidge proclaimed 37 changes in rates: 32 for higher duties, 5 for lower; and these 5 were on such unimportant items as millfeeds, bobwhite quail, paintbrush handles, cresylic acid, and phenol. In 1924, when a majority of the Tariff Commission had recommended that sugar duties be lowered, President Coolidge merely filed the report and did nothing. Consumers had no representation before the commission. The body was a football of politics and packed in the interests of the high protectionist groups. (See *American Problems Today*, by Louis M. Hacker, esp. p. 25.)

year to 3 per cent of the number of nationals already residing in the United States. Inasmuch as Great Britain, Scandinavia, and Germany had the largest numbers the act was a victory for Nordic Supremacy. By its passage the liberal immigration policy of the nineteenth century came to an end. Even Hiram Johnson's amendment, which would have excluded political and religious refugees from the penalties of the act, was defeated. "America for the Americans" was now more than a slogan in the editorials of William Randolph Hearst.

While Congress was thus setting the stage for economic isolation there were two matters of unfinished business to attend to and one matter of new business that at the time seemed destined to be of historic importance. This last was Senator Borah's brave and unexpected resolution calling for a conference on the reduction of naval armaments. Passed by Congress in May 1921, it called for the attendance the following November in Washington of representatives of the United States, Great Britain, France, and Japan. Its announcement spread a thrill of hope around the world for here, it seemed, was at last a sign of that postwar leadership expected of the United States. The two unfinished pieces of business were quickly attended to. In July, after rejecting a proposal to ratify the Treaty of Versailles without the League Covenant, Congress passed a resolution declaring hostilities with Germany at an end. In August a separate peace treaty with the former enemy was negotiated, and when Congress reconvened the following December it was ratified without much trouble. It was now time for the administration to go forward with its program for prosperity as laid down in the Chicago platform of June 1920. Although something was accomplished in this direction it was not done without considerable dissension within the Republican ranks. Harding's relationships with Congress were not as harmonious as they should have been.

President Harding, whose political hero was William McKinley, hardly fitted Woodrow Wilson's conception of the President as a man who not only "understands his own day and the needs of the country" but who has the "personality and the initiative to force his views both upon the people and upon Congress." (Wilson wrote that definition long before he became President; whether, at the end of his two terms, he was ready to revise it he never said.) The Republican leaders had chosen Harding for the reason that he was expected to be the exact opposite of the Wilsonian conception. As Dr. Butler once heard a Senator say, Harding "would, when elected, sign whatever bill the Senate sent him, and not send bills to the Senate to pass." As one historian of the Presidency remarked, not since Benjamin Harrison's day had there entered the White House "one more ready to make the President the willing servant of the Republican Party" than Harding.

Upon more than one occasion before his inauguration Harding had made it clear that he proposed to let legislation mostly be the work of Congress. But of course he did not intend to abdicate entirely. He thought that he could use the technique of McKinley and "in the quiet seclusion of the Executive Mansion . . . confer, compose differences, and bring together the departments the Fathers had taken such pains to separate." [2]

Congress made it clear that it would hold President Harding to strict accountability for his hands-off policy. The Senate was particularly quick to show its resentment over suggestions, however mild, from the White House.

When, for example, President Harding appeared before the Senate to urge that appropriations be kept within the national income, his former colleagues were wrathful and spoke harshly about his "intolerable, indefensible, and deplorable" action. One Senator charged him with trying to turn the Senate into an "amanuensis to record the vote of one man." Upon another occasion, when Harding addressed the Senate on a money bill, members of the House took umbrage. These two incidents made it clear to Harding that his mild attempt to assume executive leadership over his fellow Republicans was not appreciated.

In another instance President Harding was severely rebuked by Congress and his whole Hamiltonian concept of the government's role in business was badly shaken. This was in the matter of the infamous ship subsidy bill. President Harding proposed that government-owned vessels, left over from the war or acquired from the enemy, be turned over to private shipping companies. He suggested most generous terms and urged that large appropriations be voted to help the private companies operate them at a profitable margin. The insurgents in Congress jumped on this with surprising vehemence and after bitter debate rejected the project.

[2] W. E. Binkley, *President and Congress*, p. 219.

One historian has said: "So blind had Republican leadership become to the historical transformation of the Presidency in the 20th Century, the fact that it had become as never before the focal point of a major party's strength, that they [sic] could not see how their emasculation of the great office was impairing if not even dooming their party."

In spite of his avowed intention of letting legislation originate in Congress there was one instance in which President Harding successfully took the initiative. In his message to Congress in April 1921, he asked for an act to establish a federal budget system, as part of his campaign promise to put "more business in government." This, of course, was not an original idea with President Harding. President Taft had unsuccessfully sought such a reform and in the administration of Woodrow Wilson, after protracted action in both House and Senate, an act to provide a Bureau of the Budget, having passed the House unanimously, was killed for partisan reasons in the Senate. Substantially the same bill a Republican Senate had refused Wilson was now granted to President Harding. The Budget and Accountancy Act, creating the Director of the Budget and the Controller General of the United States, was the only creative piece of legislation of the Harding regime.

Although Harding had little if any difficulty in persuading Congress to create the Bureau of the Budget it was another story when it came to putting the budget system into operation. As the first Director of the Budget Harding chose the colorful Charles G. Dawes, a Chicago banker who was far more profane than profound. He bore the nickname "Hell and Maria." A member of several superpatriotic societies only a cut above the Ku Klux Klan in their philosophy, he was by temperament one of the first of the many neo-fascists who flourished in this era. Dawes never forgot he had been a brigadier general in the World War. He had a marked flair for publicity.

As the first Controller General, Harding chose a small-town lawyer whose financial experience was limited to a few months as head of a Marion, Ohio, bank. Harding and Daniel R. Crissinger used to steal watermelons together as boys. (Later Crissinger was appointed head of the Federal Reserve System and in 1925, under Calvin Coolidge, he was responsible, according to Mark Sullivan, for failing to raise the rediscount rates at the end of the rising market. "As a consequence of this failure, a second rising market was piled on the first, inviting the 1929 collapse.")

Dawes prepared the first budget estimates. Since his chief had said that "growing public indebtedness and mounting public expenditures" were the "greatest menace to the world today," Dawes, puffing his underslung pipe and wielding a sharp pencil, cut and cut. Harding sent the still bulky document to the House, where all appropriations originate, with a message which said in effect that the President expected Congress to make no substantial changes in the estimates. Congress was shocked. Since the days of the colonial legislatures and their conflicts with the Crown's representatives, Congress had assumed the right to say what money might be spent, and how.

The budget message was referred to the Appropriations Committee, a powerful body of thirty-five members whose chairman was James William Good of Iowa, a veteran Republican wheel horse. Extensive hearings were held, 20,000 pages of printed testimony were taken, and when the appropriations bill was placed before the House, Harding's own economy budget had been slashed by $300,000,000. Most of this was pruned, against Harding's express wishes, from Army and Navy appropriations.

Had Harding perhaps consulted more with Chairman Good, and less with his willing errand boy, Speaker Gillette, whose influence was markedly on the wane, he would have fared better. Gillette, unlike some of his predecessors, did not run Congress with a czarlike rule. Good was in a far more powerful position. But Harding ignored him.

The pruned budget was a warning that, in spite of the 1920 "earthquake," the old solidarity of the Republican Party was crumbling. The tactics of the McKinley era, when party members acted at the crack of a party whip, no longer served; and Harding, least of all Presidents since McKinley's era, did not know how to lead or crack a whip. A new and noisy, and often effective group of Congressmen, later to be known as the Sons of the Wild Jackass, were about to make their presence felt.

CHAPTER NINE

Something for the Farmer

EVERYBODY agreed that something had to be done for the farmer. Everybody had been agreeing on that since the end of the war. The farmer and his problems, real and fancied, made themselves heard on every front. Both of the major parties had been loud in their protestations of sympathy, concern, and interest in 1920 and generous in their promises. Now that the election was over and Harding was in the White House, with Mellon at his elbow, there was an obvious lessening of interest and concern. The sympathy remained. But the farmers, large and small, wanted more than sympathy. They wanted action. And being the most rugged of individualists, bred to mistrust the great financiers of the East, they intended to get it. That is, some of them did. And this intention brought more and bigger headaches to Presidents Harding and Coolidge than any other domestic problem these two great leaders had to face.

President Harding took office about eight months after American agriculture had entered upon one of the most damaging depressions in national history. A few facts and figures are necessary to understand the situation. During the prewar years from 1910 to 1914 the total American farm income ran between 6 and 7 billion dollars. During the war years from 1916 to 1918 this income jumped to 15 billions, and hit an all-time peak of nearly 17 billion dollars in 1919. That year the 1919 index of prices paid to producers stood at 250.5, which was nearly two and one-half times the prewar figure.

During the height of the Harding-Cox campaign a sharp break occurred. The July index went 10 points under the June index; the August figure was 15 per cent under July's; and the September index was 15 per cent under that of August.

As the end of election year neared there was a short flurry of industrial price declines, but these were followed by quick recovery. Between October 1919 and December 1920, the average rate of rediscount at the twelve Federal Reserve Banks was stepped up from 4.19 to 6.48 per cent, and at Kansas City up to 7.41 per cent. In the agricultural West and South the diminished issuance of bank credit which resulted from these maneuvers was felt to a far greater extent than it was in the industrial East and North. Small banks failed one after another in the agricultural Northwest, the home of the Farm Bloc and nesting place of what George Moses called "the wild asses of the plains." Bankruptcies and forced sales increased. A wave of distress reached down even into Iowa as President Harding took office.

To meet a situation which, in cold figures, can be described by the fact that corn was selling at a 25-year low and the value of 20 leading crops had dropped 38 per cent within little more than a year, several Representatives and Senators banded into a loose amalgamation which became known as the Farm Bloc. Some of its strength, but not much, stemmed from the Farmer-Labor Party, which had done so poorly in 1920.

Most of those who composed the Bloc were Middle Western and Southern agrarians, for the most part titular Republicans. But when it became obvious that the economic disturbance in the farm lands was not temporary but continuing, these were joined by a few Southern Democrats. There were few representatives of the small farmer or the farm worker among them; a great many had supported Frank O. Lowden in 1920; and they were working in the interests of the large landowners and the wealthy grain producers.

Their potential strength was seen from the very beginning of the special session. It increased as the 1922 mid-term elections approached. During this period its strength was approximately 22 votes in the Senate and nearly 100 in the House. It cut across party lines. Arthur Capper was generally considered the leader of the majority bloc of the Farm Bloc. Its policies were loosely drawn. It claimed to oppose monopoly, but what it really opposed was the means by which Eastern financial and industrial interests were seeking agricultural control.

The leaders of the minority bloc were Senator La Follette of Wisconsin, William E. Borah of Idaho, and George Norris of

Nebraska. These three sought to help the middle farmers, those in the $1000 to $4000 income group, which made up about 40 per cent of the total farm group and produced about 46 per cent of the agricultural output. It was this trio which brought the most embarrassment to the Harding administration. All three were masters of legislative strategy. They knew how to use a filibuster, and they were listened to when they spoke. They often could win Democratic support, for it pleased the Democrats to see them blocking the road to Mr. Harding's Normalcy. They drove the Old Guard into hysterical anger on more than one occasion, but the Old Guard was losing its strength. (Senators Penrose and Knox died in the early months of the administration and by 1924 old Henry Cabot Lodge, who had clung to his Senate seat by a wisp of votes in 1922, had been booed by the party he once led.)

Unfortunately the Farm Bloc, like the Republican Party, lacked definite leadership and a planned program. It was racked by sectionalism, it found no way of allegiance with labor, and its radicalism made it an easy target for the propagandists of the monopolistic press. Its leading liberals were all active isolationists at a time when international understanding would have benefited their cause. They did, however, have one strength: Senator Norris, who was in many ways the most farseeing statesman of the era, was chairman of the powerful and strategic Committee on Agriculture and Forestry.

The primary responsibility for finding a solution to the desperate farm problem lay less with Congress than with the Secretary of Agriculture. Henry C. Wallace was not a man to shirk his responsibilities. His biggest stumbling block turned out to be the man who had named him to his post. His second biggest turned out to be his fellow Iowan, Herbert Hoover. Secretary Wallace had been trying to get Harding to take a decisive step since even before the election. But Harding and his Eastern advisers were afraid to act, and they turned a cold shoulder to Wallace's proposal for a National Farm Conference at which, so Wallace hoped, Eastern conservatives, facing "distressed, roaring Westerners," might be moved towards a program of constructive action.

In May 1921 Secretary Wallace was startled to find that the purchasing power of the farm dollar was down to 78 per cent of its prewar value. At the White House he renewed his request for the calling of a national farm conference. Secretary Hoover was against the idea. Secretary Mellon was against the idea. The spineless Harding put Wallace off with the suggestion that he "ask him some other time." The fact was that there was as little harmony among the "best minds" as elsewhere within the party. Neither Wallace, Hughes, Mellon, nor Hoover was a member of Warren Harding's real inner circle, although they sometimes drank his forbidden liquor or played poker with him at the White House. (Mr. Hoover may have refused a highball, and he preferred to play bridge.) With these gentlemen Wallace was strictly on business terms. He and Hoover were ancient enemies. He and Mellon were often in opposition, especially over the latter's disapproval of the twelve regional land banks set up under Wilson.

Secretary Wallace worked vigorously for agricultural relief and reform and he was successful in his drive for the creating of the Federal Intermediate Credit Banks,[1] in regulatory laws restricting gambling on grain futures, and the placing of packers under the supervision of the Secretary of Agriculture. But the first big farm fight was initiated not by the Secretary of Agriculture, but by Senator Norris.

No one in Congress was more distressed over the agricultural debacle than Senator George Norris. "I had lived too close to the growing depression on the farms arising from glutted markets and depressed prices and high interest rates and slowly reduced fertility of the soil," he said, "to be indifferent. I had seen the bright hope of the countryside flicker and sputter and die." Norris was also not unaware of the intense suffering in Europe. He was moved by the "strange contrast" between overproduction in the United States of essential foods and clothing, and the

[1] The Federal Intermediate Credit Act was a sort of belated victory for the Wilson administration. Under its terms the Federal Farm Loan Board, which had been created to administer the Federal Farm Loan Act of 1916, was empowered to grant charters to 12 new banking corporations, each with $500,000,000 capital, to deal exclusively in agricultural transactions, and to offer loans on more liberal terms than heretofore permitted. The Beards (see *Rise of American Civilization*, II, p. 696) point to this as a retention of the "collectivist principle" — an instance in which Congress refused "to rely solely upon the beneficent working of competition and private enterprise . . . no matter how savagely Attorney General Daugherty might be prosecuting advocates of socialistic creeds."

tragedy of Europe, where there was not enough to wear, nor food to keep the people from starving.

In thinking over this situation his thoughts turned to Herbert Hoover, now in the President's cabinet. Hoover, the "great humanitarian" who had come so nobly to the relief of Belgium, would be the man to help put through the program which Norris was now working on. If his scheme was not orthodox, neither had Hoover proved his orthodoxy as yet. And if it could, as many were to suggest, be called socialistic in its implications, had not the same charge been hurled against the functioning of Mr. Hoover's own wartime Food Administration?

Norris called in Louis Crossette, who had worked for Hoover, and Carl Vrooman, who had been Assistant Secretary of Agriculture under Woodrow Wilson, and together they drafted what came to be known as the Norris Export Bill. Senator Norris introduced it in the Senate and Representative Sinclair in the House, in the opening days of the special session, after Norris and his experts had spent hectic weeks perfecting its provisions.

The Norris-Sinclair bill, in many respects, called for the reestablishment of a Food Administration. It proposed setting up a federally financed corporation which would be empowered to buy up agricultural and manufactured products, and send them abroad on the ships of the U. S. Shipping Board, already beginning to rot in idleness along the Eastern seaboard, to be sold through American selling agencies.

This proposed huge "public middleman," working without profit, was also designed to aid producers' and consumers' cooperatives, through which the bulk of the purchases of surplus goods would be made. By "socializing" the ownership and operation of elevators and storage warehouses, it was designed to reduce the costs of distribution, thus passing along savings to both producers and consumers. The bill also stipulated that the Interstate Commerce Commission should have the authority to reduce freight rates upon all products dealt in by the corporation.

The corporation would have $100,000,000 capital stock and the power to issue $500,000,000 in bonds, and it would be limited to a life of five years. Several aspects of the bill appealed to Mr. Hoover, who, by its terms, would become ex-officio chairman of the board in general charge of the business of the corporation. Norris hoped that through the intervention of Crossette, Secretary

Hoover could be completely won over to its support. He was doomed to disappointment.

Admitting that "certain aspects of the bill seemed sound," the "great humanitarian" nevertheless passed the word along to its supporters that unfortunately he could not speak openly in its favor, for fear of embarrassing President Harding.

Harding and the Old Guard, and the powerful Eastern agricultural-banking interests, were unalterably opposed to the Norris proposal. Even if it had not borne Norris's embarrassing name, it smacked too much of Wilsonian socialism for their taste.

As soon as the committee hearings started it was apparent that the bill was to meet powerful opposition. The Republican slogan, "Less government in business," was given a chance to prove its meaning. The hearings were marked with bitterness. Towards the end Mr. Hoover, who Norris always believed favored the bill in his own heart, testified against it. "I hesitate greatly," Mr. Hoover said, "at the government going into any more business." He had announced his regularity. His humanitarian days were done. And he had made Norris his implacable foe for years to come.

Many Democrats joined with the Republicans under the White House banner, and even members of the Agricultural Committee, who had been avid for its passage, "became hesitant and timid and finally veered to follow the presidential leadership," and "the agricultural bloc . . . melted away." From down North Carolina way came Senator Furnifold M. Simmons to warn that the plan would wreak havoc with the prosperity of the Southern cotton producers. He said nothing about the cotton pickers, who might have benefited. Many of his Southern colleagues were won over. The old-time protectors of the protective tariff pretended to see in the bill the possibility of the destruction of tariffs for all time. The railroad managers saw ruin, and the "resocialization" of their recently recaptured roads.

The public fight on the bill came when the heat of July had settled down in all its exasperating fury on the swamplands that are the National Capital. Senator Lodge, taking advantage of this, called for a recess. But the so-called bloc, having gone thus far, refused his request. The debate began. The President's supporters had a scheme up their sleeve. Although Vice-President Calvin Coolidge had quietly encouraged the supporters of the bill to believe that, on the crucial day, he would first recognize one of them, when that day came he slyly evaded his promise by not appearing in the chamber. In his place was Senator Curtis of Kansas, who immediately recognized Senator Kellogg of Minnesota.

This clever, tactical manipulation allowed Kellogg to present an administration substitute measure, of which he was the apparent author. This was a simple bill authorizing the War Finance Corporation, then under Eugene Meyer, the New York banker, to advance $1,500,000,000 to banks and trust companies. This, it was argued, would allow the farmers to borrow more money — enough to "ride along on" until prices improved.

But in the face of what he angrily called a "conspiracy" on the part of Meyer, Hoover, and Mellon, and which he said had been instigated by "somebody higher up," Senator Norris refused to give in. He had his heart and soul in the fight. For two days he angrily battled to put across the Export Bill and then, at the end of a long, hot, and angry speech, he collapsed. Completely exhausted, he was carried from the floor. Congress passed the Kellogg substitute and adjourned. The President announced he thought the country needed a rest.

"The defeat of that legislation," wrote Norris, a quarter of a century later, "was the greatest single disappointment of all my public service in Congress. I had grown accustomed to the ebb and flow of battle. I had seen men in highest purpose fight for legislation dear to them and had seen them bow to defeat. I myself had known what it was to lose fights. Yet I could not reconcile myself to the thought that one populous region in the world was desperate, undernourished, starving in thousands of instances, for the simple necessities of human life — and at the same time millions in another part of the world, separated by oceans and land, were suffering and agonized because of the overproduction of these same necessities."

The administration had triumphed. The return to normalcy had, somehow, been advanced. But America had also retreated farther towards isolation, had turned its back even more rudely on the world.

CHAPTER TEN

The Secretary and the Colonel

THE pattern for reaction, or normalcy, which the nation followed for nearly twelve years, was firmly molded in the two and a half years of Warren Gamaliel Harding's administration. Inasmuch as Harding was the Chief Executive, most of the blame for the damage that was wrought, and whatever credit for whatever good was done, must be his. But he was ably aided and abetted by others and by none more willingly than Andrew Mellon.

The bare outline of Andrew Mellon's ten-year stewardship of the national finances can be succinctly told. When he took office on March 4, 1921, the interest-bearing public debt of the United States was $26,061,000,000, or a per capita distribution of $228. When he resigned ten years later it had been reduced to $16,185,000,000, or a per capita distribution of $134. Let those impressive figures stand as his epitaph.

Andrew Mellon was not only a man who, as Harry Daugherty said, knew money. He was also a philosopher. Incidentally he was also an art collector and a builder. As the latter he dreamed of a gleaming National Capital filled with neo-Roman buildings built entirely of aluminum. He almost achieved his architectural ambitions and he left his tremendous collection of Old Masters to the American people, thus assuring that his name would endure at least through the first period of the Atomic Age.

Andrew Mellon's philosophy was simple. He believed that if government left business alone and if taxes were kept at a minimum business would prosper, and that if business prospered all would be well with the world. A practical man, he put his philosophy into action, and if something rather drastic had not happened in the autumn of 1929 undoubtedly a grateful people would have placed his statue opposite that of Mr. Hamilton on the steps of the Subtreasury Building in downtown New York.

A frail, timid-appearing man, with deep-sunk eyes and long, nervous fingers, he sat in the office of the Secretary of the Treasury and at meetings of the "best minds," preaching his dictum that any program of economy must be particularly generous to businessmen — and the bigger the better — and that the best way to express this national generosity was to reduce and refund.

Warren Harding, President of the United States, it was said, was completely awed by his Secretary and deeply disturbed when an irreverent Senator called to his attention the fact that, of all businessmen in the country, few personally would benefit more than the head of the Mellon family. Although the press, as a whole, was friendly to the administration it could not ignore Congressional attacks upon Harding's cabinet. These grew increasingly. Early in 1922 President Harding felt constrained to complain, at a press conference, about the "growing tendency of the newspapers to pay undue attention to Congressional attacks on Cabinet members," and went on to make it pretty plain that he wanted favorable publicity for his administration or none at all. When this became known there were angry outbursts on Capitol Hill because Harding, the great editor, was trying to "muzzle the press."

The first order of business at the first regular session of Congress in December 1921 was the first item on the Harding-Mellon plan for prosperity. This was the outright repeal of the Excess Profits Act of 1917. At the same time the administration asked a cut in the income tax and an immediate reduction in the surtax.

As matters stood profits above 8 per cent were then being taxed from 20 to 60 per cent. It was Mellon's argument that this tax, which originated in wartime, had removed all incentive from business activity. Those who had to pay such a large proportion of their profits into the Treasury in the shape of income surtaxes, Mellon pointed out, were discouraged from investing in new business and industrial enterprises. This argument undoubtedly had its sound merits and it did not cause the storm of protest that was raised when Mellon's thoughts on the income tax itself were presented.

The Mellon program demanded an immediate cut in the income tax and a reduction of the surtax from the 73 per cent maximum to 40 per cent, which would later be dropped to 33 per cent. This in itself was not so objectionable as Mellon's inept insistence that the tax reductions be stopped at incomes under $66,000 a year! Those receiving less were to pay at the old rates! Seldom in the history of the country had such an obvious piece of class legislation been put forward.

Champions of this incredibly undemocratic program were not lacking, but neither were champions of the people. Senator La Follette, as might have been expected, rushed to the aid of the Excess Profits Act and other Sons of the Wild Jackass entered the fray. Senator Reed, the Missouri Democrat, joined with the insurgents and the great fight was on.

It was La Follette who succinctly set forth the stand of the insurgents. Andrew Mellon, he said, had "brazenly and impudently" advanced the principle that "wealth will not and cannot be made to bear its full share of taxation. He favors a system that will let wealth escape. . . ."

To this Andrew Mellon replied that La Follette and the other radicals did not understand. "Anyone knows," he said, "that any man of energy and initiative can get what he wants out of life. But," continued Mr. Mellon, "when that initiative is crippled by legislation or a tax system which denies him the right to receive a reasonable share of his earnings, then he will no longer exert himself and the country will be deprived of the energy on which its continued greatness depends."

A shocked Senator La Follette declared that Mellon "ought to be retired from his post for making such a declaration," but nobody paid any serious attention to this demand for impeachment. The attack upon Mellon, however, was not without its results. Although the insurgents were unable to prevent annihilation of the Excess Profits Tax — thus saving the great corporations more than an estimated $1,500,000,000 a year and the Mellon interests alone nearly $1,000,000 in 1922 — the administration was rebuked on the matter of the income tax. Instead of cutting the maximum surtax of the highest incomes to 40 per cent, as Mellon had recommended, they were cut to only 50 per cent. The retention of the supreme surtax at 50 per cent, as Charles and Mary Beard once put it, caused "much bitterness in the hearts of those who paid the bill."

Unabashed by this mild slap at Republican policy Mellon was again to seek drastic tax reduction the following year. By 1922 the business depression had greatly improved — either through the natural cause of economics or through the destruction of the Excess Profits Tax, depending upon how you looked at such things. Joined this time with the rebels on the Republican side was John Nance Garner, the Texas Democrat. They asked Mellon why incomes below $5000 a year should not be exempt from taxation.

More than one observer likened Mr. Mellon's pat reply to Alexander Hamilton's defense of the excise tax which had brought about the Whisky Rebellion.[1] "As a matter of policy," said the man who was on a sort of sabbatical leave from the Aluminum Trust, "nothing so brings home to a man the feeling that he personally has an interest in seeing that Government revenues are not squandered, but intelligently expended, as the fact that he contributes a direct tax, however small, to his government."

There was one item on which Harding and his cabinet were agreed the government should not squander its revenues, however small and wherever levied. This was a bonus for the soldiers who had made the world safe for democracy, the same soldiers who, weary of "idealism," had helped vote the Republican Party into power. Not alone was the Republican Party opposed to such expenditure; except among the veterans themselves such a gesture of generosity met with little general approval. Estimates showed that the payment of a bonus would cost about four times what the corporations saved the first year the Excess Profits Tax was repealed.

Harding warned that if the 1922 Bonus Bill became law he would veto it. In retaliation Congress threatened to refuse to set aside any appropriations for the Army and the Navy. But, as S. H. Adams said, being "too sound a poker player not to recognize a bluff on sight the President stood pat." The bill passed both Houses by a large majority. Harding vetoed it with these words:

> Congress fails . . . to provide revenue from which the bestowal is to be paid. . . . To add one sixth of the total sum of our public debt for a distribution among less than

[1] It was about this time that Vice-President Calvin Coolidge said: "The party now in power in this country, through its present declaration of principles, through the traditions which it inherited from its predecessors, the Federalists and Whigs, is representative of those policies which were adopted under the lead of Alexander Hamilton."

5,000,000 out of 110,000,000, whether inspired by grateful sentiment or political expediency, would undermine the confidence on which our credit is builded and establish the precedent of distributing public funds whenever the proposals and the numbers affected make it politically expedient.

This was one of the few times Harding exercised the veto power on any matter of major importance. A coalition of angry Democrats and recalcitrant Republicans, their eyes on the mid-term Congressional elections, overrode the veto in the House; but it was narrowly sustained by a Senate which had carried the original bill 2 to 1.

The voice of the veteran was justifiably loud in those days so soon after the war. It was not always wrong. Listening to it in 1921, Congress passed the Sweet Bill whereby the various bureaus dealing with veterans were amalgamated into one office known as the United States Veterans Bureau.[2] To head this powerful bureau, which was entrusted with the spending of half a billion dollars a year, President Harding selected Colonel Charles R. Forbes. This choice was President Harding's $200,000,000 blunder.

President Harding had met the affable Colonel and one-time army deserter while on a Senatorial junket to Hawaii. Both he and Mrs. Harding liked him immensely. How much they really knew about him is problematic. They liked to have him around. He had a fund of jokes and anecdotes and a hearty manner. A short time after he arrived in Washington, at Harding's invitation, to head the Bureau of War Risk Insurance, he became known as the "court jester to the Best Minds" who met either at the White House or at the "Little Green House on K Street" for regular sessions of what was becoming the national pastime — poker.

[2] On April 20, 1922, the Langley Bill was passed providing for the appropriation of $17,000,000 for veterans' hospitals. This amount supplemented the $18,600,000 already appropriated by the Lame Duck Congress (1920–1921) to the Treasury Department for the same purpose. Colonel Forbes, the first administrator of the Veterans Bureau, told a Congressional committee that he could build hospitals cheaper and faster than the Treasury. On April 29 — just about the time Secretary Fall was passing the nation's oil reserves over to his pals — President Harding transferred by executive order all veterans' hospitals from the Public Health Service to the new Veterans Bureau, and at the same time gave Colonel Forbes control of the Perryville, Maryland, supply depot with its $7,000,000 worth of supplies ranging from bed sheets to trucks.

Forbes had started life as a sailor. Later he had been a drummer in the Marine Corps, and then he had enlisted as a private in the Army. That was in 1900. During his enlistment he once deserted, but he was restored to duty without trial. After duty in the Philippines he reached the rank of sergeant first class and won an honorable discharge at the end of his enlistment. He then headed for the Northwest. There he became a political ward worker and a contractor, two professions that often go well together. It was in Hawaii that he began to climb the ladder to success — and jail. In the Islands he held several appointive offices, including Commissioner of Public Works and chairman of the Reclamation Commission. It was in this latter capacity that he was the junketing Senator Harding's genial host.

The World War saw him back in the Army, this time as a major in the Signal Corps. For his services in France with the 41st and 33rd Divisions he was awarded the Croix de Guerre and the Distinguished Service Medal, and he was promoted to lieutenant colonel. After the war he went to Tacoma, Washington, to become vice-president of the Hurley-Mason Construction Company. He re-entered political activity as an energetic campaign worker for his old friend.

Forbes came to Washington on April 28, 1921, at a salary of $10,000 a year. When he took over the Veterans Bureau he had in his hands $35,000,000 to spend for new hospitals and a chance to hand out jobs to some 30,000 men and women. He showed himself adept at both: the money flowed like water, mostly to friends of Forbes, and the jobs went to his personal friends or to faithful workers for the Republican cause.

The story of Forbes's depredations has often been told in detail.[3] It is a sordid story, as sordid as any which resulted from the obscenity at Chicago in June 1920. We need not concern ourselves here with the details but rather with the over-all picture of corruption of which it is symbolic. Forbes's dishonesty cost the bureau $200,000,000 and this big-time theft was accomplished

[3] The most concise account of this and other scandals of the Harding administration may be found in *Privileged Characters*, by M. R. Werner, New York, 1935. Werner's account of Forbes's depredations is based on the official record, which may be found in *Hearings Before the Select Committee on Investigation of Veterans' Bureau*, U. S. Senate, 67th Congress, 4th Session. Government Printing Office, 1923. (See Werner, *op. cit.*, pp. 193–228.)

under the wide-open eyes of President Harding. This was one of the few scandals of the Harding administration to come to light during his incumbency. No others "broke" until after his death in 1923.

At the time Forbes became head of the Bureau most of the hospitals set aside for the veterans were suffering from a woeful lack of supplies. With a callous indifference to the welfare of the men with whom he had served in France, Forbes set out to enrich himself and his friends by declaring worthless vast amounts of material, including donations from the Red Cross, and selling them to his cronies, who thereupon resold them to the Bureau at exorbitant prices. In the purchasing of hospital sites and in the building of hospitals fraud and graft were widespread. In fact it was brought to light through the screams of unsuccessful contractors, who resented awards being given only to Forbes's paying companions. The American Legion also was vocal in criticizing Forbes's apparent lack of interest in the welfare of disabled veterans.

President Harding was first informed that things were not right in the Veterans Bureau as early as November, 1922. Dr. Sawyer had been placed in charge of the Federal Hospitalization Board, and was peeved because Forbes would not allow him to turn the hospitals into a nationwide experiment in homeopathic medicine. He visited the White House and tipped off the President to the sale of the Perryville supplies. Harding stopped the sales, but Forbes convinced him there were no irregularities involved and the trusting President lifted the embargo. Then others stepped in and, from what they told him, Harding knew that Forbes had lied to him, and must go.

According to Harry Daugherty, Harding, his heart broken over the infidelity of the court jester, demanded Forbes's resignation. The traitor asked to be sent abroad, in order to make his resignation easier. Whatever the circumstances of his departure, which took place a few days after President Harding had for the second time ordered shipments from the Perryville Depot to cease, Forbes left for Europe. Less than a month later, on February 15, 1923, he sent his resignation to the White House. A few days later Charles F. Cramer, legal adviser to the Veterans Bureau and Colonel Forbes's right-hand man — or "shadow," as he was colorfully called — also resigned his post.

As early as March, 1922, Representative W. W. Larsen, a Georgia Democrat, had pressed in vain for a Congressional investigation of the Veterans Bureau. Throughout the year various posts of the American Legion and other veterans' societies had been increasingly vocal in their criticisms of both Colonel Forbes and "Old Doc" Sawyer. Now, with Forbes's resignation announced by the White House, Congress was forced into action. On March 2, 1923, the Senate ordered the long-delayed investigation. Twelve days later the conscience-stricken Cramer locked himself in the bathroom of his home in Washington — the same house that President Harding had owned and occupied when he was a Senator — and shot himself through the head.

The Senate committee, with Major General John F. O'Ryan as its counsel, examined more than 1350 witnesses between March and October, 1923. In the latter month it opened its public hearings. As a result of the investigation Colonel Forbes and John W. Thompson, a contractor, were indicted, tried, and eventually found guilty of conspiracy to defraud the United States Government. They were fined $10,000 each and sentenced to two years in prison. The Supreme Court upheld the convictions. Thompson died before he could be jailed. Colonel Forbes spent a year and nine months at the federal penitentiary at Leavenworth.

Betrayed by his fair-weather friend, whom he, with a casualness surprising in a man trained in politics, had elevated from nowhere to an office of high trust, Harding began looking around him. What he saw was shocking. Frightened by the specter of further exposures, he began to disintegrate, mentally and physically. The strain of keeping secret the corruption of his friends and appointees was more than his mind or body could stand.

CHAPTER ELEVEN

And Something for Labor, Too

BACK in those happy days in Marion, days which he increasingly regretted he had ever left for the fleshpots of Washington, Warren Gamaliel Harding had borne the reputation of an employer who was good to the help. The men and women who worked for him in the various departments of the *Star* found him easygoing and just. He never had any labor trouble. He paid his men well in accordance with the journalistic standards of the time and place. In 1920 there had been no widespread opposition to him on the part of organized labor, although a close examination of his record would have revealed no instance of his openly championing the rights of labor.

It would be foolish to suppose that, with his nineteenth-century concepts, Warren Harding would have any large understanding of the labor problem that faced the nation in the 1920's. This was a situation nearly as drastic as that of agriculture. Not only was there unemployment serious enough to warrant Presidential intervention but there was a concerted drive to abrogate such gains as labor had made under the New Freedom and during the World War. For this Woodrow Wilson must take his share of blame. He had done nothing to halt the campaign against "radicalism" instituted by his Attorney General, A. Mitchell Palmer. This undoubtedly had grown out of an understandable nervousness over the anticapitalistic trend in Europe that came in the wake of the war. But with Palmer's open help, and Wilson's acquiescence, this had been skillfully turned into an all-out warfare against union organization throughout the country.

Now Palmer was out of the picture, his hopes of riding to the Presidency on the tail of his self-created Red Scare blasted at the San Francisco Convention in 1920. But in his place was Daugherty, who had a pathological-political case of the jitters as advanced as that of his predecessor and, perhaps, an even less well-controlled streak of sadism in his make-up. With most labor leaders still under the spell of Gomperism the unions fell easy victims to administration-supported attacks upon what, a decade later, were to be considered their fundamental and even constitutional rights. The drive against labor was powerful, well-organized, and well-financed. It was spearheaded by such organizations as the United States Chamber of Commerce and the National Association of Manufacturers. Through these agencies, and with the connivance of the administration, the so-called American Plan was put over on the American people without much difficulty.

The American Plan was the fine flower of *laissez faire* as bred in America under the stimulus, in the nineteenth century, of Herbert Spencer. It was an ingenious scheme for keeping workingmen from organizing and for maintaining low wages. Its foremost drive was in behalf of the open shop in industry. It called upon all industrialists and employers, large or small, to subscribe to what its proponents called the "hallowed American principle," which gave to every individual the "inalienable right" to enter any trade of his choosing "without interference." Under this plan the only "interference" recognized was the labor union. In the Harding administration Open Shop Associations sprang up everywhere. Anyone who dared oppose them was regarded as subversive by the "right people," from Harry Daugherty down to the foreman.

The victories of the American Plan were many. In Chicago it broke the meat packers' union. In the building trades it took perilous advantage of the corrupt practices of the union leadership. It triumphed in San Francisco, labor's so-called temple. And even in New York's well-organized clothing industry it was defeated by the Amalgamated Clothing Workers only at the cost of lowered wages.

President Harding subscribed to the principles of the American Plan as he did to all the "hallowed American principles" of Big Business. But when he took office and found between five and six million American workers idle,[1] he was faced with a political

---

[1] In 1921 the hourly wage rates in manufacturing enterprises fell 15 per cent and in 1922 they declined a further 5 per cent; in the building trades they dropped 6 per cent. The decline was general, starting with railroads and spreading next to the coal mines. Strikes were widespread in the textile, clothing, and fur industries, among streetcar operators, municipal workers

situation for which these principles seemingly afforded no answer. Nevertheless he had to do something, and so he did what he had refused to do for the worried Secretary of Agriculture. He called a conference. At the head of this conference he placed Herbert Hoover, the great engineer, who could be expected to assemble the facts and figures and even draw up a blueprint.

Herbert Hoover did not fail his chief. He came up with an idea which surprised if it did not shock the leaders of the party he had so lately joined. It was his idea that both government and private enterprise should reserve all but the most essential public works and private construction for periods of depression. Mr. Hoover argued that this not only would have the humanitarian effect of putting people to work when they needed work, but it would also save money because the work could be done in a period of low costs. Nothing, however, came of the Hoover plan, then. The depression slacked off, thanks, no doubt, partially to the administration's plea for private construction as necessary for the postwar expansion. Industry did not like the Hoover plan, for it was congenitally opposed to any restriction of operations such as the plan would entail.

President Harding and his advisers had trouble on other fronts. In 1920, with the passage of the Transportation Act, railroads had been returned to private operation. At the same time a Railroad Labor Board had been established to regulate labor conditions and to intervene when negotiations between management and labor collapsed. The board, however, claimed that it was without power to enforce its regulations against the carriers, although, in 1921, as the board was then constituted, it had few qualms about enforcing its edicts against the workers. This became particularly obvious in 1922.

In May of that year the board issued a ruling which was apparently intended to put an end to one of labor's biggest grievances against the railroads. For some time the railroads, led by General W. W. Atterbury, president of the Pennsylvania system, had openly been ignoring union regulations and wage scales affecting shopworkers by the simple expedient of farming out the majority

(in spite of the crushing of the 1919 Boston Police Strike), printers, and scores of other crafts. (See *The New International Year Book* and *The American Labor Year Book* for this period; also contemporary newspaper files.)

of its shopwork to outsiders. The unions claimed that as a result some 40 per cent of the road's own shopmen had been deprived of a livelihood.

When the board tried to end this practice General Atterbury and those who followed his precedent laughed and, in defiance of the ruling, entered upon lengthy and costly legal proceedings. Furthermore, any worker who "agitated" in behalf of the board's ruling faced certain discharge. To make a bad situation worse, the carriers now sought and received a new wage cut averaging 12½ per cent — an estimated savings to the railroads of $60,000,000 annually.

At the same time trouble was brewing in the nation's coal mines. President Harding was pressed for a solution to these problems. His answer was that the time had come to pass new legislation designed to regulate even further the already harassed unions. Even the *New York Times*, never noticeably prolabor, thought his proposal was "propaganda for industrial feudalism."

In July, 2,400,000 railway shopmen went on strike. The Railroad Labor Board at once swung into action and issued instructions to the carriers to form company unions, as the Pennsylvania already had done, and thus deprive the alleged "wildcat" strikers of their seniority rights. Disorders, accidents, and some scenes of violence and sabotage resulted.

After the strike had been in progress for a fortnight President Harding, having consulted with his Attorney General, issued a proclamation directing "all persons to refrain from all interference with the lawful effort to maintain interstate transportation and the carrying of the United States mails." Although the striking shopmen had been waging their fight singlehandedly (the other railroad brotherhoods preferring to negotiate their own agreements with the roads in exchange for keeping men at work) they ignored the proclamation.

As far back as January Secretary Hoover[2] had injected himself

---

[2] There was little to comfort the cause of labor during the Harding administration. President Harding upon one occasion urged state governors to help the operators open the mines by having the state militia protect scabs and strikebreakers. Various conferences sponsored by the government purportedly to iron out differences between the workers and the mine and railroad operators invariably took the side of the employers. Ironically, the antilabor policies of the administration were laid down by Herbert Hoover, the Secretary of Commerce, who intervened many times in matters which

into the picture. In that month he had called a conference in the hope of averting the threatened strike. He was accused of trying to set up a "super railroad labor board" — with himself in control. Although he denied this, he opposed a plan of the United States Chamber of Commerce which would have created a Commissioner General of Transportation but which, not being under the Commerce Department, would have removed him from the scene. Now, at President Harding's suggestion, he called a secret meeting to which he invited fifteen of Wall Street's leading bankers. Only eight attended, and they rejected his proposals. Meanwhile attempts to settle the strike by arbitration collapsed when the roads adamantly refused to restore the workers' seniority rights.

Harding had fumbled the ball. Hoover had failed to recover. Now it was up to someone else. And that someone else was Attorney General Daugherty, who took the ball, shut his eyes, and with a federal judge of his choosing running interference, plunged for a touchdown.

In Chicago, where he went in the dead of night, Daugherty stood before James H. Wilkerson, a federal judge who owed his appointment to President Harding and to Daugherty himself. Although Daugherty, it is said, accused the shopmen of committing 17,000 crimes, Judge Wilkerson needed only the conspiracy clause of the Sherman Antitrust Act to issue one of the most vicious labor injunctions ever handed out in American history.

By the terms of Judge Wilkerson's temporary injunction the shopmen were restrained from interfering in any manner with the operation of the roads. They were enjoined from combining to interfere with railroad transportation or to interfere with any person employed by the roads or desirous of such employment. They could not aid anyone by "letters, telegrams, telephone, word of mouth, or otherwise" to do any of the forbidden acts. They were warned to keep off railroad property and not to try to induce anybody to stop work in railroad shops "by threats, violent or abusive language, opprobrious epithets, physical violence or threats thereof, display of numbers or force, jeers, entreaties, arguments, persuasion, rewards or otherwise." Picketing

---

seemingly should have been the concern of the Department of Labor. Puddler Jim Davis, the Secretary of Labor, was ineffective, one of the weakest members in Harding's (or Coolidge's) cabinet.

was forbidden. Union officials were restrained from issuing strike directions or saying anything that might keep a strikebreaker from work. They were enjoined from using union funds to do any of the things forbidden in the injunction writ.

Wilkerson's injunctive violation of the constitutional rights of the shopmen broke the strike.

At first violent resentment swept the ranks of labor, but the leadership of the American Federation of Labor, as usual, advised caution and thus prevented what, at a later date, might have flared into a general strike.

One group of intelligently managed carriers, led by farsighted Daniel Willard of the Baltimore and Ohio Railroad, arranged a separate agreement with its shopmen, restoring the situation to what it had been before the strike. General Atterbury's Pennsylvania, however, exacted a more rigorous peace. On that line 175,000 shopmen lost their precious seniority rights. The workmen were, on the whole, badly defeated and left to find what comfort they could in the thorough disgrace of the Railway Labor Board, which soon ceased to function.

The attitude of Big Business toward labor prevalent in the early 1920's was vigorously supported by the White House. The 1922 coal strike is a case in point. In none of the disturbed industries had there been more employer trouble (usually called "labor trouble") than in the vital coal fields. During the years 1921 and 1922 this industry had more strikes than at any other similar period in the past. For these the feudal-minded operators were wholly to blame. Working conditions and wage rates among the miners were a national disgrace. Attempts on the part of the miners to remedy the dreadful situation were met with violence. The so-called forces of law and order were marshaled against the workers. West Virginia was continuously a bloody battlefield. Even President Harding realized that the situation called for drastic measures, and, in his fumbling way, he did what he could.

Then, as now, the leader of the miners in their struggle for a living wage and decent working and living conditions was John Llewellyn Lewis.[3] Politically he was a Republican. At one time Governor Frank O. Lowden had tried to make him Secretary of Labor for Illinois. During the World War he had helped keep

[3] John L. Lewis, vice-president of the United Mine Workers, was at this time acting president.

the miners in line at their pitiable $5-a-day wage while profiteers grew rich and shipbuilders wore silk shirts. When, in 1919, the miners sought a 60 per cent increase, the six-hour day, and the five-day week, President Wilson had coldly reminded them that the nation was still at war and that their no-strike pledge was still to be observed. In the face of Wilson's stern warning John L. Lewis, following the instructions of the United Mine Workers Union, called the men, 400,000 strong, from the mines.

In perspective it is apparent that the miners were in a stronger position than they realized. A similar strike threat hovered over Great Britain, threatening its entire coal industry. There was postwar chaos in the German pits. The United States, for these and other reasons, dominated the coal markets of the world. Economically the miners were justified in making their demands. They had kept their pledge. The operators could not have held out very long. But they had a strength behind them which the miners could not have combated without precipitating what would have amounted to a revolution. They had the government, its courts, its army.

Attorney General Palmer hastened to a friendly court and obtained an injunction against the miners. It characterized the strike as a "national menace" and ordered its cancellation within seventy-two hours. Faced with the temper of an administration that was hostile to them, threatened with the force of arms, the leaders of the strike took counsel. Led by John Lewis, who a few days before had angrily condemned President Wilson's strangulation of his efforts, the leaders retreated. The men were ordered back to work. What could John Lewis do except what he had done, what could he say except these words:

"We will obey the mandate of the court. We do so under protest. We are Americans. We cannot fight our government."

A commission of arbitration granted the miners a 27 per cent pay increase but failed to shorten the eight-hour day.

Now, in 1920, John L. Lewis, who had become the president of the UMW, set out to organize the miners in the West Virginia fields. There his organizers were met with armed guards, private detectives, the local police, and even the militia, all working for the operators. A civil war between the miners and the operators seemed a possibility until President Harding sent in a detachment of the United States Army to restore order. But order thus restored is seldom lasting. A year later the miners, now 600,000 strong, again struck.

Harding was in a quandary. He realized that public sentiment lay on the side of the miners, but, as he put it one night while having a highball in his bedroom with the reporter Mark Sullivan, "The goddam operators are so stiff-necked you can't do anything with them." He was right. The coal barons were so stiff-necked that they kept the industry at a standstill for nearly a year. Although Lewis managed to stave off a wage cut for some of the miners, the strike does not go down in history as a great labor victory. The fault seems to lie at John Lewis's feet. He made too many concessions to the operators. He signed agreements in one field which weakened union strength in another. There were too many "trades." In later years it was recognized that his failure to "organize the unorganized" was his most egregious fault. There were, he whined, "twice too many mines and twice too many miners." Still under the influence of the Gompers philosophy, John Lewis failed to recognize the power in great numbers. It was not deliberate sabotage: neither John Lewis nor labor as a whole was ready for the sweep of industrial unionism that was to come some years later. The United Mine Workers of America might at that moment have become labor's most unified threat if it had not taken John Lewis so long to decide what he wanted to do. For this he cannot be blamed. When the strike ended, union membership among the miners again began to fall away, and control over vast regions of the mining country was wrested from John Lewis's control through antiunion injunctions, through the easier method of armed intimidation. It was not until ten years later that he was fully to realize the economic and strategic lessons of 1922.

With the strikes of the miners and the shopmen causing widespread concern, the cautious Harding, ever mindful of the political implications of any situation, sought to win back some of the waning support he had among labor. Following the Wilkerson injunction, his Attorney General had engaged in wild and demagogic attacks upon the Reds, whom he accused of hounding him from the very depths of Moscow for having done his American duty. So wild were his accusations that honest people everywhere were disgusted. There was even an abortive attempt in the House to impeach him. It came too soon, although in the charges brought against him he was accused of "deliberately conniving at the looting" of the Navy's oil reserves. Following the issuance of the Wilkerson injunction Daugherty had screamed: "So long as and to the extent I can speak for the government of the United States, I will use the power of the government within my control to prevent the labor unions of the country from destroying the open shop." This was too much even for the Harding administration. Some counterpropaganda was needed.

President Harding supplied it. He turned to the United States Steel Corporation, as Theodore Roosevelt and Woodrow Wilson had done before him, knowing full well that he had nothing politically to lose in such an attack. No other industry was more invulnerable than Steel. It had long withstood the attacks of reformers and, under the presidency of that feudal overlord, Judge Elbert H. Gary, it stood above government or public opinion. Harding, however, had no intention of attacking it with the Big Stick, but with the conciliatory Harding smile, the firm Presidential handclasp.

In the steel industry gruesome conditions prevailed. The twelve-hour day and the seven-day week were in effect. Worse still, the twelve hours were stretched out every fortnight to twenty-four. Steelworkers almost never had a day off.

When the American Federation of Labor had mildly suggested a conference, with President Wilson's blessing, to look for ways to alleviate these intolerable and inhuman conditions, Judge Gary had answered with a firm rejection. "The twelve-hour day must go," he said (for the newspapers). "The public demands it." But he had no intention of doing anything about it. Nor did President Harding now have any intention of taking drastic action. To do so would have run counter to his political philosophy. Besides, Judge Gary was his friend. He had found a job for Harding's paramour when the Senator from Ohio felt that Nan Britton's presence in Washington might prove embarrassing. The Judge was not worried.

It was also not in consonance with Harding's belief in less government in business, or with his theory that the Executive should not initiate legislation, to ask Congress to act. Instead, he invited fifty of the nation's leading steel manufacturers to come to dinner at the White House and talk it over. Judge Gary inveigled forty-one rather startled magnates into accompanying him to the friendly meeting. Afterwards the White House issued a cautious statement which made the bold assertion — the most radical to issue from that source during Harding's tenure — that the twelve-hour day must go "if, and when, practicable."

The committee charged with discovering when this millennium might arrive soon came to the conclusion that it was quite impracticable to abolish the twelve-hour day. Judge Gary sighed and spoke to the newspapers. Something must be done, he said, "at the earliest time practical," but everyone must realize that such a step would "involve many factors."

Perhaps because he well knew that he was being made the goat of the issue, Harding did not let the matter drop. It simmered in his mind for a year. Shortly before he left on his fatal trip to Alaska in the summer of 1923 he sent word to Judge Gary that the twelve-hour day would be the topic of one of his contemplated speeches. The Judge had just publicly announced, for U. S. Steel and the whole industry, that "abolition of the twelve-hour day . . . is not now feasible." Harding had made up his mind that he would be a candidate for re-election in 1924, and realizing that he might need an issue to obscure the scandals of the Veterans Administration and such others as might well come to light almost any time, he undoubtedly felt that here was one ready made.

Judge Gary apparently felt so too. His committee issued what, for them, was a conciliatory report, although it made no definite commitments. Harding seized the advantage and read the report in a speech at Tacoma in which he said, "I would be proud, indeed, if my administration were marked by the final passing of the twelve-hour working day in American life." On August 2, 1923, on behalf of the American Iron and Steel Institute, Judge Gary announced the end of the twelve-hour day. But the announcement was buried deeply inside the newspapers the next day. There was little room. For the newspapers were crowded with black-bordered mourning for the President's death and dramatic accounts of the swearing in of Calvin Coolidge as President of the United States.

CHAPTER TWELVE

Tidal Wave at Mid-Term

HARDING was the willing servant of those reactionary forces that day by day in every way, to paraphrase that eminent philosopher, Dr. Émile Coué, who arrived with his magic formula from France early in 1923, were making America a better and better place to live in. He deliberately allowed one branch of the government, the executive, to fall to a new low. He failed to exhort the second branch, the legislative, to decisive action on behalf of the people. And he carefully arranged matters so that the third, the judiciary, would, for more than a decade, stand jealous guard over the power and prerogatives of the monopolists of Big Business whose tool he was.

No other of Harding's contributions to normalcy had as far-reaching an effect as his repacking of the Supreme Court. Already listed far to starboard, with each opportunity — and he had four — he made certain that the ship of justice did not return to an even keel. Through death and retirement he was allowed to place on the supreme bench four implacable apostles of what the Beards once called the Hamilton-Webster-McKinley school: Chief Justice William Howard Taft; Associate Justices Pierce Butler, George Sutherland, and Edward Terry Sanford. Two of these lived to spend a snarling old age in desperate, but eventually futile, warfare against the liberal reforms of the New Deal.

When President Harding took office the Supreme Court was presided over by that fine old rock of reaction, Chief Justice Edward Douglass White. This eminent jurist had by sheer force of will power clung to the bench until he had seen the dark and dreadful skies clear with the defeat of President Wilson. As Taft once chuckled, Chief Justice White had said that "he was holding the office for me and that he would give it back to a Republican administration."

When this was accomplished Chief Justice Taft headed a court to which he himself as President had commissioned five of its nine members. This was later to be increased to six when Charles Evans Hughes returned to the bench he had deserted in his unhappy search for the Presidency. Arraigned in hopeless dissent against these firm defenders of the faith were Associate Justices Oliver Wendell Holmes and Louis Dembitz Brandeis.

Without exception the court was composed of nineteenth-century men. Those on the right were still living under its impetus and were impelled by its economic, political, and juristic concepts. The two strong men on the left were also nineteenth-century men. Justice Holmes was a nineteenth-century liberal, one of the finest flowers of his age. Justice Brandeis was the exhorter of a philosophy of economic liberalism that had come into being in those days of industrial expansion which preceded the dawn of the century to whose first forty years he was to contribute so generously of his intrepid mind and spirit.

As President of the United States the Chief Justice had given the country a colorless administration that sat like a mossy rock between the flashy colors of Roosevelt and the less flashy but more intense hues of the New Freedom. In the years to come he was not to change color. It was Taft's court which was to declare the child labor amendment unconstitutional, that was to make void the minimum wage law for women, that was to set aside the provision of the Clayton Act providing for jury trials in contempt cases, and that was to uphold the notorious Lusk "gag law" of New York.

Perfect complements to Chief Justice Taft in their social, economic, and political views were the three Associate Justices whom President Harding appointed in 1922. In that year Justices Clarke, Day, and Pitney resigned and Justices Sutherland, Butler, and Sanford took their places. Of these three appointments one was purely political.

George Sutherland had been in politics nearly all his adult life. A native of Buckinghamshire, England, he was brought by his parents to this country when he was fifteen years old. His family settled in Salt Lake City, Utah, where he was admitted to the bar at the age of twenty-one. When Utah was admitted to the Union thirteen years later he became a member of its first State Senate. After serving there four years he went to the House of Representatives in Washington and later, beginning in 1905, he served two terms in the United States Senate. There, as an ally of crusty, penny-pinching Reed Smoot, he voted consistently against all liberal or reform legislation. A strict party man, he was credited with swinging Utah into the Taft column in 1912. He called liberals and progressives "insurgent soothsayers." President Harding admired him and was greatly impressed by his political philosophy. As a result of his work during the 1920 campaign, when he was one of Senator Harding's closest advisers, he was known as the "Colonel House of the Harding administration." Even after his appointment to the court he was frequently consulted on matters of policy by President Harding, who had at first intended to nominate him as his Attorney General. His appointment to the Supreme Court, so obviously a political plum, aroused some resentment, but there was little open opposition in the Republican-dominated Senate and he was easily confirmed.

The Senate, or at least the Liberal Bloc of that august body, did not take as kindly to Pierce Butler. There was good reason for their opposition. Pierce Butler's whole career — he was fifty-six years old at the time of his nomination — had been spent defending some of the country's most powerful railroad interests. As general counsel for the Chicago, St. Paul, Minneapolis and Omaha Railroad he had played an important role in major legal battles involving the railroad industry and the government. He was without question one of the country's most able railroad lawyers, and as such was a deep-dyed conservative in his political and economic views. After his elevation to the court he was a stanch defender of all conservative legislation. His appointment met the determined opposition of Senators La Follette, Norris, Norbeck, and Heflin, who could not conceive of his serving the ends of justice in the light of his reactionary record. A bitter fight ensued in the Senate but he was finally confirmed. After he became a Justice he assiduously refrained from taking part in such railroad cases as he had been involved in before joining the court. But on all other issues he took a firm stand on the far right. It fell to him, also, several years later to write the decision in the Teapot Dome case, wherein Harry F. Sinclair's lease of the nation's oil lands was denounced as a fraud, and former Secretary of the Interior Fall was termed faithless — faithless to President Harding, the Republican Party, and the people.

The least imposing of the three Associate Justices, but one faithful until his death in 1930 to the code of the man who appointed him, was Justice Sanford. He had been a federal judge ever since he had served as Theodore Roosevelt's Assistant Attorney General. During his years on the highest bench his output of decisions was limited. But he wrote the decision, to which Justices Holmes and Brandeis added notable dissents, upholding the conviction of Benjamin Gitlow in New York, who had been found guilty of publishing a communist manifesto. He also wrote the decision upholding the Pocket Veto.

Pierce Butler and George Sutherland, Willis Van Devanter and James C. McReynolds, remained on the Supreme Court, doing their best to uphold the outworn philosophy of Warren Harding and William Howard Taft well into an era when their economic and social theories were outworn. The presence on the bench of Butler, Sutherland, and of Taft until his death in 1930, was in many respects Harding's most lasting contribution to history.

The Senate fight against Pierce Butler, as well as other attacks on administration measures in Congress, was symptomatic of an undercurrent of disappointment felt by a large section of the public over the manner in which Warren Harding was traveling the road back to normalcy. As the mid-term elections of 1922 approached it became increasingly obvious that the Republican Party was in difficulties. That summer more than one newspaper warned editorially that there must be a rehabilitation of the Republican Party in the nation or there would be a third-party movement in 1924.

The Democratic Party had not yet recovered from its smarting defeat in 1920. No new leader had developed within its ranks. James M. Cox was dead and done for politically. A call of the roster of outstanding Democrats revealed no one, unless it was perhaps William G. McAdoo, who could whip the party into shape for a smashing victory in 1924. The party itself had evolved no new program to counteract Harding's reactionary trend. The scandals of Harding's friends and appointees had not come into the open. The Democrats assumed that the next two years might see Harding so alienate the farmer and labor that they could ride to victory. And their hopes soared after the results of the November election were in.

The election proved that the people were turning from Harding and his crowd. But the more astute observers were aware that their attitude was a negative one. Although they turned away from the Republicans there was no proof that they approved the Democratic Party's vague program. Nevertheless they shifted in such numbers that it threw a bad scare into the White House and in the inner circles of Republican leadership. When the votes were counted the Republican majority in the House had dwindled to a small fraction. In the Senate the Republican majority was cut by two thirds. This meant that Republican control of Congress had vanished; that, with the insurgents and progressives newly encouraged, the administration could expect to make little headway with any legislative program of its own, but would have to busy itself in restraining the rebels from passing anti-administration measures.

In states like Montana, Colorado, Nebraska, Iowa, North Dakota, Oklahoma, and Minnesota liberal candidates were elected against the power of party machines. In Iowa Smith W. Brookhart defeated a conservative. In North Dakota, where he had the aid of the Nonpartisan League, Lynn Frazier was victorious, and in Minnesota, where he foreswore allegiance to the older parties and ran on a Farmer-Labor ticket, Henrik Shipstead also won a Senate seat. In Wisconsin Robert M. La Follette was returned to the Senate and saw his choice for governor also elected. Even Victor Berger, the Socialist, recaptured his seat in the House. In Pennsylvania, where Boies Penrose lay less than a year in his grave, Gifford Pinchot was elected governor after a campaign in which he attacked the Penrose hierarchy, the Old Guard, and the entire Harding administration. There were Democratic gains in Ohio and the Democratic Party carried New Hampshire. And in New York a "man of the people," Alfred E. Smith, was re-elected governor on the strength of his liberal program by a plurality of 400,000. In Massachusetts, Henry Cabot Lodge, the living symbol of Old Guardism, barely squeaked by. As the *Literary Digest* expressed it, the Old Guard, "deaf and blind to the teaching of recent history," watched control slip from their fingers.

Against what had the people rebelled? They had shown their disgust with the Fordney-McCumber tariff; they had expressed disapproval of the administration's fumbling and imperialistic foreign policy (of which more later); they had disapproved Harding's veto of the bonus; they had shown their defiance of Big

Business and Harding's complacency towards its demands; they had rebuked his inept handling of the farm crisis and his evasion of the unemployment problem (Mr. Hoover's committee did not report until the following year); they had shown their disgust at Mellon's tax program, and their bitterness at the administration's smashing of labor unions by injunction and armed force; and they had uttered a rebuke to Harding's reactionary Supreme Court.

Although the 1922 election was a Democratic resurgence, it was, nevertheless, an election of negatives. The people who had so loudly spoken their disgust with the administration at Washington had voted for no positive program. For such a program had been offered them neither by the Democratic Party nor by the Progressives. Among the latter there was little cohesion of purpose or unanimity of aims. The American Federation of Labor was still opposed to independent political action. The railroad brotherhoods, who had met early in 1922 to discuss "progressive political action," shied away from organizing an independent party and, having agreed to give their support to "labor's friends" in the two major parties, took action in but a few scattered places. The Conference for Progressive Political Action helped Burton K. Wheeler in Montana, but did little else.

If any major figure emerged from the election in 1922 it was old Fighting Bob La Follette. In that year he became the acknowledged spokesman of the independent bloc of progressive legislators in Washington. But, as he said a few months after the election, "There is no Progressive Party or Progressive bloc. There is, however, a Progressive group that has agreed to meet together, to move together, and to appoint committees that shall study certain matters for the common good. It is clearly understood that this group shall not act as a caucus or attempt to govern the action of its individual members."

As spokesman for this loosely knit organization Senator La Follette was far from ineffective. He and the others — they changed from time to time and often from measure to measure — watched the administration with keenly suspicious eyes. Often this group was able to stand in the way of reactionary legislation, and if they did not always succeed in defeating it they at least were able, as one observer put it, to keep the spotlight of publicity shining on abuse.

Bob La Follette was outspoken in his criticism of the Harding administration, but his criticism stemmed from memories of the Populist movement of thirty years before. He was bitter in his hostility to monopoly, and this was the key to his political sentiments. He was both an idealist and a militant reformer who had no desire to destroy the capitalist system but who dedicated his life to making it work with fuller justice for all the people. At the same time he was a hardheaded politician and one of the ablest tacticians in the Senate. His outlook, however, was circumscribed and he inherited a Jeffersonian distrust of labor, which kept him from fully seeing the value of a political alliance, if such were possible, between the farmers, the workers, and the middle classes. Because of this La Follette failed to build an organized and disciplined opposition which might have been victorious in 1924.

In spite of his shortcomings La Follette stood firmly on the side of liberalism. He never slackened his condemnation of the financial oligarchy that had, as he said, succeeded the slave power as the great special interest in control of government. He exposed the tariff as the creation of the lobbies of special privilege. He showed how the monopolies were continually merging in defiance of the antitrust laws with the connivance of the Harding administration. He was bitter in his mockery of the State Department's imperialism of oil, especially in Mexico. He denounced the reactionary decision of the Supreme Court which declared the child labor amendment unconstitutional. And he showed up the reckless trend of the entire Harding-Coolidge-Hoover era when he sarcastically suggested that all acts of Congress should carry a rider saying that "this Act shall not apply to any individual or corporation worth $100,000,000 or more."

But La Follette and those who gathered under his banner, although they spoke bravely of restoring and perpetuating the control of the people over their government, could offer no effective program to bring this about. They went little beyond urging a national campaign for "direct open primaries for all elective offices, including the Presidency, and for effective Federal and State corrupt practices acts."

CHAPTER THIRTEEN

Harding Looks for Peace

"YOU didn't want a surrender of the U.S.A.; you wanted America to go on under American ideals. That's why you didn't care for the League *which is now deceased.*"

A burst of applause greeted Warren Harding's obituary of the League of Nations which he delivered to a group of his fellow townsmen at Marion who were celebrating his election as President of the United States. With those words he established the foreign policy of his administration and with those words he set the pattern for isolation that was to last throughout the decade.

In spite of President Harding's insistence that the League was dead, it showed surprising signs of life. From its headquarters at Geneva it continued to function. The great and small powers who had subscribed to its charter were wholehearted in their determination to make it work. They went ahead confident, perhaps, that if they succeeded the United States would find it unprofitable to remain withdrawn. This attitude, of course, was somewhat embarrassing to the United States. But that great statesman, Charles Evans Hughes, was loyal to the administration of which he was third in command, and he doggedly and literally pursued the policy enunciated by his chief.

At the start of the administration the State Department, through Ambassador Harvey in London, expressed its total unwillingness to receive communications from the League. It made no exceptions even to communications relating to strictly nonpolitical matters or to humanitarian problems which long had been the moral concern of the United States. So strictly did Mr. Hughes's State Department construe the policy of complete withdrawal that it left unanswered in its files proposals to change the Covenant to meet American objections. It was not until the *New York Times* revealed this situation that Secretary Hughes arranged to receive and answer nonpolitical communications, not directly, but through the United States legation at Berne. Because of Hughes's ostrichlike attitude the United States, which long had been considered a leader in such matters, deliberately blocked the League's program for international opium control and measures for organized health.

The Harding administration fostered a policy of deliberate isolation. It made every attempt to kill the League of Nations by its insistence that it was already dead and by sneering at its efforts to organize for world peace. The Hearst press cheered Harding on. Newspapers like the *Boston Evening Transcript*, and other arch-Republican organs, were shrill in their denunciation of any word or action that might be interpreted as likely to help draw the United States unwittingly into the League. This meant especially adherence to the World Court.

The signing of the separate peace treaty with Germany took the United States officially out of the World War and ended our association with our wartime allies. But much as the timid Harding might have desired it, neither this nor his policy regarding the League could hide the fact that we were still a part of the world. Even one as myopic as President Harding could not fail to see that the United States stood in dangerous rivalry with the two other great naval powers of the world, Great Britain and Japan.

There was, of course, a large segment of the population who honestly subscribed to a policy of isolationism as not only traditionally American but necessary to our welfare. Perhaps none expressed this belief better than Senator Borah. "If I have a conviction throughout my life with which it has been possible for me to be consistent at all times," said the man who was soon to become the chairman of the Senate Foreign Relations Committee, "it has been the conviction that we should stay out of European and Asiatic affairs. I do not think we can have here a great, powerful, independent, self-governing republic and do anything else. I do not think it is possible for us to continue to be the leading intellectual and moral power in the world and do anything else. I do not think we can achieve the task now confronting us, that of establishing here an industrial democracy as we have achieved a political democracy, and do anything else."

And so the United States went about its business, with Borah working for industrial democracy, and Harding working against it. And Harding was able to say truthfully a few months before his death:

"I have no unseemly comment to offer on the League. If it is serving the old world helpfully, more power to it. But it is not for us. The Senate has so declared, the Executive has so declared, the people have so declared. Nothing could be more decisively stamped with finality." It was sad, but it *was* the truth.

But there were still oceans, and navies, and Great Britain and Japan. Even President Washington, who, in a phrase so often repeated, had established the ancient American fear of entangling alliances with the Old World had not expected the United States to live in a vacuum — although his policies were often perverted to seem as if he did. Nor did Senator Borah, the honest isolationist, require that we have no dealings with the other nations of the world. He recognized the fact that the United States was already entangled in two major international problems that would still remain, no matter how deeply we buried our head in the sand.

The first problem, and the most pressing, was our inescapable economic rivalry with Great Britain. The second was the situation in the Far East. One was not separate from the other. In the Orient two serious situations could not be ignored by the Western powers. The first and most serious was the rise of Japan as a rival to the Western colonial powers in the Pacific. The second was China's valiant effort to establish a free national life despite disorganization within its vast borders and threats of aggression from without.

The Chinese empire had long been crumbling. At the turn of the century the Boxer Rebellion had brought about intervention by the Western powers. Since then a succession of uneasy phases had resulted in the establishment of the republic under Sun Yat-sen, whose almost impossible task was to find ways to pacify the warring feudal chieftains and build protection against foreign encroachment, most notably Japan's. As a reward for having joined the Allies in the first German war against mankind, Japan — despite Wilson's vigorous objections — had claimed the former German provinces of Shantung and Kiaochow, as well as many special privileges in China. China's protests and the refusal of the Western powers to accede to Japan's complete domination of

China's economy had finally induced Japan to lessen her demands, but at the time President Harding assumed office the situation was more than uneasy.

Looking across the Pacific and the Atlantic from the plains of Idaho, Senator Borah beheld a "spectacle of competitive armaments in a world at peace." This violent display,[1] rather than the specific disturbances in the Far East alone, led him to plead for Pacific action. Apparently without previous consultation with President-elect Harding, Borah arose in the Senate in December 1920 and introduced a resolution calling upon the President to invite Great Britain and Japan to a conference to discuss the reduction of the world's great navies, our own included. Later, after the new administration was in office, Borah's resolution was incorporated as an amendment to the Naval Appropriations Act of 1921, and was enthusiastically passed by the Senate in May and by the House in June.

At first the Harding administration was far from enthusiastic over Borah's proposal. But when it saw it was meeting with public approval it quickly got behind the plan. The halting or destruction of huge navies fitted into the administration's call for economy in government. Then there was the threat that Great Britain would take the initiative if the United States failed to do so, an act that would have robbed the administration of much welcome prestige. And so it was that the State Department, in the summer of 1921, optimistically invited the governments of its four leading naval rivals, Great Britain, Japan, France, and Italy, and those of the Eastern colonial powers, Holland, Belgium, Portugal, and China, to send representatives to Washington in November to discuss disarmament and the preservation of peace. A suggestion that Russia also be invited was bitterly and successfully opposed by Herbert

[1] The separate peace with Germany incorporated the Versailles section calling for Germany to disarm as a step toward universal disarmament. Instead of arms limitation a huge naval race began. This was generally brought about by increasing Japanese-American tension. The Hearst press and other jingoistic newspapers screamed about the Yellow Peril. Vast publicity was given the building of Japan's so-called monster battleship, *Mutsu*, which was usually described as the most formidable warship ever built. At the same time the United States was racing to complete its 1916 naval program, which would make us more powerful (in new vessels) than even the British navy. It was freely predicted that Japan would strike against the Philippine Islands before 1923, or before her naval strength was outdistanced by our own.

Hoover. Germany was not invited for fear her presence would anger France.

The Washington Conference was in keeping with President Harding's inaugural insistence that the United States, in spite of its rejection of the League, was ready at all times to "associate with the nations of the world, great and small, for conference and counsel, for the suggestion of plans of mediation, conciliation, and arbitration." The calling of the conference was widely hailed as a gesture of sincere desire on the part of the administration for the United States to take its place in world leadership. It opened, amid appropriately sentimental ceremonies and great hopes on the part of the people everywhere, on Armistice Day, 1921.

Secretary of State Hughes, who headed the American delegation that was composed of Senator Henry Cabot Lodge, Elihu Root, and Senator Oscar W. Underwood, ranking Democratic member of the Committee on Foreign Relations, was elected chairman by the delegates. Secretary Hughes had carefully kept his intentions secret. When he addressed the first session he electrified the world.

Without mincing words the tall and stately statesman called for a naval holiday to last not less than ten years, during which time there should be no further building of capital ships. He also advanced a plan for the scrapping of certain older ships, which he named, and of capital ships under construction, and the restriction of capital ship replacements by an agreed maximum of tonnage. Hughes also proposed a naval ratio of 5:5:3 for the United States, Great Britain, and Japan.

Such a blunt and pointed statement of the American position, coming so unexpectedly, gave the United States a greatly to be desired vantage point. Throughout the world Hughes's statement was met with fervent approbation, although all the old admirals howled in dismay. Japan was on the side of the admirals, and decidedly unhappy. The ratios finally arrived at left her in a seemingly inferior position. She was not, however, entirely the loser, for she demanded upward revision of the tonnage estimates of the other powers and thereby managed to save the *Mutsu*, her largest warship.

As a result of the Washington Conference a Five-Power Naval Treaty was arrived at which gave a trusting world new hope for lasting peace. This treaty provided for a ten-year naval holiday, after which replacements would be permitted at the ratio of 5:5:3:1.75:1.75 for the United States, Great Britain, Japan, France, and Italy, respectively. Under this treaty the United States, Great Britain, and Japan were to scrap seventy vessels, built or building, or 40 per cent of their capital ships. The United States alone had to scrap thirty vessels.

All was not easy sailing at the conference. More than once France threatened to bring it to an ignominious end. She aroused suspicions that militaristic ambitions motivated her, especially when she demanded twice the tonnage of capital ships allotted her. France finally capitulated, however, although she remained adamant on several other important points. There were many reasons for this, such as the refusal of the United States and Great Britain to ratify a treaty of alliance with France for protective action in case of an attack by a resurrected Germany. The French diplomats, being realists, seemed to think that national security should come before international disarmament. Then France demanded a minimum submarine tonnage that would be greater than the combined total of the United States and Britain. Since she was adamant in this, Britain refused to reduce her quota of destroyers and other auxiliary vessels that could be used in antisubmarine warfare. But in spite of France's realistic attitude the treaty was eventually signed.

Also arrived at, as a result of the Washington Conference, was the so-called Nine-Power Treaty dealing with the Far East. This reaffirmed the Open Door policy in China by pledges to respect the independence, sovereignty, and "administrative integrity" of that unhappy land. The treaty also called for the elimination of "imperialist spheres of interest" in China, and for Chinese control of the tariff system.

The Four-Power Treaty, also negotiated at this time, which was mainly the work of Henry Cabot Lodge (as the Nine-Power Treaty was primarily the result of Elihu Root's diplomacy), abrogated the Anglo-Japanese alliance, substituting for it a pledge that the United States, Great Britain, Japan, and France would respect one another's rights in the Pacific. Of particular significance today is the inclusion in this treaty of America's pledge not to fortify our Pacific possessions. This left Hawaii our westernmost outpost and left the Philippines exposed to Japan. A separate agreement was made at this time between Japan and China, restoring economic privileges in the Shantung peninsula and modifying certain of the iniquitous twenty-one demands previously made on China.

On the whole the conference was considered successful and quite a feather in the Harding cap. The main criticism leveled against it was for its failure to deal with land armaments and to put an end to naval expansion in submarines, cruisers, destroyers, and aircraft. The conference did bring to an end the Anglo-Japanese alliance; it did put a stop, temporarily at least, to certain of the more costly aspects of the armaments race; and in certain respects it brought a momentary halt to Japan's expansion in the Orient. Far Eastern relationships that were to last a decade were fixed at the Washington Conference. Later, when world stability crashed, American foreign policy had to undergo deep changes, but for the time being good work had been done.

The most significant lesson the American people could have learned from the conference was the fallacy of isolationism. America's traditional dislike for alliances, entangling or otherwise, was rudely shaken by these treaties, which effectively advanced America's increasingly imperialistic aims. President Harding was forced to say, when he sent the treaties to the Senate for ratification, that "nothing in any of these treaties commits the United States to any kind of alliance, entanglement, or involvement." This pusillanimous utterance caused many to insist that, if his statement was true, the treaties were therefore meaningless and accordingly valueless. To this Harding could only say, "Let us accept no such doctrine of despair as that!" Warren Harding, as so often in his career, was caught in a web of his own confusion.

It was not to be expected that the treaties would go through the Senate without meeting opposition, nor did they. Some of the opposition came from groups which were chronically hostile either to Great Britain or to Japan. They called the treaties a surrender. Big Navy supporters loudly objected to scrapping ships already afloat or about to go down the ways. Then there were those who had long been urging Congress to fortify our Pacific bases who now saw in the treaties an end to their long, vain dreams of a Far Eastern Gibraltar. But public opinion, on the whole, ignored these objections and there was little apparent reason why the necessary two thirds of the Senate should not vote in favor of ratification.

Many observers felt it would be comparatively easy even to

secure unanimous approval. But Senator Lodge, who felt it his sacred duty to jealously guard the fate of all treaties, reasoned that this would be bad political strategy. It was his burning desire to make certain that the world recognized the Washington Conference as a great Republican victory, as one that stood in sharp contrast to Woodrow Wilson's and the Democratic Party's failure with the League. It was necessary for him to secure a few Democratic votes to meet the two-thirds majority; but he did not wish to have the Democrats unite in support of the treaties. This was his old game, the kind he liked best to play. It was also probably the last time the old gentleman from Massachusetts would be allowed to play it. And so, whenever it appeared as if the Democrats were about to cast too many votes, he would drive them back with the opposition by well-calculated speeches and malicious thrusts. At last he was able to see the treaties ratified by the narrow margin he desired. It was a shameful performance, but one typical of Lodge, who, to the bitter end, held party prestige above all else.

One other problem plagued the Harding administration: the matter of reparations and war debts. The President set the pattern of refusal to recognize any link between the two, but in reality he had inherited this policy from Woodrow Wilson. It was handed down to Calvin Coolidge, whose administration bore the brunt of this perplexing problem.

Warren Harding did his best to help America run away from the rest of the world. He did not invent, but he deliberately fostered, the dangerous policy of withdrawal and isolation. Too confused to understand, or want to understand, the problems of international relationship, he let others take over where a stronger President would have exerted leadership. The result was disastrous, as the coming years were to show.

CHAPTER FOURTEEN

A President Goes West

NINETEEN twenty-three was a year of hope and promise. The depression which had plagued the country since 1920 ended. If agricultural prices were still depressingly low, a bright ray of sunshine beamed on the industrial scene. The automobile industry, already the index of prosperity, was expanding with amazing rapidity. A new industry, radio, was helping to cut the widespread unemployment that had reached the five million mark less than two years before.[1]

[1] Radio became a Big Business in the early 1920's. In 1920 Dr. Frank Conrad discovered the entertainment value of broadcasting records and by the following year Westinghouse had established KDKA, the first commercial station, to stimulate the sales of its manufactured sets. KDKA made history by broadcasting the results of the election on November 2, 1920. By 1923 radio was a well-established industry. There were many broadcasting stations and many competing manufacturers of sets.

Large-scale capital was required to build, equip, staff, and operate the growing radio chains. Lobbyists were required to secure the best channels, and soon three chains had a monopolistic control of the airwaves.

As early as 1922 radio had become so important that Herbert Hoover, as Secretary of Commerce, called the first annual Radio Conference. He said: "It is inconceivable that we should allow so great a possibility for service . . . to be drowned in advertising matter." The radio industry was well represented at the conference, but it was mostly concerned with the manufacture and sales of sets, and did not envision, as Mr. Hoover did, the future fate of radio as the hucksters' greatest gold mine. The conference recommended that "direct advertising . . . be absolutely prohibited and that indirect advertising be limited to the announcements of the call letters of the station and the name of the concern responsible for the matter broadcast."

In 1927 the Federal Radio Commission was formed, as a result of hearings by a House committee which investigated the industry. Advertising abuses, rather than monopoly, was the first topic taken up by the Commission. (See *Private Monopoly*, pp. 101ff., and *Radio's Second Chance*, pp. 140–145.)

At the first conference Secretary Hoover laid down a principle for radio that bears frequent repetition:

"The ether," he said, "is a public medium and its use must be for the public benefit. The use of radio channels is justified only if there is public benefit. The dominant element for consideration in the radio field is, and always will be, the great body of the listening public, millions in number, country-wide in distribution."

The great boom of the 1920's, the boom that was to take the name of the sour-faced Yankee presiding over the Senate, had begun.

Under such circumstances it might have been expected that the man in the White House, the brotherly man with the broad smile whom everyone liked, would be beaming with confidence and happiness. But he was not. He was nervous and jumpy, his handsome face sagged with some inner strain, his hands shook, and there was a haunted look in his eyes.

In February, Harding was a guest at the Gridiron Club dinner in Washington. Ray Stannard Baker, who attended, found him a "large, benevolent-looking, vague, tired human being . . . there seemed to me to be nothing sure, strong, clear, about him or his speech. His voice dripped with good intention pleading for sympathy. . . . He declared that a new war in Europe was an utter impossibility: the people would not stand for it. And this at a time when the French were in the Ruhr and the Turks laying mines off Smyrna. Like so many Americans, he simply closed his mind to disagreeable facts and bolstered his optimism with gushing enthusiasm about the greatness of America. Not a word of vitalizing leadership, not a suggestion of courage, vision, power. It was pathetic; you were sorry for the man, sorrier still for the country."

One day Nicholas Murray Butler called on him and found him seated behind a desk piled high with letters and documents, his head buried in a litter of papers awaiting his signature or study. "I knew," he sighed to his visitor, "that this job would be too much for me." Poor Harding! He was perhaps the most hardworking of Presidents, but this was due not so much to his many duties as to his incapacity for clear thinking, or the making of decisions. A short time later Albert J. Beveridge more than suspected that the people were beginning to think that "he amounts to nothing," and that they were disgusted with his weak and procrastinating ways. He even feared that "public indifference" might drive Harding from office in 1924.

In this year of hope and promise Warren Gamaliel Harding was a worried man.

The causes of his worry were many but not, as might well have been the case, certain reports that had come to him from those experts whom Herbert Hoover had employed to investigate unemployment. One of these, at least, contained a clear warning that should have disturbed his complacency. If President Harding ever read it, he showed no signs of understanding it. He made it public; and both he and the public promptly forgot it. But it would have been well if both President Harding and Vice-President Coolidge and all the people had pondered over the long report of a professor of economics at Columbia University.

Herbert Hoover's Committee on Unemployment had, after two years of serious study, issued three reports. The one on unemployment proper, as we have seen, came too late to do any good for the thousands of jobless who were looking around corners for prosperity. But Wesley C. Mitchell's report of business cycles, their nature and effect, pointed to the future. It is not without its irony that the decade which ended with the crash of 1929 should have begun with Professor Mitchell's description of the business cycle and a warning of its human consequences. Few people paid any attention to its clear proof that "unless Government and business took proper measures, revival and prosperity would inevitably be followed by crisis and depression." [2]

No, it was not the inevitable consequences of the return to normalcy that were tearing down the fibers of the President, whose primary political aim seemed to be to keep government and business as separate as possible. His trouble was that he knew too much of what was going on behind the scenes of his administration. He knew the extent of the graft and corruption that his friends and appointees had brought to Washington; the graft and corruption that was to stamp his administration as the worst the nation had ever endured. He also knew (it is almost certain) that Mrs. Harding had discovered at last his long affair with Nan Britton, the mother of his child. He knew these things and he was scared. For, once they came out into the open, he would face irreparable disgrace.

The exposure of Colonel Forbes's Veterans Administration, with its attendant suicide of Charles Cramer, had been sensational enough. But because this was generally believed to be an unfortunate and isolated instance, there was little suspicion that greater crimes were waiting to be exposed. Indeed, Warren Gamaliel

[2] A condensation of this important report may be found in *The Shaping of the American Tradition*, by Louis M. Hacker, 1947, pp. 1039ff.; and the complete report may be found in *The Report of a Committee of the President's Conference on Unemployment: Business Cycles and Unemployment*, 2 vols., McGraw-Hill, 1923.

Harding had never been more popular than he was in that halcyon spring. There were few to pay any attention to occasional hints in Congress that it might be well to look into the leasing of oil lands to Harry F. Sinclair and Edward L. Doheny, gentlemen whose names had not yet taken on the sinister implications they were to assume a few months hence. Nor did the mysterious suicide of Harding's old pal of his hunting and fishing days in Marion, the ineffable Jess Smith, which occurred in May, shock any except a few cynical journalists, whose hints of what was behind this strange affair were quickly discounted.

Early in the summer of 1923 President Harding left the heat of Washington on what was to be a triumphal tour of the West and Northwest and would take him into Alaska, the farthest north any President had ever ventured. He planned to make a number of major speeches which would deal with America's place, as he conceived it, in the postwar world. The newspapers reported that he appeared very tired as he boarded his private car, the "Superb," but this was blamed on the early summer heat, the exacting winter he had been through, what with the Washington Conference, Congress, and the other usual strains of office, as well as on the fact that he had composed twelve of his nineteen proposed speeches before closing his desk.

The journey to Alaska and back was an important one to Warren Harding. It was, first of all, of primary political significance. The national party conventions of 1924 were just a year off. He was making his first bid for a second term in the White House. He was concerned with placating the farmers, who were showing signs of increasing restiveness. He also felt it necessary to discuss the international situation, which had again risen to plague the administration. Both of these questions, he knew, might well be issues in 1924, and, in the face of the 1922 mid-term election results, it was none too early to begin campaigning.

Warren Harding tackled the second of the two issues in his first speech, at St. Louis. Harding, as we have seen, was under obligations to at least thirty-one famous Republicans who had supported his candidacy as a way into some form of world organization. Millions of Americans had also hoped that the administration would not completely abandon all the nation's past pledges "to the dead, to the world, and to the future." In February Harding had taken cognizance of these aspirations and, in defiance of the bitter-enders, had proposed our adherence to the World Court.

At this time he had implied that the organization of a rival court to the Permanent Court of International Justice (World Court), already established in connection with the League of Nations, was as impracticable as to construct another League. Secretary Hughes had backed him up by preparing a set of four reservations. These would have allowed the United States to join the World Court without involving it "in any legal relation on the part of the United States to the League," but at the same time giving it equality with those nations which were members of the League. This suggestion had gone to Senator Lodge's bitterly hostile committee, which called the Court a "League Court" and quickly squelched the Harding-Hughes proposal that we join it. An attempt to bring the proposal out of committee was defeated in May, and there it remained when President Harding spoke in St. Louis.

As might have been expected the shifty Harding shifted his position once more in this speech. He was at heart a bitter-ender, or perhaps he merely felt more severely under obligations to these implacable foes of League or Court than to any other elements in the Republican Party. Whatever the reason President Harding, who had said in February that the Hughes reservations would "wholly free the United States from any legal relation to the League," now was not so sure he was right. In his St. Louis speech he insisted that the Court must be changed until it was "so constituted as to appear and to be, in theory and in practice, in form and in substance, beyond a shadow of a doubt, a World Court and not a League Court." Having thus again revealed the confusion of his own mind, he headed west toward the parched plains.

The rains fell ahead of him. Lands with which the drought had raised havoc turned green. As the Superb rolled onward he did not see the real conditions of the farm lands and, as Russell Lord recalls, local boosters, prating about God's country, kept him from knowing the real situation. Had he preceded the rains he might have been moved the more deeply to consider the necessity for farm relief. Secretary Wallace joined the party en route and later Secretary Hoover came aboard the train. As he headed towards the great Northwest the price of Chicago wheat broke to $1.00 a bushel and three days after that disastrous decline the conservative

New York Times, in a special dispatch, reported that grass-roots Republicans feared "a rising radical tide" among the farmers. Harding went to Alaska.

Even at the start of the trip Old Doc Sawyer had been worried about the President's condition. He knew that Harding was a sick man. Those who accompanied him on the journey realized this, too. He had "gone on the wagon," he could not sleep, his eyes were hollow, his blood pressure was alarmingly high. In San Francisco he was stricken with what was described then as an attack of ptomaine poisoning, presumably from some crab meat he had eaten aboard the vessel that was returning him from Alaska. There he was put to bed in the Palace Hotel. His illness turned into what was diagnosed as pneumonia. The headlines were alarming for several days and a country awaited anxiously for reassuring news. Mrs. Harding remained constantly by his bedside. On August 1 he released a speech he had prepared for delivery: a defense of his St. Louis straddle on the World Court. The next day, August 2, he died. The cause was given as apoplexy.

Later many rumors arose as to the real cause of his death. It was suggested, in the absence of an autopsy, that he had been poisoned, presumably by his wife, perhaps by both Dr. Sawyer and Mrs. Harding, to save him from obloquy. Those who were with him on the trip recall it with "pity and horror." They knew, or suspected, that he was a broken man. He was almost beside himself with anxiety. The Presidency had grown too much for him. His friends had betrayed him. His inherently weak character failed to stand the strain. In Northampton, Massachusetts, Calvin Coolidge, pausing on his way to his father's meager home in Plymouth, Vermont, gave an interview which the *Times* headlined, "Harding Worn Out, Coolidge Holds." That probably was more nearly the truth than the melodramatic and never proved or disproved stories of murder or suicide that later gained great currency.

Harding *was* worn-out. He should never have been President. He had neither the mind nor the moral stamina for the exalted position. He looked like a president, but he was a little man, a small-town editor, a small-town politician, whose prepossessing façade was a false mask for the emptiness inside. Yet the people did not know it, then. They loved this tall, large, handsome man. They mourned for him with that outburst of emotion and sentimentality of which the American people are always so capable.

They mourned for him as they had mourned for no man since the death of Abraham Lincoln. They didn't know.

Calvin Coolidge went on to Plymouth, to pose for pictures in the August hayfields, to sit and talk with his father, to rest. Another little man, in his shirt sleeves, enjoying the summer coolness of the foothills of the Green Mountains. A pinched little man, who had risen to the most anonymous job in the government, the Vice-Presidency of the United States. Late in the night he was aroused from his bed in the little farmhouse to be told that President Harding was dead. He sought and found a Bible. He sought and found the words of the Presidential oath. The oil lamp was lighted in the living room. A few people, those who had brought the news in the night, stood silently around. John Coolidge, his old father, a justice of the peace, read the oath. In his dry, Yankee twang Calvin Coolidge repeated it and became, there in the mountain midnight, President of the United States.

Three years after Harding's death a man who had watched him being nominated, who knew how that nomination had been bought, and who yet went out and voted for him, was to write:

> Harding's story is the story of his times, the story of the Prodigal Son, our democracy that turned away from the things of the spirit, got its share of the patrimony ruthlessly and went out and lived riotously and ended it by feeding among the swine. God what a story! The story of Babylon is a Sunday school story compared with the story of Washington from June 1920, until July 1923.

William Allen White's words came closer to the significant truth than the words that Bishop William Manning spoke when the nation was hushed at the death of its unrevealed President:

"If I could write one sentence upon his monument it would be this, 'He taught us the power of brotherliness.' It is the greatest lesson any man can teach us. It is the spirit of the Christian religion. In the spirit of brotherliness and kindness we can solve all the problems that confront us."

That Warren Harding was a kind and brotherly man none could deny. But the problems his very best qualities failed to solve were to plague the nation for a decade more.

"May God ever give to our country," the good Bishop went on

in the hushed Cathedral of St. John the Divine, "leaders as faithful, as wise, as noble in spirit, as the one whom we now mourn."

The leader whom God gave to our country in August 1923 was Calvin Coolidge. For the next five and a half years this silent and myopic Puritan sat above Babylon as the American democracy turned more and more from the things of the spirit and the dreadful decade of cynicism and materialism boomed onward towards depression and doom.

CHAPTER FIFTEEN

Scandals—and Scandalmongers

THE sudden death of President Harding was the most fortunate thing that could have happened to the Republican Party in the summer of 1923. Had he lived he would not have been able to withstand the merciless battering he would have received when the full extent of the scandals of his administration became known. They would have been laid, and rightly, at the door of the White House. The Republican Party would have gone down with the man who was its leader.

Death changed all that. A wave of emotion swept the whole country as rapidly as the teletypes flashed the tragic news. It swelled to incredible heights in the days between his dying, his lying in state at Washington, and his burial in Marion. People in every walk of life thought of the man, so suddenly taken from them, as a martyr to the rigors of office. Even those who opposed his policies assumed a sudden affection for the man they had taken on trust. They knew so little about him. And this little had been built into a legend which press and pulpit in sepulchral tones made final and irrevocable. *Nil nisi bonum.*

It was not until many months later that facts began to pierce this legend and people began to wonder whether Warren Harding had been "one of the knightliest, gentlest, truest men who ever lived in the White House," as Harry Daugherty said he would come to be known when "the last obscene literary scavenger has uttered his dying howl." But by then it was too late to matter. Let the dead past bury its dead. Calvin Coolidge was in the White House, the stock market was booming, all was right with the world. Or at least with that corner of the world with which the American people seemed determined exclusively to be concerned.

The facts that pierced the legend were ugly; but they came out piecemeal and in the confusion of long-drawn-out hearings and trials. And the people did not seem to care. Frederick Lewis Allen perhaps best described the attitude of the mythically average American when he wrote: "A commuter riding daily to New York from his suburb . . . observed that on the seven-o'clock train there was some indignation at the scandals, but that on the eight-o'clock train there was only indignation at their exposure and that on the nine-o'clock train they were not even mentioned."

The most amazing thing about the exposure of corruption under President Harding is how this was turned, not against the Republican Party, but against those who made the disclosures. As Mr. Allen said, ". . . the harshest condemnation on the part of the press and the public was reserved, not for those who had defrauded the government, but for those who insisted upon bringing the facts to light. Senator Walsh, who led the investigations of the oil scandals, and Senator Wheeler, who investigated the Department of Justice, were called by the *New York Tribune* 'the Montana scandalmongers.' The *New York Evening Post* called them 'mudgunners.' The *New York Times,* despite its Democratic leanings, called them 'assassins of character.' In these and other newspapers . . . one read of the 'Democratic lynching-bee' and 'poison-tongued partisanship, pure malice, and twittering hysteria,' and the inquiries were called 'in plain words, contemptible and disgusting.' " [1] And, to make doubly sure the people did not take seriously these revelations of thievery and deceit, the inevitable practice of blaming the Reds was freely indulged in. The internationalists, Socialists, and Communists were, of course, at the bottom of this vile effort to undermine the United States Government and the American way of life.

Secretary of the Interior Albert B. Fall, the once impecunious New Mexican rancher whose confirmation by acclaim Senator Lodge had engineered in the Senate, was the first to draw the fire of the inquisitors. For a decade Fall had lived just this side of bankruptcy, but since his appointment to Harding's cabinet he had shown signs of affluence. His New Mexico ranch began to expand, blooded cattle ranged its fields, new ranch houses sprang up. In October, just two months after Harding's strange death, Senator Thomas J. Walsh, a Montana Democrat who had been quietly probing Fall's apparently recent rise to riches, called for a

[1] Frederick Lewis Allen, *Only Yesterday.* New York, 1931, pp. 154-155.

148

public hearing to look into the unusual circumstances surrounding the leasing of two naval oil reserves to private corporations.

By slow but vigorous examination of many witnesses, Walsh revealed that Senator Fall had accumulated nearly $125,000, although his annual salary was only $12,000. Senator Walsh set out to prove that there was a connection between this and the proved fact that Secretary Fall had convinced President Harding and Secretary of the Navy Denby, almost at the start of Harding's administration, that the two Navy-held oil fields should be transferred to the Department of the Interior. This Harding had done by executive order. Secretary Fall thereupon leased the reserves at Elk Hills, California, to Edward L. Doheny, the multimillionaire president of Pan-American Petroleum Company. Doheny told the Walsh committee that the transaction should bring a profit of at least $100,000,000 to his company. By a strange coincidence, Walsh brought out, Doheny's son had given Secretary Fall a black bag containing $100,000 at practically the same time the transfer to Pan-American had been made. This was covered by an unsecured note. Fall never could explain its origin.

When Senator Walsh looked into the lease of the Teapot Dome reserves in Wyoming he found further corruption. Fall had leased this vast field, which had been set aside by President Wilson's order for the use of the Navy, to Harry F. Sinclair, another millionaire oil magnate. The lease had been made in 1922 without competitive bidding. Digging deeper, the indefatigable Walsh discovered that Fall had been bribed in this instance also. This time it was shown that $223,000 in Liberty Bonds had been transferred from a Sinclair corporation to Fall's son-in-law and that Fall had been made an outright gift of $85,000 in cash and a herd of blooded cattle for his ranch.

Reluctant though he was to make any move that would bring disgrace to the Republican Party, President Coolidge, the apostle of law and order, could not ignore this unpleasant situation, even if it was known that Fall had "loaned" a substantial part of his bribe to the Republican National Committee. He was forced to take action. Upon the advice of Harlan Fiske Stone, dean of the Columbia Law School whom he later placed on the Supreme Court, President Coolidge chose the able Owen J. Roberts and the picturesque Atlee Pomerene as special counsel to prosecute the oil cases. He thus went over the head of his Attorney General,

Harry M. Daugherty, who was himself heading for disaster.

Sudden lapses of memory on the part of Fall, Doheny, Sinclair, and their many pals in high and low places, when they took the witness stand, made the prosecution difficult. Sinclair was thrown into jail for three months and fined $1000 for contempt of the Senate when he refused to answer Senator Walsh's questions, and later, during the trial of Fall and Sinclair, for having the jury followed by detectives, he was again jailed six months for contempt of court. But he was never punished for bribing Fall, nor was Doheny. Both were acquitted after protracted court proceedings.

Secretary Fall, strangely enough, was found guilty of accepting the bribes, and he was sentenced to one year in jail and a fine of $100,000. More important than this punishment, however, was the eventual cancellation of the leases and the return of the oil fields to the government. The investigations and the trials brought much publicity and tarred many close friends of Warren Harding with the brush of suspicion. A shadow that has not yet been removed was cast on Harding himself. It may have been that he was unaware of what was going on, at least until within a few weeks of his death. The sudden knowledge of his friends' treachery undoubtedly hastened his end. But it was Harding who had known and admired Fall, who had ignored his past record, and who had taken him from the Senate to be his adviser. The ultimate blame was his. He should have known.

Caught in the midst of the mess was Secretary of the Navy Edwin Denby. The stuffed shirt of the cabinet, he was the victim not of his dishonesty but of his stupidity. He resigned his cabinet post. But Attorney General Daugherty, now widely suspected of corruption equal to Fall's, refused to quit his office. The suspicions failed to die down, and President Coolidge kept silent. Then, at long last, another Harding scandal broke wide open. And Daugherty was definitely caught in the web.

During the war many pieces of enemy alien property were seized by the government. When Harding became President he appointed Thomas W. Miller to the office of Alien Property Custodian. Among the properties in Miller's charge was the reputedly German-owned American Metal Company, whose assets in 1921 were put at $6,500,000, including interest. As a result of Senator Burton K. Wheeler's relentless probing it came out that one

John T. King, a character in New York's political underworld and a friend of Harding's old pal Jess Smith, had received $441,-000, which he was supposed to pass on to the right parties, who would see that the German interests got American Metal. Some $50,000 of this amount was passed to Miller; another $50,000 went to Jess Smith, who had an office in Daugherty's Justice Department and who lived in Daugherty's home. Before the case went to trial, however, the mysterious King died and Jesse, who hated guns, bought one and supposedly killed himself with it.

President Coolidge could not side-step this, either. A formal investigation of the Attorney General was called for. Daugherty refused to testify. He said his testimony might incriminate him. But he did issue a statement in which he indicated that his relations with the late President, whose personal attorney and cabinet officer he had been, and with other high officials, were highly confidential. His inference was that he was trying to protect Harding's memory. And so Thomas Miller alone stood trial. He was convicted and jailed.

Although Coolidge hesitated and hated to take action, even he was now forced to admit that Daugherty must leave the administration. He made him resign, and replaced him with Harlan Fiske Stone, who had won an able reputation as dean of the Columbia Law School and who, like Coolidge, was a Yankee born and bred. After Daugherty had left, further revelations showed how Jesse Smith had acted as an intermediary between crooks, bootleggers, and favored buyers and Daugherty's department, if not Daugherty himself. It was also disclosed that Daugherty, through his special agents in the Department of Justice, had created a sort of "government by blackmail."

This unsavory mess had little or no effect upon the silent, sour, unhappy man in the White House. He had sat in Harding's cabinet, a member ex officio, from the beginning. Rigorously honest in money matters, one who gave more than lip service to his belief in law and order, and no tyro in the hard school of politics, he can hardly have been unaware of the moral character of his associates. He sat at the same table in the White House with Fall and Daugherty and he knew what sort of men they were. He cannot have been unaware of Jesse Smith, the willing stooge for Daugherty and Harding's onetime fishing companion. He was present when Colonel Forbes was caught in his dishonesties. He saw these men on close terms with Harding. But he was not responsible for them. He could have done nothing about them, except at the cost of wrecking the Republican Party to which he owed everything he was in public life. And so he kept his silence. He would have dearly liked it if, when he became President, he could have washed his hands of the whole matter. But the mess was too sticky for that.

In his time people spoke often and freely about "Coolidge luck." He had always been lucky. It was a lucky chance that brought the Vice-Presidency his way. His luck now held. The country was on its upward climb. Business was good and getting better and, as he once said, "the business of America is business." This sentiment was the sentiment of those who ran the country. Nobody wanted to do anything to stop that. Except those misguided Democrats who were stirring up the mess. As the historian Allen said, the people, high and low, had voted for Normalcy and they still believed in it.

The days of the great reaction had set in when Calvin Coolidge moved to the White House, and the most that most people required of him was that he "should keep his hands off business (except to give it a lift now and then through the imposition of favorable tariffs and otherwise) and be otherwise unobtrusive. They did not look for bold and far-seeing statesmanship at Washington; their idea of statesmanship on the part of the President was that he should let things alone, give industry and trade a chance to garner fat profits, and not rock the boat."

And so the people, with few exceptions, shut their eyes to the unholy spectacle of corruption and their ears to the damning words that were filling page after countless page.

CHAPTER SIXTEEN

Courage, Faith, and Tolerance

IN June 1920, Dwight W. Morrow, a partner in the firm of J. P. Morgan and Company, wrote to a friend who had asked him his opinion of Calvin Coolidge. They had met twenty-nine years before at Amherst College where they were classmates. Said the son of a Pittsburgh schoolteacher about the son of a Plymouth, Vermont, storekeeper:

> I am sure Coolidge would make a *good* President; I think he would make a *great* one. He has had a very unusual experience, but the country and the world need to utilize the experienced. He has real courage entirely free from bluster. He has faith, — a profound faith in the fundamental soundness of democracy, and that faith has begotten, as it did in Lincoln's case, a great faith on the part of the people in him. He has tolerance, and when we think of the next four years either in our domestic or our foreign problems, an indispensible quality is toleration. He has knowledge, and there never was a time when it is more true that knowledge is power. Finally, he has character, and not only this country, but the world, is hungering for a leader with character.

There was very little that was true in the Morgan partner's enthusiastic encomium. Calvin Coolidge did not make a great President and there are many reasons for saying he did not make a good one. Calvin Coolidge had political experience, but it was limited and provincial and it hardly fitted him for the role of world leadership expected of a President of the United States. Calvin Coolidge had faith, but it was faith in the perfection of outmoded dogma, and he had no faith in democracy as conceived by Jefferson, Jackson, or later by Franklin D. Roosevelt. It is true that the people had faith in him; but after 1929 they realized their faith had been blind. Calvin Coolidge did not have tolerance, nor was tolerance the indispensable quality for the solution of the domestic or foreign problems he had to face. Calvin Coolidge had knowledge, but it was knowledge of little things; in matters of greatest concern to the welfare of the people he was abysmally ignorant. Calvin Coolidge had character, but it was a small character, a mean and warped character.

There was one thing in Calvin Coolidge's favor: he did not look like a president. With his sandy hair, the suggestion of freckles, the thin mouth, the sharp, angular face, and the cold blue eyes that made up his physiognomy he looked more like a holder of mortgages in a county seat than he did like a President of the United States. When, as he often did, he posed as the pitcher of hay or an Indian chief, he looked (and probably felt) ridiculous. He had a somewhat misplaced reputation for taciturnity. When he spoke it was with a Vermont twang, which pleased a people whose roots were mostly rural, but it was no more pleasant to listen to on the radio than the equally honest East Side accent of Al Smith.

These petty characteristics — the pinched face, the nasal voice — were indicative of the inner character of the man. Except in his personal relationships he was one of the chilliest personalities ever to appear on the American political scene. He could grow nostalgic, even poetic, about the granite hills of Vermont, which he loved; he could pause (without photographers) at his mother's grave while on the way to the Presidency; he could barely hide his deep anguish at the death of his son. Occasionally, to his intimates, he could unburden himself of his doubts, suspicions, and worries. But as a public figure he was, as William Allen White revealed in *A Puritan in Babylon*, almost a pathological case — cruel, frigid, distrustful, sour, loathing people and human contacts.[1]

This man who had, as another biographer once said, a brain that functioned without words, was born and raised in a cold, small town in the Vermont hills. He was educated in a small but good Vermont academy and at Amherst College in Massachusetts.

[1] Nor does a careful reading of Claude M. Fuess's carefully documented and semiofficial biography, *Calvin Coolidge, the Man from Vermont*, change this verdict. Fuess cites instance after instance — albeit with a more friendly interpretation — of his cruelty, frigidity, his granitelike humor, his distrust and avoidance of people, which are only added evidence of the correctness of this judgment.

In both of these he learned what he had always instinctively known: the virtues of thrift and the rights and liberties of the individual. He was not taught to worship wealth, but he early learned the Hamiltonian theory of the impeccability of the rich, the wise, and the good. At no time in his life, from childhood on, did he question the propriety of the squire, the banker, the successful man. From his college days he was the willing servant, the faithful retainer, of the moneyed interests of Massachusetts. He could not be bought. He did not have to be. He believed, and believing he obeyed.

Although trained to be a lawyer Coolidge was never markedly successful at his chosen profession. Politics as a living and as a way of life interested him more. He came up through the ranks, first as a ward heeler in Northampton, later as city solicitor and clerk of the courts. After serving in the lower house of the General Court of Massachusetts (as the legislature in the Bay State is grandiloquently called) he became Mayor of Northampton. He then moved up to be a state senator. Always cautious and reliable, his career as legislator was undistinguished. He was chairman of the legislative committee which in 1911 was appointed to settle the textile strike in Lawrence, Massachusetts. The attitude of this tolerant man was to be found in a letter he wrote at the time: "The leaders are socialists and anarchists, and they do not want anybody to work for wages. The trouble is not about the amount of wages; it is a small attempt to destroy all authority whether of any church or government."

It was while president of the Senate that Calvin Coolidge unburdened himself of this delightful social philosophy: "If any man is out of a job it's his own fault. The State is responsible for sending Democrats to Washington who have arranged the tariff laws with very harmful results. The State is not warranted in furnishing employment for anybody so that that person may work. Anybody who is not capable of supporting himself is not fit for self-government. If people can't support themselves, we'll have to give up self-government." He had a plan, however, to relieve the situation. "My plan," he said without a smile, "is for a Republican administration to enact adequate tariff laws to open the shops and factories so that things will take care of themselves."

Calvin Coolidge was president of the Senate and later lieutenant governor of the Commonwealth. He followed the Massachusetts tradition by being elected governor. As governor he attracted little attention outside Massachusetts and probably would never have gone to higher office, unless perhaps to the Senate, had it not been for one event. (The Senatorship was probably not for him; he was in the opposite camp in the Republican ranks to Senator Lodge, who at that time was probably powerful enough to keep Coolidge in his "proper place." Lodge hated him. Although the Coolidge family of Boston was distinctly Brahmin, the Vermont cousins were, in Lodge's opinion, of no account. When someone asked him in 1920 if he knew Coolidge he coldly replied, "Only as long as has been necessary.")

The event which catapulted him to national fame was the strike of the Boston policemen in 1919. The policemen had defied the general order of Police Commissioner Edwin U. Curtis, a lifelong Republican politician, by asking and receiving a charter for a union from the American Federation of Labor. They had the full support of organized labor in Massachusetts. Commissioner Curtis, in the face of this defiance of his orders, had either to resign or to give in. A stubborn man, he charged the police with insubordination. The police refused to disband the union, which they had formed to better their economic situation. They were poorly paid, housed in disgraceful conditions in rat-infested station houses, forced to work long hours, and otherwise abused. The sympathy of the public was with them at the start.

Nineteen officers were tried for insubordination and found guilty but they refused to withdraw from the union. Democratic Mayor Andrew J. Peters at first sided with the Republican commissioner, who had been appointed by the Governor under the peculiar Massachusetts law which thus places the ultimate control of the Boston police force in the Governor's hands. This meant that Coolidge sooner or later would have to intervene. A citizen's committee, headed by James J. Storrow of the powerful banking house of Lee Higginson and Company, was formed to study the situation. Their conferences with the union came to an impasse. The police reaffirmed their determination to strike if their right to retain their charter was not allowed.

Meanwhile the Governor, who was "tired of seeing people," went on a tour of the state institutions. He felt that the police were acting like mutineers on the high seas, but he was willing to let others solve the desperate situation without his interference, if they could. The committee at last decided that the best way to reach a solution was to submit the matter to a neutral board of arbitration. Coolidge refused, coldly and flatly, to declare himself in favor of this compromise. Then Commissioner Curtis, in a stilted letter to Mayor Peters, made it clear he would not budge. The union was the issue, he said, not the working conditions of the men. He suspended the nineteen policemen. Coolidge was touring the state.

When he was reached by Storrow and others he again refused to accept the compromise plan of the committee and at the same time refused to mobilize the militia, saying the matter was safe in Curtis's hands. The policemen then met and, by a vote of 1134 to 2, decided to go on strike.

By the day set for the walkout Coolidge had returned to Boston. He stated that he had no authority to interfere with the actions of the Police Commissioner and Curtis said, "I am ready for anything." Coolidge evidently believed this, for, in spite of great pressure, he did not alert the State Guard. The police left their posts as planned. The police stations were deserted. That night rioting broke out in downtown Boston, stores were looted, and staid Boston took on the aspects of a city in the throes of a revolution. Many citizens thought that this was true. In that wild night public opinion was turned against the police.

Governor Coolidge, well aware of the rioting, still did not call out the troops. Mayor Peters summoned officers of the militia to City Hall and, worried by reports that railroad men, firemen, telegraphers, and others might join in a sympathetic strike, took advantage of a special act and removed Curtis from command of the police. Curtis went to Governor Coolidge, but still Coolidge did nothing. On the second night of the strike the criminal element took over the city. Rape and robbery and riots made a shambles of Boston, especially in the region of Scollay Square. Volunteer troopers armed themselves with badges and blackjacks and succeeded in restoring some measure of order by the next noon.

As Mayor Peters now said, there had been "no co-operation from the Police Commissioner and no help or practical suggestion from the Governor" during the two days and nights of lawlessness. On the third day Governor Coolidge called out the entire State Guard, issued an executive order taking over the police, and restored Curtis to command under his own, Coolidge's, direction.

In the meantime Samuel Gompers, president of the A. F. of L., who had been in Europe, returned and sought to bring about the reinstatement of the policemen pending arbitration. Coolidge coldly replied that Commissioner Curtis had decided the men had abandoned their sworn duty and that he would support him in his declaration that their places were now vacant.

To this Gompers said: "The question at issue is not one of law and order, but the assumption of an autocratic and unwarranted position by the commissioner of police, who is not responsible to the people of Boston, but who is appointed by you. Whatever disorder has occurred is due to his order in which the right of the policemen has been denied, a right which has heretofore never been questioned."

As Claude M. Fuess has said, Coolidge was thus offered his opportunity and grasped it with unerring sagacity. He replied: "There is no right to strike against the public safety by anybody, anywhere, anytime!"

Those words, and those alone, made Calvin Coolidge, the cautious, uncertain, groping Governor of Massachusetts, a national figure overnight. Few stopped to analyze his part in the strike. Few cared to point out that if he had acted sooner, if he had followed the advice of James J. Storrow and other fair-minded citizens, it is very probable that there might never have been a strike of the Boston policemen in the autumn of 1919.

Commissioner Curtis, whose stubborn blindness had caused the walkout, refused to take back a single policeman who had left his post. When Governor Coolidge, who had just been renominated by a large Republican majority, was asked to reinstate what Fuess has called "at least the more innocent strikers," he refused. "That way treason lies," he said.

Calvin Coolidge, in his *Autobiography*, declared that his chief mistake was in not calling out the State Guard on the afternoon the police had set for abandoning their posts. He never admitted that his major blunder was in leaving Boston the day the issue came to a head and in refusing then to back the citizens' committee, whose tireless efforts for arbitration undoubtedly would have averted the strike, the bloodshed, and the heartbreak that his cautious inaction brought about.

The second term of Governor Calvin Coolidge was without incident. In July 1920, as we have seen, he was chosen by a rebellious Republican Convention to take his place as Vice-President on the ticket of Warren Gamaliel Harding.

Calvin Coolidge, who had never traveled more than a few hundred miles from Massachusetts in his whole life, moved into a suite of four rooms in the New Willard Hotel in Washington with his gracious, charming wife, Grace Goodhue Coolidge. He was paid $12,000 a year, the most he had ever earned. He had a car, a chauffeur, and two secretaries. And he had nothing to do except preside over the Senate. He was never close to the administration, although President Harding did have him sit in at cabinet meetings. There he seldom opened his mouth, offered no advice, and accordingly embarrassed nobody. In those days he was often morose and moody. The newspapermen found him exceedingly eccentric. They printed stories, often made up, about his taciturnity and his Vermont dry humor. Otherwise he came very close to being the forgotten man of the administration.

As presiding officer he watched with approval the passage of the Fordney-McCumber tariff bill, Mr. Mellon's tax bill, and the establishment of the Bureau of the Budget. He thought no Congress in history showed more "important and far-reaching accomplishment" than the Sixty-seventh. But although he later said he derived much entertainment and information from his duties he was bored and unhappy much of the time. He tried to alleviate his boredom by becoming a sort of official diner-out for the administration. When asked why he, who sat so silently through his meals, went to so many dinners, he replied, "Got to eat somewhere." When not dining out he read, mostly the standard histories, biographies, and works on economics. He said, "I read a great deal and listened to much," and he made many more speeches than people, listening to the myth of his silence, realize. He wrote some articles for the magazines, in a brittle style which caused Heywood Broun later to say that he was "the least gifted author the White House has known in many generations," although his short if platitudinous sentences were a relief beside Harding's pompous phrases.

In expressing his own personal philosophy of life Calvin Coolidge also expressed his beliefs in the function of government which he was to foster during his stay in the White House. As far as it went his passionate faith in the virtues of thrift was a good way of life, as he had learned in his childhood in Vermont.

But, as history shows, it somehow did not work when transferred to the running of national government. Calvin Coolidge said: "There is no dignity quite so impressive and no independence quite so important, as living within your own means."

In presiding over the Senate Calvin Coolidge came to know men he had not had a chance to know in Boston. He became friendly with Senator Borah, Charles Curtis, James Wadsworth, Reed Smoot, and the other Old Guardsmen whose prestige and power were rapidly slipping away. He watched in action Democrats like Oscar W. Underwood, Joseph T. Robinson, Claude Swanson, Carter Glass, who were holding the fort for the conservative wing of the Democratic Party. He once said about this period of his life: "Presiding over the Senate was fascinating to me . . . I was entertained and instructed by the debates . . . the country is safe in [the Senate's] hands." He changed his mind after 1924.

Those Eastern Republicans, who had watched with pleasure Coolidge's quick rise to national prominence, had faith in him. They knew he would never let them down. At a period when agricultural distress and unemployment were the real issues, Calvin Coolidge blandly told reporters that the two important problems facing the country were taxation and finance. He could never conceive of the anarchistic doctrine of using taxation to aid the victims of economic depression.

As Vice-President, Calvin Coolidge made many speeches. Almost without exception they were run through with a single thread of thought. The title of one speech might well have gone for them all. He seldom failed to work into his addresses some reference to "The Power of the Moral Law." An examination of these utterances gives rise to the belief that Calvin Coolidge was a thwarted preacher, that he would have been happier in the pulpit than in the hurly-burly of Washington. His father had named him well when he called him John Calvin.

In one of these speeches he expressed his fundamental tenet as conclusively as he ever did, even after moving into the White House when his speeches attracted more attention.

"The world today," he said, "is filled with a great impatience. Men are disdainful of things that are, and are credulously turning to those who assert that a change of institutions somehow brings an era of perfection. It is not a change that is needed in our Constitution and our laws so much as there is a need for living in accordance with them. . . . It is not our institutions that have failed, it is our execution of them that has failed. . . . The life of the nation is dependent not on criticism but on construction, not on tearing down, but on building up, not in destroying but in preserving."

Calvin Coolidge would have been happier if he had lived in seventeenth-century America instead of the twentieth century. Like Miniver Cheevey he was born too late.

Always he sprinkled his Vice-Presidential addresses and lectures with moral warnings. Although he once boldly admitted that "the age of science and commercialism is here" he was forever saying, "We do not need more material development, we need more spiritual development. We do not need more intellectual power, we need more moral power. We do not need more knowledge, we need more culture. We do not need more laws, we need more religion. We do not need more of the things that are seen, we need more of the things that are unseen."

Since Calvin Coolidge could not have things as they were, he was willing to settle for keeping things as they are. But one finds it rather difficult to accept his moral preaching in the light of his hesitation and silence about the scandals of his late chief's administration. Nevertheless he did express the religion of those he served by his warnings against destructive criticism, against tearing down. The press and the public followed him there.

As Warren Harding had his Daugherty so Calvin Coolidge also had his Warwick. One man planned his career, worked to bring the plan to fruition, saw it succeed beyond his wildest hopes. He was Frank Waterman Stearns, who always thought Calvin Coolidge was as great as Washington and Lincoln combined.

A Boston-born gentleman of *Mayflower* stock, Frank Stearns had entered his father's drygoods firm of R. H. Stearns and Company, whose Tremont Street store was the favorite of all the better Boston families who still looked with suspicion upon E. A. Filene's bigger and more garish emporium. He was a graduate of one of the city's better private schools and of Amherst College in the class of 1878. Sixteen years Coolidge's senior, he had not known the Vermonter when the latter was in college. His first association with him, when Coolidge was in the State Senate, was an unhappy one. But once he got to know Coolidge he became obsessed with the idea that here was a Great Man whom he, Stearns, would someday make President of the United States. He asked nothing material in return.

A short, stout, pudgy man with gray hair and a mustache, Stearns could have passed for a country doctor, but instead he was one of Boston's most successful merchants. He was reticent and sincere and he presided over his department store with benevolence. Aside from the store his great interest was Amherst College, of which he was for many years a trustee. Born and bred in the Republican tradition, he had had little if anything to do with politics until he was in his late fifties, and then he would probably have had no active association with party affairs if it had not been for his Great Obsession.

Stearns's original acquaintance with Coolidge came when he sent a friend to the Senator to ask his help in defeating a bill which Stearns felt was detrimental to Amherst College's finance. Coolidge at first ignored the plea and later curtly told the emissary he could do nothing about it. Stearns was pretty much annoyed. But three years later Dwight W. Morrow sang his praises to the merchant. Stearns looked him up at the Algonquin Club. Coolidge said, "How d' do." Later he invited Stearns to visit him "up on the Hill" someday, and for some reason Stearns did. Coolidge was affable and Stearns was greatly impressed with the way the President of the Senate could say "No!" to three state senators who approached him in Stearns's presence. Stearns wrote and asked Coolidge for his photograph.

The friendship ripened quickly after that. Stearns gave a dinner to Coolidge to which a host of Amherst people were invited and from that time Stearns became a sort of joke among his friends because he was always talking about what a great man Coolidge was and how far he was going. Only Dwight Morrow and a few others agreed. Stearns became Coolidge's closest adviser and most ardent press agent. He shepherded him through the governorship and was at his shoulder that hot July day when luck came Coolidge's way and a man from the state of Washington nominated him for Vice-President.

In this office Coolidge remained closer to Stearns than any other person. They saw each other frequently and corresponded faithfully. He was a much needed comforter. Many of Coolidge's letters to the Boston merchant revealed a strong streak of pessimism and irritation. He said he was suspicious of everybody he met — and this feeling, which he carried all his life, was probably responsible for his unwillingness to make conversation. He was afraid that even his smallest utterances might be used against him. As Stearns told him it was rather a shame that Coolidge did not "get more comfort" out of his successes. He had to warn him sternly to be nicer to people, to try to show that he was interested in them. To which Coolidge replied: "I do not think you have any comprehension of what people do to me. Even small things bother me." That he was neurotic there can be no question.

Congress was not in session from March 4 until the following December in the crucial year of 1923. Vice-President Coolidge left the heated Capital in June at about the same time President Harding started on his fatal journey to the West. His first port of call was his old college at Amherst, where he was to be among the distinguished guests and alumni at Commencement. He, too, was by now a trustee. He arrived there in time to become involved in the nation's major academic *cause célèbre*, the Meiklejohn case.

Alexander Meiklejohn was president of Amherst. He was a great liberal, a thinker, and a passionate believer in academic freedom at a time when civil liberties of all kinds were undergoing violent attack. Calvin Coolidge sat on the platform near him when President Meiklejohn, goaded into passionate speech by the reactionary actions of the board of trustees, delivered a bitter speech attacking those who opposed his liberal theories of education. It was a brave if ill-considered speech. Although Coolidge said nothing at the time he was obviously antagonistic to President Meiklejohn's defiant words. A short time later the trustees met. They voted to remove Meiklejohn from office by voting him a year's salary and requesting his resignation. Calvin Coolidge was one of the trustees who supported this move. At the same time the trustees elected Dr. George D. Olds, an old friend and favorite teacher of Coolidge, to act as President during this year and to become president the following June. Dwight W. Morrow was in general charge of the Meiklejohn removal, but Coolidge had his full share in the meetings that led up to this action.

From Amherst the Coolidges motored to Plymouth. The Vice-President was completely unmoved by the attacks in the liberal press which his part in the Meiklejohn affair had engendered. He

163

did not mind being called a "midget statesman" by Oswald Garrison Villard in the radical, if not anarchistic, *Nation*. A small group of reporters went with him as far as Ludlow. When Harding became ill others piled into that dreary little Vermont village, which boasted the only "hotel" in the region of Father John's home. The photographers had a field day picturing the Vice-President mending a sap bucket and pitching hay. When Harding apparently was recovering most of the journalists left. Of such little consequence was the Vice-President considered by the press of the country that, on the night of Harding's death, only three New York reporters and one from Boston were still stationed in Ludlow. One of these, Roy Atkinson of the *Boston Post*, was the first to receive word of the tragedy in San Francisco.[2] He aroused the others, who made a mad dash by automobile over shameful roads to the Plymouth farmhouse. Standing silently and with no photographer present they heard Calvin Coolidge take the oath of office and, following a precedent set by John Tyler in 1841, assume the Presidency.[3]

[2] Since the author of this book, as an apprentice on the *Post* that summer, was the one who flashed the word to Roy Atkinson, he will stick by this version against all others which give the credit to another newspaperman. One of the more amusing things in Coolidge's biography is the effort that has gone into getting an "accurate" account of what really took place the night Harding died. Roy Atkinson's story, telephoned shortly after the swearing in and written by the late Clifton B. Carberry, managing editor of the *Post*, is unquestionably the most accurate. Roy Atkinson was a great reporter of the old school; he was there, he took notes, he knew what happened.

[3] The Constitution does not say the Vice-President shall *become President*; it merely says, and this ambiguously, that "the powers and duties [of the President] shall devolve on the Vice President." If Coolidge had wanted to break precedent in 1928 he might have insisted he had *not* been President between August 1923 and March 4, 1925, and therefore had served only one term as President. But, of course, he did not choose.

CHAPTER SEVENTEEN

Down the Middle Road

MANY people thought that Calvin Coolidge was a lucky man, but he felt that an unseen hand had reached out in the darkness of night to make him, as he said, an "instrument in the hands of God."

A seventeenth-century orthodox Christian with simple and unbending faith, he moved into the White House to carry on God's will. He was deeply moved by the way it had happened but he was fundamentally unchanged by the sudden event. Nothing could change Calvin Coolidge. He was then, and was ever to remain, the same inflexible Vermonter, hill-hemmed and narrow, that he had always been.

The Republican Party rejoiced that, at this moment of crisis, it had a man upon whom it could absolutely depend. Big Business, a little jittery over the way things had been going, was happy indeed. Andrew Mellon thought it an act of God that Calvin Coolidge was in the White House; he knew he would have no trouble handling him. Herbert Hoover may have been disappointed in the appearance of a man who might delay his own chances for the Presidency, but he was undisturbed by the ascendancy of a man who expressed Coolidge's philosophy. Senator Lodge's shock at hearing the news mattered little, for he was to be dead in little more than a year and his power in the party was already dwindling. Calvin Coolidge was, as the *Literary Digest* so aptly put it, the High Priest of Stability, and his prescription of "confidence, reassurance and optimism" was just what the country needed.

The *Nation*, of course, could hardly be expected to take this view of things. If it did manage to make a historic evaluation of the new President, its words then were looked upon as the snarl of the radical Left.

"And now the Presidency sinks low indeed," that weekly said. "We doubt if ever before it has fallen into the hands of a man so cold, so narrow, so reactionary, so uninspiring, so unenlightened, or one who has done less to earn it than Calvin Coolidge. Every reactionary may today rejoice, and every liberal may be correspondingly downcast."

When Calvin Coolidge sat down at Warren Harding's desk in the White House there were just ten months to go before the national conventions would be held in the summer of 1924. The insurgents and progressives in Congress held the balance of power. But still the Republican Party was nationally dominant and with Coolidge at the helm its hopes rose measurably.

Calvin Coolidge made no changes in the cabinet of which he had been the silent associate for two and a half years. As we have seen he chose to ignore the scandals of the Harding regime until driven by public opinion and the fulminations of the Sons of the Wild Jackass to do otherwise. The Democrats were sure they had unbeatable campaign material in the exposures now taking place. But Coolidge was imperturbable. He spoke of the "errors in judgment" of Fall, Forbes, and the rest, but he did not bring the power of the Presidency or the Moral Law to bear upon the mess. Even with his closest friend, Frank Waterman Stearns, he kept silent. He hoped things would blow over. Senator Borah hardly waited for Harding to be in his grave before he was saying that nobody but Coolidge could be nominated or elected in 1924, but he privately thought the chances would be better if Coolidge got rid of Daugherty and told him so. Coolidge said he thought such an act would be looked upon as a repudiation of President Harding and greatly resented. Thus expediency won over the moral law until further expediency forced Daugherty to go.

One of the first official acts facing the new President was to find a successor to George B. Harvey as Ambassador to Great Britain, this estimable diplomat having resigned shortly after Harding's death. At first Coolidge wanted Elihu Root to accept the post, but Root was too old and ill to undertake it. Frank O. Lowden was Coolidge's second choice, but the unsuccessful contender for the 1920 nominations would not accept the post. Then, much to the disappointment of Dwight Morrow and his fellow Morgan partner, Thomas Cochran, both of whom were to be

166

close advisers of Coolidge, he offered the appointment to Frank B. Kellogg. The Morgan men, and others in the party, thought the former Senator from Minnesota, who had been defeated in the 1922 debacle, was too radical. He had helped prosecute the Union Pacific Railroad and the Standard Oil Company during the Roosevelt "trust-busting" era, but as a Senator his political viewpoints had come to be similar to those of Coolidge. On the League issue he was a "mild reservationist," but otherwise he had shown few liberal tendencies. Coolidge was a little disturbed that this appointment was not well accepted by Morrow and Cochran, but the faithful Stearns told him that "no President ever had two more valuable or more unselfishly devoted friends" than J. P. Morgan's two partners. Coolidge replied that he thought the matter would "work out all right." It did.

The only other problem that immediately occupied the President's attention, other than the signing of the Five-Power Treaty in mid-August, was the threat of the anthracite coal miners of Pennsylvania. He called upon the operators and miners to meet with a Federal Coal Commission which President Harding had appointed. With John L. Lewis appearing for the miners, the conferences reached an impasse, but all Coolidge said was, "Tell the people there will be fuel." He then appointed Governor Pinchot as a special mediator. Pinchot's plan was acceptable to neither side and the strike was called. Coolidge said nothing, except that he had been advised he had no authority to seize and operate the mines. In mid-September a compromise agreement was reached and the strike ended with the miners receiving the substance of their demands. From his first essay at Presidential caution Coolidge emerged as neither hero nor villain of what might have been a most dangerous situation.

When Congress convened in December, President Coolidge was ready with a message which had the virtue of brevity and a certain historic interest as the first such message broadcast by radio. In the four months he had been in his accidental office, Coolidge, who had a shrewd sense of publicity values, had built up his carefully nurtured reputation as Silent Calvin. It was therefore with more than the usual interest that the country awaited what was to be his first public statement of importance.

In this first state paper Calvin Coolidge discussed many topics of vital interest to the people of the United States and of the world. He made clear his stand on the League of Nations, the World Court, Russia, the soldiers' bonus, taxation, and agriculture. There was nothing in his address to cause the uneasy ghost of Warren Harding to turn in his grave. Its philosophic basis was well expressed in words that were becoming familiar through frequent repetition:

> We want idealism. We want the vision which lifts men and women above themselves. These are virtues by reason of their own merit. But they must not be cloistered. They must not be impracticable. They must not be ineffective. The world has had enough of the curse of hatred and selfishness, of destruction and war. It has had enough of the wrong use of destruction and war. For the healing of the nations there must be good-will and charity, confidence and peace. The time has come for a more practicable use of the moral power, and more reliance on the principle that right makes its own might.

We want idealism and vision, he said, and proceeded to outline a program which contained little that was idealistic and nothing that was constructive.

Calvin Coolidge again pronounced that, as far as the administration in Washington was concerned, the League of Nations was as dead as Harding had said it was. But, even as Harding had done upon one occasion, he advocated American participation in the World Court. He endorsed the proposals to this end then pigeonholed in the Committee on Foreign Relations of which the aging Henry Cabot Lodge was still the jealous chairman.

"As I wish to see a court established, and as the proposal presents the only practical plan on which many nations have ever agreed, though it may not meet every desire, I therefore commend it to the favorable consideration of the Senate." Thus the World Court was placed high on the Coolidge administration's agenda and it might have been expected that Coolidge would use the prestige of his office to press for its approval. He did nothing of the kind.

When the proposal for ratification of the World Court protocol finally reached its most critical stage on the Senate floor, President Coolidge was amazingly reticent. He put up no personal fight for its passage. Instead he remained silent and sent no word, even indirectly, to those Senators who were valiantly struggling to put across what they had every reason to believe was a measure close to the administration's heart. On the very day when a word from the White House might have turned the tide President Coolidge sat at lunch with a group of prominent editors. They went back to their homes, pleasantly impressed with the President, to write glowing words about him. But, in the face of his lack of encouragement even to those who went to the White House to consult him, the World Court measure was defeated.

Turning to the problem of war debts Coolidge expressed himself as opposed to their cancellation, but he did not take a stand against some form of adjustment to be worked out later. His real attitude towards collection of the money owed to the United States by our former European allies was best expressed in the famous, if apocryphal, laconicism, "They hired the money, didn't they." If, as is likely, he never did say that, it was nevertheless just what he might have said, as Mrs. Coolidge once remarked.

Upon one important topic President Coolidge spoke with that spirit of tolerance which Mr. Morrow had detected in his make-up. His attitude toward Soviet Russia was one of unexpected amelioration. Shortly before he delivered his message Lenin had announced the New Economic Policy which was widely interpreted, especially by those who wished to resume commercial relations with Russia, as a modification of doctrinaire Marxism. To Coolidge this policy showed what he called "encouraging evidences of returning to the ancient ways of society."

Although he bluntly said that the favor of the United States was not for sale, he admitted that he was willing to make concessions in the interest of closer collaboration between the two countries. As one who never deviated from the moral law he declared that he took this stand "for the purpose of rescuing the Russian people." He then posited three essential requisites for any change in American policy: (1) compensation for American citizens who had been deprived of their property through Soviet confiscatory decrees; (2) recognition by Lenin's government of the debts of the Kerensky government; and (3) abatement of what he called the active spirit of enmity to American institutions. Once these conditions had been met, he continued, "our country ought to be the first to go to the economic and moral rescue of Russia."

To this section of the Presidential address the Soviet government made quick reply. Anxious to take what steps it could to resume normal trade conditions, Russia announced its willingness to enter into negotiations with the United States upon the conditions laid down by President Coolidge. Foreign Commissar Chicherin did not know our Secretary of State.

Blunt indeed was Mr. Hughes's answer to Russia's bid. His curt note had none of the conciliatory tones of the Coolidge message. "There would seem at this time," he said, "no reason for negotiations." Let the Soviet government first take the steps outlined by the President; steps, he added, which called for no conference. For until they were taken no negotiations could be undertaken. "Most serious is the continued propaganda to overthrow the institutions of this country. This government can enter into no negotiations until these efforts directed from Moscow are abandoned." Whereupon Secretary Hoover, who once had said that the ambition of his life was to crush out Soviet Russia,[1] sighed with profound relief; and so did Attorney General Daugherty. Calvin Coolidge never returned to this subject. In fact, no further gesture in this direction was made until Franklin Delano Roosevelt entered the White House a decade later.[2]

On matters of domestic policy President Coolidge spoke with more assurance than he did on foreign affairs, with which, until Harding's sudden death, he had had no concern and on which he had spoken or written only rarely. He was on familiar ground when he said, "Of all the services which Congress can render, I have no hesitation in declaring this one to be paramount." He was, of course, speaking of taxation, and he put himself squarely behind Andrew Mellon's plan. This plan proposed to cut in half the levies placed upon the highest incomes. It was Mr. Mellon's con-

[1] Cited in *Dinner at the White House*, by Louis Adamic, p. 197.
[2] Secretary Hughes's successor, Frank B. Kellogg, "was if possible even more conservative in his approach to the problem. He saw the bogey of communist propaganda on every hand, at one point hysterically warning the Senate of rampant Bolshevism in Mexico. With the advent of the Hoover administration, what had become a fixed and settled policy was again reaffirmed by Secretary Stimson." (*The Road to Teheran*, by Foster Rhea Dulles, p. 175.)

Two years previously, on March 31, 1921, Secretary of Commerce Herbert Hoover told Maxim Litvinov: "The question of trade with Russia is far more a *political* one than an *economic* one so long as Russia is under the control of the Bolshevik." (Cited in *The Great Conspiracy*, by Michael Sayers and Albert E. Kahn, p. 142 *n*.)

tribution to the moral law, for he believed that, since the wealthy, by subterfuge and other means, evaded the payment of the current rate of 50 per cent of their incomes, it was far better to set the rate at a point which these wealthy, good, and wise citizens would think was fair. Remembering his earlier mistake, he now asked that taxes on incomes under $4000 be sliced in half, and that those under $8000 be reduced by from 6 to 8 per cent. Taxes on inheritances and gifts, he felt, should be abolished. Of all this Coolidge heartily approved.

It is no wonder that the press of the country went into paeans of praise the day after this message was delivered. Businessmen were ecstatic. Wall Street responded with a Boom! As William Howard Taft said, President Coolidge's message was "great in the soundness of its economic statesmanship . . . great in its very quiet directness." Nor was Calvin Coolidge exaggerating when, several years later, he recalled that "no other public utterance of mine has been given greater praise."

There were, of course, some who were not carried away by its quiet directness or by its economic statesmanship. Among these were the fighting members of the Farm Bloc who were disheartened by Coolidge's animadversions on agriculture. Here he set himself with granite firmness against any suggestion of governmental aid for the farmers. Calvin Coolidge himself was no farmer, although he liked to posture as one when the photographers came around in the summer, and he was always ready to help pitch hay. From his rural, but not strictly agricultural, Vermont background he was sure that the farmers wanted no system of governmental relief. Like the worker who couldn't get a job the farmer who couldn't make it pay wasn't worthy of self-government. Therefore, the farmer should not depend upon the governmental fixing of prices. "Simple and direct methods put into operation by the farmer himself," said the economic statesman, "are the only real sources for restoration." He was to hear from that later on.

The approaching convention and election were very much in President Coolidge's mind when he made his first important speech. He was not at all shy in making plain the fact that he keenly desired the nomination. Only a few days after delivering his message to Congress he admitted to Washington newspapermen that his hat was in the ring. It was not long before everyone who could read political signs was climbing on the political bandwagon. They agreed with America's greatest individualist and industrialist, Henry Ford, who was the first to crow: "The country is perfectly safe with Coolidge. Why change?"

But if Coolidge had his eye on 1924, so did Congress have its collective and sometimes speculative eye on the same goal. It was inclined to try the nerve of the new President. Such recalcitrants as Senators La Follette, Ladd of North Dakota, Norris and Brookhart, who had a high stake in the coming elections, especially sought to humiliate Calvin Coolidge and build up issues for the campaign. They had their own legislative program, near the top of which was Farm Relief. Next to it was defeat of the Mellon plan.

On the latter they were forced to adopt a compromise, cutting the surtax to 40 per cent, which was, of course, a partial victory for Mr. Mellon. They abolished the surtax on incomes under $10,000 and the normal rate of taxation was lowered from 4 to 2 per cent on the first $2000. But on the other hand the maximum estate tax was raised from 25 to 40 per cent and a new gift tax was established. President Coolidge's anger was raised nearly to the veto point by the inclusion of a so-called "publicity clause," which called for the publication of income tax returns. Coolidge denounced this invasion of personal privacy, which had been inspired by a desire to help halt dishonesty in filing returns, but which was quickly exploited beyond its original purpose by the newspapers. Even the dignified *New York Times* printed long columns of tax returns when they became available. This law remained until 1926.

The most violent assault on the administration came with the introduction of the first McNary-Haugen farm relief bill. Drawn up by George N. Peek, president of the Moline Plow Company, and sponsored in the Senate by slim, intense, scholarly Charles L. McNary of Oregon and in the House by Gilbert N. Haugen of Iowa, it was all that President Coolidge hated most. Briefly explained, it was a bill designed to raise prices on raw materials by segregating the exportable surplus so that the domestic market would not be adversely affected by world prices. The government was to be compensated for losses incidental to this scheme by an "equalization fee" levied on the raisers of the raw material.

Even such a mild attempt at artificial price raising shocked orthodox Republicans. It was to rise again more than once to plague President Coolidge after 1924, but now the Farm Bloc stumbled and the bill was defeated in June of that year by a vote of 223 to 153 in the House. From the beginning the several McNary-Haugen bills aroused wild opposition in Wall Street, essentially because they threatened the country with arbitrary price-fixing by the government rather than by the edicts of private monopoly. This opposition was to grow stronger later on, but Wall Street and the other Eastern centers of private enterprise had little to fear. President Coolidge had no intention of ever letting such anarchy become a law.

Although he was saved from having to put up a fight against the farm bill and from the attendant embarrassment of having it come up before a Senate recalcitrant at backing his policies to the full, President Coolidge suffered one major legislative setback. Against his warnings Congress passed a Soldiers' Bonus Bill. President Coolidge promptly vetoed it. But 1924 was an election year, and the soldiers represented many votes. The House passed it, 315–17, and the Senate, 59–26, over his veto. In this rebellion against the administration the so-called radicals were not to blame. Leading the fight to override the President were these faithful Old Guardsmen: Henry Cabot Lodge in the Senate and Speaker Longworth in the House.

On the whole Calvin Coolidge weathered his first months in office without experiencing any overwhelming difficulties. He kept to the middle road; he kept his mouth shut; he waited for November with great hope and complete faith in Calvin Coolidge, the instrument in the hands of God.

CHAPTER EIGHTEEN

Reaction, Rum, and Romanism

NOBODY was very much excited about the Republican Convention that met in Cleveland, Ohio, on the tenth of June, 1924. There was nothing to get excited about. The Republican Party and its national chairman, William M. Butler of Massachusetts,[1] hand-picked by Calvin Coolidge himself, had everything well in control. Coolidge's old friend, Frank Stearns, was on hand, as happy as could be, to see that everything went off according to schedule. Things were not as they had been four years before when the hungry hordes struggled for power. The old Senate cabal was in the background. Senator Lodge, who had presided so haughtily in 1920, was not consulted on anything and as the convention proceeded was booed by the delegates who were almost 100 per cent for Calvin Coolidge, whose veto on the bonus bill Lodge had voted to override. Jim Watson and Senator Brandegee, who had swaggered their way through the smoke-filled rooms on the night that Harding was lifted from obscurity, were ignored. It was Calvin Coolidge's convention all the way.

Even in the writing of the platform the Old Guard was not consulted. This led some observers to rejoice at their departure, to talk about the resultant revitalization of the Republican Party. They saw a new era of enlightenment. Their cheers were prema-

---

[1] William M. Butler had for many years been attorney for W. Murray Crane, the Republican boss of Western Massachusetts, and long the intra-party enemy of Henry Cabot Lodge. Calvin Coolidge was a product of the Crane machine, through whose ranks he had risen to the governorship. Until it began to appear that he might someday be President, Coolidge had few political friends or backers, except Stearns, in the eastern part of the State. His mild support of the League, which led him to his endorsement of the World Court, stemmed from his association with Crane, who had died shortly after waging an unsuccessful battle for the League at the Republican National Convention in 1920. (See *The Gentleman from Massachusetts*, by Karl Schriftgiesser, pp. 354–358.)

ture. For the surrender of the old gods meant little. The new gods may not have been Senators, but they thought the same, they demanded obeisance to the same decalogue. That they had been replaced by businessmen who were comparative amateurs at the game of politics did not mean that the outlook of the party had been shifted. The man they were working for was no amateur; a politician who had risen through the party machine, he knew his way around. And so did his faithful secretary, C. Bascom Slemp, who as a Republican Congressman from Virginia for fourteen years had long controlled Republican patronage in the South. With Slemp to guide them, the drygoods merchant from Boston and the textile magnate from New Bedford (who had some political experience in Massachusetts) had nothing to worry about.

The platform that was presented to the convention was a dull and dreary document. It was as platitudinous as any ever evolved by a Republican platform committee. The ancient phrases lumbered through its uninspiring length: rigid economy, reduction in taxes, cherished traditions, protection as a national policy, American standards of life, a spirit of independence and self-reliance, private initiative, respect for law, unyielding devotion to the Constitution — they were all there. It said nothing that had not been said four years previously except that, at Coolidge's insistence, it contained a mild endorsement of the World Court. It, of course, met with Coolidge's full approval, for in its endorsement of the Mellon tax plan, the protective tariff, limited aid to the farmers, and the other reactionary party policies, it backed up what was to be Coolidge's most outspoken statement during the campaign: "I am for economy and after that for more economy."

The convention successfully side-stepped the scandals of the Harding administration. Some mention had to be made of them and Theodore E. Burton of Ohio, in his "keynote speech," dismissed them by deploring the "unworthy motives and grasping avarice" of a few individuals and by assuring the public that any suggestion that there was "widespread corruption" in the government was just so much enemy propaganda.

The convention opened on a Tuesday and by Thursday morning it was ready to nominate Calvin Coolidge. This was done at tedious length by a former president of Smith College. It was seconded eight times with appropriate oratory from delegates strategically placed geographically. A Vermont delegate added to the Coolidge legend by telling the delegates that up in his country all the Coolidges were known as people who never wasted time, words, or money. This speech, straight out of the sap bucket, was especially well received. Then the voting began, since there were no other nominations. What might have been a unanimous vote was spoiled by the Wisconsin and the North Dakota delegations, who cast their 28 and 6 votes respectively for Senator La Follette, and by some recalcitrants from South Dakota who cast 10 votes for Hiram Johnson. In spite of these rebellious voices the chairman ruled that the nomination was made unanimous.

There were few nominations for Vice-President. Borah had indignantly refused to take second place to Coolidge, and Governor Lowden made it plain that, despite the wishes of many at the convention, he did not want it either. On the third ballot General Charles Gates Dawes was nominated. The convention was then adjourned. Its three-day length made it one of the shortest national conventions on record.

The Democratic Convention, held in Madison Square Garden in New York, was something else again. It lasted from the twenty-fourth of June to the tenth of July, and during those hot and hectic days more than 100 ballots were cast before the assembled Democrats were able to choose a candidate.

In the four years of the Harding administration the Democrats had failed to put back the pieces shattered by the earthquake of 1920. No party had been as badly split since the Whigs were driven to disintegration in 1852 as was the Democratic Party in 1924. It had no single leader. It had no real program. And it was trying to go in too many directions at one time. The tragic elements of the times affected the party of the democracy while sliding off the back of the Republicans. Everything — Prohibition, religious prejudice, sectional strife, the Ku Klux Klan, economic trends, even the weather (it had been reasonably cool in Cleveland, it was unmercifully hot in New York), mitigated against the Democratic Party. Its lack of cohesion was appalling and yet —

In the sullen, angry, and passionate maelstrom that was the Democratic National Convention of 1924 two of the leading issues of the day, issues which the Republicans ignored, were courageously brought to the fore and subjected to the glaring light of publicity. It was in Madison Square Garden that the Klan, and all its vicious implications to the spirit of democracy, received its deathblow. And it was in this same jam-packed, sweaty, noisy arena that Prohibition was first subjected to the political attack that eventually led to its repeal. And from this same arena emerged two great political figures, each of whom was to be Governor of New York and one of whom was to be President of the United States and the greatest leader of the democracy since Andrew Jackson. As of 1924 the Democratic Convention was a fiasco, but historically it served a high purpose for which the American people should be grateful.

The cleavages that cut deeply into the party's structure were many. At Madison Square they were exposed not only to the light of publicity but to the healing effect of the air. For this was the first national convention ever to be heard over the air waves. For most of the sixteen days of its continuance thousands of American citizens sat glued to their earphones as the Democrats harangued and balloted. It was years before the strident cry, "Alabama casts twenty-four votes for Underwood!" with which the dreary repetition of the roll call began, ceased to echo in countless eardrums.

The fundamental fault of the Democratic Party in 1924 was that it wanted to be like the Republican Party. It forgot its historic heritage as the people's party and wanted to be the Party of Prosperity, too. It listened to the siren call of normalcy and turned its back on reform. It threw aside the social and economic ideals of Woodrow Wilson, although the casting off did not come without a struggle. The Democratic Party was still the party of the Solid South. And in 1924, as in some vast sections even today, the Solid South would have no part of Northern progress. Its resistance to this was manifested through its sheet-clad night riders, those apostles of White Supremacy and storm troopers of native fascism, who sprang from the clash between its growing industrialism and its ancient slave-labor philosophy. Its leaders pitted the poor whites against the poorer blacks. Its tenant farmers and migrant workers were submerged. Its Negroes were restless. Primed by their exploiters, the exploited hated the North, with its foreigners and Catholics and Jews and its restiveness over the Prohibition which the Bible Belt had foisted on the nation.

The great Northern Democratic machines in New York, Hudson County, Boston, Chicago, were unanimous in their opposition to Prohibition and the Catholic-hating Klan.[2] Thus they turned to the one man in the party courageous enough to speak out against these two national evils. In Alfred Emanuel Smith, who was a Roman Catholic rather than a Congregationalist, and who spoke with an East Side accent rather than a Down East drawl, they had found a hero. That he deserved this worship his record amply revealed. But this same record did not impress the South. There, the party turned to William G. McAdoo, who was the darling of the Klansmen, who was Dry, and who spoke with old-fashioned (albeit hypocritical) fervor against Big Business. One further difference between the South and the North existed, although it lay beneath the surface: with the invasion of the South by industry, its ancient advocacy of Free Trade (which had helped make the South solidly Democratic) was on the decline.

The Democratic Party in 1924 was at its lowest ebb. Although there was no one then to recognize its full historic import the dramatic interest of one event at Madison Square Garden did not pass unnoticed. This was the reappearance in public life of Franklin Delano Roosevelt, crippled but indomitable, who stood in his steel braces and delivered one of the happiest nominating speeches any convention anywhere had ever listened to. With felicitous phrases expressing his inbred faith in the liberal meaning of the Democratic Party, Roosevelt called upon the convention to nominate Alfred E. Smith. The Happy Warrior, he called him, and the phrase that might well have been applied to Roosevelt himself lasted longer than the reputation of the man of whom it was then so truly spoken.

Al Smith was ending his second term as governor in 1924. During those years in Albany, where he had served his long

[2] The "bosses" of seven important and pivotal states of the East and North Central sections were Irish Roman Catholics. These states were Illinois, Indiana, Maryland, Massachusetts, New Jersey, New York, and Pennsylvania. "The Brennans and the Taggarts, the Hagues and the Olvaneys were much in evidence. A strange study in contrasts, the convention brought together, though not in harmony, bourbons from the deep South, many of them in wing collar and with flowing mustache, rough-hewn Irish bosses from the Northern cities, ranchers from the west, discontented farmers from the prairies." (See *The Progressive Movement of 1924*, by Kenneth Campbell MacKay, pp. 99–100. Columbia University Press, 1947.)

political apprenticeship, he had made himself by his integrity and liberal spirit one of the really outstanding political executives in the country's history. His was a record of which any chief executive of any state in the Union might justifiably be proud.

The lean, ruddy-faced, gray-templed Al Smith, with his neat clothes and his hair parted carefully in the center, his ever-present cigar and his winning smile, had come a long way from the days when he worked in an East Side fish market. He was a product of Tammany Hall. He knew everything there was to know about big city politics. But in the years of his learning he had not become corrupt. The higher he moved in the inner circles, the greater his integrity became. He stood with poise and dignity before the people who loved him and he wore a brown derby so that they would know he had not forgotten he was one of them. His greatest pride was that there was nobody who could honestly say that the ex-fishmonger, the man who had "taken orders from Tammany and who now gave Tammany its orders," did not know how efficiently and honestly to run the greatest state of all forty-eight.

First elected in 1918, Al Smith had gone to Albany intent upon proving that good government could come from the sidewalks of New York. He did not fill the public offices with political hacks. He put men who knew how into posts they could handle regardless of their political affiliation. He kept the doors of his office open to the public, and these included businessmen as well as beggars for favors. He faced a sneering and hostile Republican legislature whose attitude, as he said, was that he was a political accident who would disappear from public view within two years. They tried to ignore him. But when they tossed aside his Reconstruction Committee, appointed to study the problems created in the state by the World War, he went directly to the people and forced the lawmakers to accept it. And in spite of Republican opposition he created his Industrial Commission to settle strikes, he reformed state employment agencies, and he organized other improvements throughout the state. His program, for which the Republicans would give him no money until he had gone across the state speaking in its behalf, included education for children, adults, and immigrants and the reorganization of the state government along efficient and economic lines. He appealed to businessmen on the grounds of economy. Women supported him for his stand on broader education and because he had placed many women in positions of trust in the government.

As governor, Al Smith showed that he possessed that tolerance which was so lacking in Calvin Coolidge. He made Sunday baseball possible in such communities as wanted it, and he did the same with motion pictures. It was his belief that no people had a right "in law or morals, where they constitute a minority, to impose their views upon the majority." The fascistic Lusk Bill, which would have formed a gestapo to investigate New York's teachers, who, under its edict, would have had to take a special oath of allegiance, he vetoed with these words: "The traditional abhorrence of a free people of all kinds of spies and secret police is valid and justified and calls for the disapproval of this measure."

In 1920 he was a victim of the Republican sweep, but he staged a remarkable comeback in the 1922 election, receiving the largest majority then ever accorded a New York governor. At once he called in his advisers — for, it is true, he originated very little of the legislative program he engineered — and with their help put through as many farseeing reforms as New York ever witnessed. Out of them came a housing commission, a rent control law, civil service for women, salary increases for the state's teachers, children's courts, the rebuilding of state hospitals, state aid to keep fatherless children at home, and improved labor codes.

In one other instance Al Smith took a liberal stand that endeared him to most thinking people. An avowed and devout Roman Catholic, he nevertheless firmly believed in the constitutional separation of Church and State. In April of this election year, when he was about to be a candidate for the nomination, he stood courageously against measures originated within his Church to impose a censorship of moving pictures. With similar courage he helped defeat the so-called Clean Books bill which the Catholic Church was seeking to pass. He said and believed that no form of censorship could be tolerated in a democracy, for censorship, as he saw it, was "not in keeping with our ideas of liberty and of freedom of worship or freedom of speech."

Of all whom the Democrats had to offer none was better qualified for the Presidency than Alfred E. Smith. He knew as little about agriculture as Calvin Coolidge and perhaps as little about the rest of the world as the former Mayor of Northampton. But he had a habit, when he was ignorant of a subject of which he needed knowledge, of calling in the best experts. What they had to teach he had the mind to absorb. He was not a profound thinker and he was no more apt to seek out causes than was the expedient Coolidge. But, once he had been told, he had the uncommon ability of putting the case into the simplest, most understandable of terms; and once he was convinced of the rightness of his cause, he would never give up fighting for it. If he could not convince the legislature by an array of cold facts and figures he would go on the radio and tell the people. It was not until the political fates had embittered him years later and time had passed him by that he forgot the people. Had he worshiped God in a wooden church instead of in a cathedral he might have been allowed to offer them the use of his integrity and brilliance in 1924.

But the Ku Klux Klan was at Madison Square Garden in all its hooded might. And the Klan cared nothing for Al Smith's record, his vote-getting ability, his tolerance, his passion for good government for the people. To the Klansman he was a Catholic and a Catholic to a Klansman was as a Jew to Adolf Hitler. The Southern delegates turned on him with a fury that brought a disgrace to the Southern wing of the Democratic Party which it has never been able to wash out. Joined with the Klansmen were those other potentially fascist-minded citizens who wore, instead of the white robes, the white ribbons of the Anti-Saloon League. Had not Al Smith dared to support as governor the New York State referendum wherein the state was empowered to ask Congress to modify the Prohibition laws? They knew he was a Wet, in spite of his declarations that the Eighteenth Amendment, as part of the Constitution, had to be enforced regardless of the people's will. And so, with all the strength and funds at the Drys' command, with Wayne B. Wheeler of dreadful memory taking personal charge, Smith's bid for the nomination was bitterly fought. Thus Rum and Romanism became the issue, although not then as viciously as it was to be in 1928.

Al Smith's stubborn persistence that he could break down the opposition lasted for two weeks. But at last he realized that the deadlock could never be broken. Already a record had been smashed. On the seventieth ballot the vote had been 415 for William Gibbs McAdoo and 323 for Smith. It was obviously impossible for either man to win. McAdoo realized this. On the ninety-sixth weary ballot both Smith and McAdoo withdrew their names, but the bitterness between them was such that neither would yield to the other. Their strength was thrown to John W. Davis, who had climbed to and stayed steadily in third place. All this the public had heard through their cramped and sweaty earphones, until they were as nearly disgusted with Democracy as were the heat-sickened delegates themselves. A sigh of relief greeted the nomination of Davis on the one hundred and third ballot. Nobody paid much attention then to the fatigued naming of Charles W. Bryan, brother of the Great Commoner, as Vice-Presidential candidate. The Governor of Nebraska was too obviously placed on the ticket as a sop to the West, where the naming of a Wall Street lawyer to lead the ticket might not be well received.

The acrimonious, dissension-ridden convention, the longest since that faraway time in Charleston, South Carolina, when the Secessionists bolted from Stephen A. Douglas and threw the election to Abraham Lincoln in 1860, hardly presaged victory for the Democratic candidate. The delegates went home with their wounds. The party as such had achieved no coalescence. It was still sectionally rent, still unorganized, and its National Committee was still composed of men at loggerheads with each other. Nor did they leave behind a platform built of good political intentions. This had been prepared well in advance of the convention and it reflected none of the issues so bitterly brought to the fore in the sweltering Garden. It bore no condemnation of the Ku Klux Klan, whose repudiation had been achieved to a great extent by the defeat of McAdoo. Nor did it go back, as Davis would have liked it to go, to the spirit of Woodrow Wilson. Instead, in mild terms, it asked for a public referendum of the League of Nations. It took cognizance of the Republican trend towards the sanctity of private enterprise by urging the nationalization of the merchant marine, and it rebuked imperialism by favoring independence for the Philippines. Otherwise the document was as dull and meretricious as that which the Republicans had scribbled at Cleveland.

CHAPTER NINETEEN

The Democratic Gentleman

JOHN W. DAVIS was fifty-one years old when he was nominated for the Presidency in Madison Square Garden in July 1924. For forty-seven of those years he had done nothing for which he could be attacked in the political arena. A true Jeffersonian Democrat, he had a long and impressive record as a liberal. His name had been connected with the writing, passage, and defense before the Supreme Court of legislation which liberals and labor alike held in high repute. As Solicitor General during the administration of Woodrow Wilson he had fought the good fight. But in 1920, with the passing of Democracy from Washington, he had gone to New York to become a Wall Street lawyer. J. P. Morgan and Company, the Erie Railroad, Standard Oil, and the New York Telephone Company were among his clients.

In spite of his associations Down Town, in spite of his Manhattan town house and his Long Island estate, John W. Davis would probably have made a good President. His democratic instincts were inbred in him. He held the political concepts of Jefferson and Woodrow Wilson in high regard. The contrast between him and Calvin Coolidge was the same contrast that existed between James M. Cox and Warren Gamaliel Harding. Intellectually he was far superior to the Vermonter. He was a scholar and a gentleman and he had come farther from Clarksburg, West Virginia, than Coolidge ever got from Plymouth, Vermont. Unlike Al Smith he was not a "man of the people," but he had the same high understanding of their rights and privileges and needs that characterized the Squire of Hyde Park, who was later to succeed where both he and Al Smith failed.

John William Davis's father was a lawyer and a politician. Born in Clarksburg, West Virginia, the son of a saddle maker, the elder Davis stuck to the region of his birth. When the Civil War came he was among those who helped keep his part of Virginia loyal to the Union and later helped establish the new state of West Virginia. He served his district in Congress for four years in the 1870's. His wife, John William Davis's mother, was a remarkable woman. A native of Baltimore, she had been graduated from the College for Women there and, although she reared five daughters and one son, she never gave up the pursuit of knowledge. She wrote poetry, fought for women's rights, painted, played the piano, read Latin and Greek for enjoyment, and spoke French and German. She transmitted her love of knowledge to her only son, who grew up in a rambling, comfortable, book-filled house.

Politics was a passion with Davis's father and next to politics came the law. It was foreordained that John Davis would become involved with both. His first formal instruction came from private tutors but at fourteen he was sent to a boarding school in Monticello, Virginia, and this childhood nearness to Jefferson's home seems to have had an influence on his life. After two years in this environment he entered Washington and Lee University at Lexington, Virginia, where he played football, sang in the glee club, and studied well enough to be graduated within three years.

When the family fortunes were adversely affected by the panic of 1893 young Davis helped earn his way through law school by tutoring. He also spent a year as a clerk in his father's law office in Clarksburg. Then, following a year at the law school of his college, he returned to become his father's partner. After practicing for a year he accepted an offer to teach law at his alma mater. He was back with his father in 1897, a poised, tall, handsome young man of twenty-five, whose greatest attributes were an inquiring mind, a command of concise English, and a personality which endeared him to all who came in contact with him.

Although his father had immersed himself in politics his experiences in postwar Washington had been unpleasant and he constantly warned the younger man to avoid political entanglements. But in 1898 John Davis was nominated for the state legislature against his and his father's wishes and elected by a 200 majority in a traditionally Republican district. Although he served as county chairman of the Democratic Party for the next twelve years he refused to run for office, even when offered the nomination for Congress and for the governorship of his state. He enjoyed his law practice, at which he worked hard and studiously. He had married one of the girls he had tutored while studying for his profession and had one daughter. But his wife died a year after his marriage. Saddened by the tragedy, he threw himself even more seriously into his work, a lonely man with graying hair and a face lined beyond his years.

It was John Davis's philosophy that as a lawyer it was his duty, "just as it is the duty of the priest or the surgeon," to serve anyone who came to his office. Thus he was counsel both for the local glass factories and for the glassworkers' union; for the coal companies and the miners' union; and neither side thought this strange, for he served each with equal objectivity.

When the Democratic state convention met in 1910 John Davis attended mainly for the purpose of preventing his nomination for Congress. The pressure put upon him was tremendous and he telegraphed his father for final advice. The older man wired back two definitely negative replies, but these were kept from Davis by a man who was insistent that he accept the nomination. By this ruse he was inveigled into running for Congress and he was easily elected, for he was equally admired by both Democrats and Republicans.

After his nomination in 1924 the Republican press was almost as fulsome in its praise of Davis as was its Democratic rival. This may have been because it would have been hard indeed for the Republican papers to speak harshly of a Morgan and Company lawyer, but the admiration expressed for his character and abilities seemed genuine.

In Congress, where the Democrats were in the majority, Davis was placed on the important Judiciary Committee, an honor for a freshman Representative. There he did work which should have mitigated greatly in his favor in 1924. John Davis wrote the final draft of the Clayton Antitrust Act. He was author of its famed section forbidding the courts to enjoin workers from striking and of the clause which forbade judges to jail strikers for contempt of court without a jury trial. His speeches before the committee and on the floor, which had great effect in bringing about passage of the act, were of that brief, penetrating quality which later led Chief Justice White to say to President Wilson: "The Court thinks so much of John Davis that when he appears for the government the other side hardly gets 'due process of law.'"

Re-elected in 1913 he returned to his congenial work on the Committee on the Judiciary with the definite ambition of securing a vacancy on the United States Circuit Court. Although political friends pressed Woodrow Wilson for the appointment the President, who did not know him, passed him by. But shortly thereafter he and Wilson became acquainted and the President was so impressed with the West Virginian that he appointed him Solicitor General. He served five years in this post. He broke a long-standing record with the number of his personal appearances before the Supreme Court, where he was unusually successful in his defense of the progressive measures of the New Freedom.

Although he lost his plea for the child labor amendment, which the court found unconstitutional, he won his defense of the constitutionality of the Adamson "eight-hour" act. It was Davis who convinced the court of the President's right to withdraw from public sale lands known to contain oil or minerals necessary for the national defense. He prosecuted the Steel Trust under the Clayton Act which he had written. And he brought many an industrialist and banker, including J. P. Morgan, John D. Rockefeller, Andrew Carnegie, and Charles M. Schwab, before the bar of justice. So successful was he, and so highly regarded by the members of the highest bench, that he would have been named to the Supreme Court had a vacancy occurred.

In 1918, while in Switzerland as American High Commissioner for exchange of prisoners with Germany, President Wilson asked him to succeed Walter Hines Page, who was ill, as Ambassador to Great Britain. He did not feel he could afford the post, but when he counted his assets he found he had enough available funds to carry him through two years. No American ambassador had ever been as friendly towards the British as his predecessor. It was no wonder that, as the *Outlook* reported, the British were chagrined at the assignment to the proud Court of St. James's of an ambassador of whom they knew nothing. (Solicitors General seldom get their names in headlines!) But they quickly got over it for they found him "handsome, suave, soft of voice, precise in phrase, dignified without assertion, well informed without pedantry, a lawyer without legalism . . . easy, shrewd, sympathetic, candid." Or, as the King said, "one of the most perfect gentlemen I have ever met."

John Davis returned to the United States in 1920. He had long since remarried. He had liked the social and professional life of Washington and London. He had outgrown Clarksburg. With his party badly defeated he had no place to go politically and so he accepted an offer from the same New York law firm from which Grover Cleveland had gone to the Presidency. It was not long before he headed the firm. He became counsel for the New York Rubber Exchange, for J. P. Morgan and Company, for the New York Telephone Company — a Wall Street lawyer without peer. His standing as a corporation counsel brought him the presidency of the American Bar Association in 1922.

Two years previously, at San Francisco, Davis had been mentioned as a possible nominee and had, indeed, received enough token votes to mark him definitely as in the running for 1924. In 1923 friends in Clarksburg began building him up. Their activities, spearheaded by Clem Shaver, an astute politician with wide acquaintanceship, produced results. Davis protested, as usual, but Shaver and his friends would not listen. Davis had written in *Party Government in the United States* that he felt as did the early Americans: that no man should openly seek the office of President, perhaps the most powerful in the world, but that the office should seek the man.

He knew that his three years in Wall Street had built a barricade that would be difficult even for one of his integrity and past record to hurdle. But as he said, no one of his clients had "ever controlled or ever fancied he could control" his political conscience. He knew he had served his clients, whether the Glassmakers' Union or J. P. Morgan, faithfully; but at the same time he had always maintained his own independence of mind. He asked, "If one surrenders his own philosophy to win an office, what shall he live by after the office is won?"

At the opening of the convention he realized his chances were very slim indeed. Al Smith controlled at least a third of the delegates; McAdoo had half of them in his hand. John Davis was just another "favorite son," and the weary delegates cheered his name a scant five minutes when it was placed in nomination by the West Virginia delegation. He had only 31 votes on the first ballot.

The newspapers, whatever their political affiliation, had nothing but praise to speak of this man whom the arch-Republican *Boston Evening Transcript* described as the outstanding and straightest thinking Democrat of his day. He was, as everyone agreed, a man

187

who might well be the one to take Calvin Coolidge's measure. And perhaps he would have done this, even in spite of his Wall Street connections, even in spite of his running mate, whom many thousands confused with William Jennings Bryan, if it had not been for Robert M. La Follette.

CHAPTER TWENTY

We Will Gather by the River

WHILE the Democrats were wrangling and bickering in New York, and the Republicans throughout the country were sitting smugly back awaiting the results of that long-drawn-out exhibition of democracy at its noisiest worst, a strangely inspiring event was taking place in Cleveland. There, in the same municipal auditorium where the Coolidge steam roller had done such effective work, a motley crowd of men and women from all parts of the country came together on Independence Day. They were not gathered to listen to inspirational addresses about the Founding Fathers but, as most of them honestly thought, to draw up a new Declaration of Political Independence which would free the people from allegiance to either of the blundering and outworn major political parties.

Officially this meeting of nearly a thousand "broad-shouldered men and earnest women," as one newspaper reporter described them, was the Convention of the Conference for Progressive Political Action. Unofficially it was the gathering by the river of the representatives of some five million Americans who, having heard faint rumblings of thunder on the left, had renewed their dreams of creating a brave new world. They had come filled with disgust at the Republicans' treatment of the farmer and the worker and empty of any hope that the Democrats would offer anything better. Now they were determined that out of this meeting would come a definite program and a definite candidate and, perhaps, even a new party, all of which could be used to smite the forces of reaction that had a stranglehold upon America in 1924.

Those who came to Cleveland with these lofty aims were not like the delegates who had jammed the same auditorium to place the accolade of Babbitry on Calvin Coolidge. Nor were they like the old line of politicians from the Southern plantations and the

Northern slums who were tearing at each others' throats at old Madison Square Garden. A New York reporter called them "a gathering of students" whose average age was under forty, whose collective mien was serious, whose crusading zeal was evangelical. They bubbled with enthusiasm, this diverse gathering of idealists, socialists, single-taxers, college boys and girls, farmers, railroad men, workers, disguised communists, and lunatic fringers, as they sang "Onward, Christian Soldiers" and succumbed to the revivalist spell that the spirit of Fighting Bob La Follette cast upon them.

Jacob Coxey, who had once led his "army" on Washington, was present; so was a bearded editor from New Jersey who had sworn in the 1890's not to cut his whiskers until Populism was triumphant; so was an ancient from Milwaukee who had seen Lincoln nominated and who believed the nomination of La Follette would rank with that event in history. There were bohemians from Greenwich Village, long-haired and horn-rimmed; and hitch-hiking members of the Young People's Socialist League; and a delegate from Boston with a resolution for a plank in the platform compelling Klansmen to wear their sheets twenty-four hours a day. (He also wanted the Volstead Act suspended ten days a year: "That would give the Drys plenty of fresh arguments for abstinence . . . and the Wets a chance to express their true sentiments.") There was a migratory worker named James Francis Murphy who came to Cleveland intent upon nominating himself for the Presidency.

With such as these the correspondents had much fun. Representatives of most of the press filled their dispatches with ridicule in labored efforts to disparage both the convention and Senator La Follette. But even the La Follette-hating *New York Times* had to admit there was "nothing artificial" about the gathering; and the *Herald Tribune* made it clear that nine tenths of the eccentrics attracted to Cleveland would "cool their heels outside this convention." The more comprehending reporters, like Clinton W. Gilbert, whose *Mirrors of Washington* had punctured many a stuffed shirt three years before, saw behind the eccentricity and clearly reported that despite the obvious lack of money and organization the convention represented a serious undercurrent of revolt with which both major parties might have to reckon before November. It was quite possible that what the dissident voters in 1920 had so miserably failed to accomplish might be achieved this year. There was also a possibility that a third party worthy of the name might also here be born. No astute political observer took the Cleveland affair lightly and the more astute managing editors of the reactionary press, taking it very seriously indeed, sought to fight it from the start with the effective weapon of mockery.

The Conference for Progressive Political Action was the result of a demand that had been growing since 1920 for a united front of liberals. Four groups played an important role in its formation. As a result of the kicking around they had received since the war, the Railroad Brotherhoods had become politically conscious. So had the farmers, or at least those who had found representation in the Nonpartisan League before its disappearance as a national organization in 1923. As early as 1921 the Socialists, convinced by the vote of 1920 that they alone could not be effective politically, had begun to make overtures to other progressive groups, hoping eventually to establish a permanent third party. For a time, as the historian Edward M. Sait put it, it seemed as if the Socialist Party were ready to "sacrifice its revolutionary myth to the realities of American economic life and — like the Independent Labor Party in its relation to the Labor Party of Great Britain — accept a place on the left wing of a farmer-labor party." The fourth group was the old Committee of Forty-eight.

The first meeting of the Conference for Political Action was held at the invitation of fifteen railroad brotherhoods in February 1922. This Chicago conference brought together progressives of every size, shape, and description. There were labor men, farmers, and scores of others not attached to any organized group, among the three hundred who answered the call. At least fifty international labor unions were officially represented. The recognized leader among them was William H. Johnston, president of the International Association of Machinists. The organizations represented, and seriously hopeful of accomplishment, included the Committee of Forty-eight, the Socialist and Farmer-Labor Parties, the Nonpartisan League, the National Catholic Welfare League, and the Church League for Industrial Democracy. Not a great deal was accomplished, however, beyond the forming of a Committee of Fifteen whose purpose was to help build up local organizations. A national convention was called for December 1922. The organizations invited to attend this were carefully selected to keep out the more "radical" elements of the country, especially the Communists.

It was pretty impossible for such divergent groups as met in Chicago to arrive at any conclusions; and no platform, or even program for future action, could be agreed upon. A Committee on Declaration of Purposes was formed and eventually it issued an uninspiring "Address to the American People" which blamed "the apathy of the people and their division upon false issues" for the fact that "the control of this visible government has been usurped by the 'invisible government' of plutocracy and privilege" and, after listing fifteen instances of usurpation, pledged themselves to organize for the coming campaign in every state and Congressional district.

Chairman Johnston reported that "although the time was ripe for progressive political action," nevertheless the organization of a third party would have to await further developments. Perhaps the most important result of the meeting was that it brought the full support of *Labor*, the official newspaper of the standard railroad unions with a circulation of about 400,000 copies. This gave the C.P.P.A. a much-needed outlet for its propaganda.

When the second meeting was held in December 1922, the Progressives were greatly cheered by the results of the mid-term elections, although their own tangible effect upon them was difficult to apportion. They had been effective mostly in the farm states and in Colorado and Arizona. Two important issues faced this convention: (1) should it accept the support of Communists? and (2) what should be done about the immediate formation of a third party? The first was solved by the vote of the delegates not to accept the credentials of representatives of the Workers' Party. On the second there was a diversity of opinion. The farmers, true to the principles of the Nonpartisan League, were opposed to a third party, their idea being to work for their ends in the primaries of the two major parties. The Railroad Brotherhoods did not favor a third party at this time. The Socialists, however, did; and there were many more or less independent delegates who also were thus inclined.

For the first time at a C.P.P.A. meeting lines were drawn sharply. On one side were the Trades-Unions and the Brotherhoods; on the other were the Socialists and other Third Partyites. The Brotherhoods carried the day. A brief six-point or "postcard" platform was adopted, calling for public control of railroads, mines, and public utilities; direct election of the President and Vice-President and extension of the direct primary to all forty-eight states; enactment of the Norris-Sinclair farm relief act; increased taxes on high incomes and inheritances and payment of a soldiers' bonus through an excess profits tax; and legislation for better labor laws for women.

The next meeting of the C.P.P.A. was held in February 1924. By this time American labor had been greatly encouraged by the seeming success of the Labour Party in England under Ramsay MacDonald and the farmers by the electoral victories of the National Progressive Party in Canada, which had succeeded momentarily in disrupting the two-party system above the border. Chairman Johnston reported $16,500 in the treasury, mainly from contributions from railroad unions, miners, and machinists. But the most important action was calling the convention now taking place in Cleveland "for the purpose of taking action on nomination of candidates for the offices of President and Vice President." Still no action had been taken on forming a third party, nor was any to be taken in 1924. Although newspapers spoke openly of a third party, there actually was none in that year.

During these years the Communists, having heard from Moscow and accordingly softened their cries for a world revolution, had begun to emerge from the underground into which they had been driven in this country. A Workers' Party was formed in 1921. Within a short time, in its zeal for a united front, the party began its new policy of infiltration into other groups. The C.P.P.A. ignored its demand, sent to the Chicago conference, for moving toward a "common ground" on which all labor unions and every "political party of the workers" could fight together. This meat was too raw for the C.P.P.A. At the conference's second meeting, in Cleveland in 1922, the Workers' Party was refused attendance on the grounds that it was "un-American." But when the Farmer-Labor Party in 1923 invited groups interested in promoting an alliance of farmers and workers the Communists turned out in droves. They came openly as delegates from the invited Workers' Party and secretly from a score or more of smaller organizations and were present in such strength that they dominated the meeting. According to Robert Morss Lovett they also wrecked it when they formed the new Federated Farmer-Labor Party, from which many A. F. of L. labor groups soon withdrew to return to their policy of Gomperism. According to Benjamin Gitlow, the Communists had direct orders from Moscow to prevent the endorsement of La Follette, and they hoped to accomplish this by "kidnaping" the 1924 Cleveland convention as they had kidnaped the Farmer-Labor group the year before.

But La Follette had no use for Communists. "To pretend that the communists can work with the progressives who believe in democracy," he said, "is deliberately to deceive the people." He openly repudiated both the Farmer-Labor Party and the Communists, and "emphatically" protested against their being "admitted to the councils of any body of progressive voters." Thus the Communists were effectively barred from "taking over" the Cleveland convention, for this was to be La Follette's convention almost as much as the one a few days before had been Calvin Coolidge's own. One hundred strong-armed guards were stationed in the municipal auditorium to help Chairman Johnston ward off the vociferous storm troopers from the Kremlin who were expected to appear, their pockets undoubtedly filled with Moscow gold.

The greatest organized strength in the conference came from the Railroad Brotherhoods, and this at a time when labor in general was in a weakened condition. Since 1920 labor had been subjected to withering assaults. In 1924 it was definitely on the defensive. The conservative press fostered the assaults which, as we have seen, had the full approval and open support of the Harding administration. The Red scare was not yet ended. Foreigners were no more liked than they ever were, as the high tariff propagandists well knew. The American Federation of Labor was as scared as business at the "threat of Bolshevism." Thus it was that by 1923, when recovery showed signs of appearance, labor had been robbed of most of its wartime gains. Alone among the powerful unions the Brotherhoods had managed to solidify their position and become even more powerful in the postwar era.

No more individualistic unions existed than the Brotherhoods. They had first been organized as benevolent societies when the big insurance companies had refused to gamble on the lives of men working the trains. As they grew they refused to affiliate with the A. F. of L. They had expected better things of Warren G. Harding than he gave them, and when he allowed Attorney General

Daugherty to run wild during the shopmen's strike of 1922 they lost faith in the Republican Party as it was then constituted. They were ready for political action. But they wanted no part of a third party, any more than old Sam Gompers did. At first they supported William Gibbs McAdoo, the Democrat who was favorable towards labor, but they dropped him when it was revealed that he had taken a lawyer's retainer fee from the oil-stained Doheny. Now they were turning towards La Follette and it was their solidarity as much as anything that gave a semblance of unity and direct purpose to the gathering at Cleveland.

On the eve of the convention the National Committee of the C.P.P.A. announced that it had formally asked Senator Robert M. La Follette to be a candidate for the Presidency. This was a strategic move to forestall any implications that a third party was in the making. La Follette had made it plain that he would only run as an "independent" and his backers at Cleveland were insistent upon following his wishes. By announcing in advance the invitation for him to run they dispensed with any possibility of a nomination from the floor. The Socialists were forced to give in to this, but only after the concession was made that, after the election, another convention would be called for the sole purpose of considering the formation of a permanent third party.

With pretty girls passing the collection plates (they raised $3000 towards expenses) the convention may have had many of the features of a revivalist meeting, but there was a "self-imposed discipline" as well as a buoyant enthusiasm that carried it rapidly forward. The railroad men, the La Follette machine from Wisconsin, the farmers from the Dakotas and Minnesota, co-operated fully. There were some clashes between this amalgamation and the Socialists and certain Farmer-Laborites, but these were soon smoothed over. On the afternoon of the second day the independent candidacy of La Follette was endorsed and a platform adopted — both by acclamation. The National Committee was empowered to select a Vice-Presidential running mate. No third party was formed, but from that day to the end of the campaign the progressive movement was known everywhere as La Follette's party.

There was considerable conjecture in the press over whom the National Committee would choose for Vice-President. Several names from labor's top ranks were suggested and there were reports that Associate Justice Louis Dembitz Brandeis had been urged to run. But when Burton K. Wheeler bolted from the Democratic Party with the remark directed at Davis — "I cannot represent any candidate representing the House of Morgan" — and openly endorsed La Follette, it was a foregone conclusion that Wheeler would be the man. At the time of his acceptance he summed up the situation with these words: "I find myself unable to support either of the Republican candidates, who frankly admit their reactionary standpat policies, or the Democratic candidate who may claim in well-chosen phrases that he is a progressive but whose training and constant association belie any such pretension. *Between Davis and Coolidge there is only a choice for conservatives to make.*" But even like thousands who felt inclined to support La Follette and Wheeler, but who, on election day, could not tear themselves away from party fidelity, Wheeler could not disassociate himself entirely from the Democratic Party. "I am a Democrat, but not a Wall Street Democrat," he said, and announced that he would support the local Democratic ticket in Montana and that especially would he support Thomas J. Walsh for re-election to the Senate.

The platform adopted at Cleveland seems today far less radical than it appeared in 1924. It began with the assertion that the "great issue" was control of government and industry by private monopoly and its outstanding planks were clearly directed towards correcting this evil. The platform had the virtue of brevity and it was pleasantly lacking in ambiguous or platitudinous phrases. Instead it was a model of its kind.

In straightforward language the Progressive platform called for these reforms: The right of Congress to overrule decisions of the Supreme Court; the direct nomination and election of President and Vice-President; extension of the initiative and referendum to the federal government, with provision for a popular referendum for the declaration of war except in case of actual invasion; government ownership of the railroads; and abolition of the use of the injunction in labor disputes.

Towards the end it tacked on a plank on foreign policy, as meaningless and directionless as anything the Republicans or Democrats had offered. Here it merely called for "revision of the Versailles treaty," although it also advocated abolition of conscription and the reduction of armaments. The League went unmentioned, but a careful reading of the plank revealed it as an attack on the League. In reality it was a weak attempt to reach a compromise between Eastern intellectuals, who favored international co-operation, and Henrik Shipstead's Western isolationists, who were an important segment of the Progressive movement.

As had both the major parties so did the Progressives handle the Ku Klux Klan issue like a hot potato. It was so hot no mention was made of it. Later La Follette was to make up for this uncourageous omission by being the first of the three candidates to speak with unmitigated fervor against the Klan and all it stood for and thus force John W. Davis and Charles G. Dawes to attack it. The great moralist, Calvin Coolidge, did not mention the Klan once during the campaign.

In their speeches La Follette, and to a lesser extent Wheeler, sought to make monopoly and reform the two great issues of 1924. By doing so they were following intellectually honest dictates, but they were at the same time making a political mistake. Had the Progressives turned their big guns on the simple issue of "Thou shalt not steal," as one of their own strategists suggested early in the campaign, they would probably have forced the Republicans to take the defensive. Instead, the Republicans turned the fight against monopoly into the specter of Bolshevism seeking to destroy the American way of life.

CHAPTER TWENTY-ONE

From the Plains and Mines

FOR the first time since 1912, when Theodore Roosevelt led some 4,000,000 Americans astray in the wilderness,[1] the people had in the race for the Presidency a third candidate whom they could take seriously. Senator Robert M. La Follette, with his long record of fighting the people's battles, with his gift for oratory, and with his proved ability as a political strategist, was not a man his enemies were likely to look upon without misgivings. In his own heart La Follette knew he had no chance of winning the fight, but the presence of his name on the ballot, as he and Calvin Coolidge and John W. Davis well knew, was a distinct threat to the election's being a cut-and-dried affair. Even the most sanguine Republican at thoughtful moments found his smug assumption of a Coolidge landslide disturbed by the presence of this "radical." There was always a possibility that he might force a deadlock of the Electoral College. And if he managed to lure too many people to his side he would be a definite threat to orderly two-party procedure in 1928. It was all right to sneer at La Follette but not to laugh at him. Not too much, anyway.

For more than forty years Bob La Follette had been making his influence felt one way or another on the American people. In his home state of Wisconsin and in Washington he had raised his voice against most of the evils of the American way of life. In 1913, the year after Teddy Roosevelt had so ingloriously stolen his thunder, he had made clear the philosophy underlying his part in the struggle for Reform — that Reform to which the American people had seemingly said farewell in 1920. "Within the changing phases of a 25-year contest," he wrote in his *Autobiography*,[2]

---

[1] 4,126,020 to be exact; and so scattered that they won him only 88 electoral votes.

[2] Published in 1912.

"I have been more and more impressed with the deep, underlying singleness of the issue. It is not railroad regulations. It is not the tariff, or conservation, or the currency. It is not the trusts. These and other questions are but manifestations of one great struggle. The supreme issue, involving all the others, is THE ENCROACHMENT OF THE POWERFUL FEW UPON THE RIGHTS OF THE MANY. This mighty power has come between the people and their government."

Although Robert M. La Follette was considered a dangerous radical by millions of Americans who saw him mocked and lambasted daily in the newspapers of 1924, the description was hardly accurate. He subscribed to none of the "isms" then prevalent. He particularly abhorred Communism and he held Socialism in but little higher regard. He was intensely proud of the fact that his grandfather had owned the farm in Kentucky next to that of Abraham Lincoln's father. His American roots went back to the middle of the eighteenth century when John La Follette, a Huguenot refugee, fled the religious persecutions of his native France. They were deep in the soil of the Middle Border when he was born in a log cabin in the Wisconsin township of Primrose in 1855.

His youth was one of typical pioneer hardships, neither more nor less than those endured by most boys growing up on hard-worked farms of his generation. He worked his way through the University of Wisconsin, where he met his wife, Belle Case, whose close association with him in his public career is a true epic of American womanhood. In 1880 he was admitted to the bar and that year was elected district attorney over the candidate backed by the boss of Dane County. Four years later he was elected to Congress on the Republican ticket. The youngest member of the Forty-ninth Congress, he served three terms until defeated in the Democratic sweep of his state in 1890. He returned to private practice in Madison where he soon resumed his fight against the political bosses of the Republican machine in the state. With the support of the liberals and Populists he received the Republican nomination for governor in 1900.

Although he won the election, the Stalwarts, as the Old Guard was called in Wisconsin, controlled the legislature. Against their determined opposition he inaugurated a program for reform of the state government. Soon his "Wisconsin Idea," as it was called, was attracting national attention. (We have seen how James M. Cox, as Governor of Ohio, borrowed from it.) The idea was based on four major principles. The first was a system of direct-primary nominations protected by law. The second was an equal tax on corporate property with other property. The third was the regulation of railroad charges to insure fair competition and to prevent the roads from passing their taxes to the public. The fourth was establishment of expert commissions to regulate railroads and other public interests.

Always imbued with an unquenchable faith that the people will do the right thing when they know what they are being asked to do, Governor La Follette took his program directly to them at county fairs, Grange meetings, sessions of Chautauqua, and in every other way possible in those days before radio. The people listened and liked what he said. Most of his program was enacted into law along with other progressive measures, such as better insurance laws, remodeled banking laws, extended civil service provisions, and a long-range conservation program.

In 1905 Governor La Follette sought wider fields. Resigning from the governorship, he went to the Senate, to be re-elected three times by the people of Wisconsin. On the Senate floor, in many battles that have become a thrilling part of American history, he worked to extend the fundamentals of the Wisconsin Idea through national legislation. His fights against the railroad monopolies were epic. The Senate never had a better friend of conservation of national resources. His attacks upon the Old Guard bosses of his own Republican Party made him a proudly hated figure among the reactionaries. With his white shock of hair and his great ability to furnish cold facts with the maximum of oratory he became one of the most watched and listened-to men in Washington, even if he often was fighting for a lost cause. Moved by a passionate belief in the rightness of his thinking, he inspired deep love in those who followed him and deep hate in those who opposed him. Tyrannical, egotistic, impatient, he was not an easy man to understand. But his utter sincerity was appreciated on all sides, and his fiery zeal for reform kept him year after year at the forefront of the endless battle against "the encroachment of the powerful few upon the rights of the many."

His followers were far from confined to Wisconsin and other regions where George Moses's "wild asses of the desert" played.

In 1908 he had received a score of votes at the Republican Convention and, in 1912, until Theodore Roosevelt appeared out of the African jungle, it was La Follette who had headed the Progressive revolt. By stealing his thunder and filching his program (which he had no deep intention of following) the incredible Teddy had driven him off the reservation and ridden to his own deserved political disaster. Later La Follette's opposition to America's entry into the World War, which he looked upon as the further folly of imperialism, had cost him some of his following; but it also had endeared him to others. In the dismal days of Harding's return to normalcy his star shone brighter than ever. It was around his stalwart old figure (he was sixty-nine in 1924) that the liberals and Progressives gathered in the brave effort to keep the government from falling irrevocably into the "hands of the few."

It was only natural that those who had not become victims of the mental inertia of the times should turn to La Follette in 1924. He who had worked so hard through so many years knew that he had little more time left. He decided, as Harold Ickes put it, that it was "then or never for him" and so he girded himself for what he must have known was to be his last great battle. The ferocious old lion quivered with anticipation as he saw the corruption of the Harding Republicans being exposed. He headed for the political jungle with joy in his heart.

If Fighting Bob La Follette was the one natural choice of liberals to head an independent ticket there likewise was no other choice for a running mate than the younger but equally pugnacious Burton K. Wheeler. He, too, had won his spurs fighting for the rights of the many against the powerful few. And in his case the powerful had been powerful indeed. His fights had been spectacular. Perhaps he did not own the deeply inbred philosophy of the older man, but he had the same spirit, the same ambition, and the same fighting heart. His life had been adventurous and stormy and in the course of it he had licked both poverty and disease with the same courage that he was later to summon against the great Anaconda Copper Company, of Wall and State Streets and Montana.

Burton K. Wheeler, so closely associated with the rowdy West, was born in the small manufacturing town of Hudson, Massachusetts, in 1882. A victim of asthma and threatened with tuberculosis, he had headed west after his graduation from high school. He got as far as the University of Michigan, where he earned his way as an itinerant bookseller and dishwasher. When his doctors warned him against returning East, he settled in the wide-open mining town of Butte. His Yankee conscience was jarred by the brutal way Anaconda Copper dominated the city and the state. His first law cases, in defense of miners, showed him how deeply Anaconda had corrupted. He entered politics with the determination to do something about it. In 1910 he was elected to the state legislature on the Democratic ticket. He fought for the repeal of laws which enabled the company to escape payment for injuries received by miners and was at once tagged a dangerous radical for his pains. He joined forces with Thomas J. Walsh, Anaconda's ancient enemy, and helped send him to Washington when Anaconda's hold over the senatorship was broken by the amendment allowing the direct election of Senators.

Tom Walsh reciprocated by recommending Wheeler's appointment as United States Attorney for the District of Montana. Here he sailed into political corruption with a vengeance and struck vigorously at Anaconda. He refused to prosecute wartime strikers on the specious charges of being seditious persons and concentrated his attention upon grafters in high places. He even advocated government ownership of natural resources and railroads, a subversive suggestion in Anaconda-owned Montana. He opposed American entry into the war. In many ways he made himself thoroughly obnoxious to the copper monopolists. In 1918 he was plainly told to quit, or Tom Walsh would be knifed by the Democratic Party. He resigned. But he did not quit. In 1920, with the backing of the Nonpartisan League, he won the Democratic nomination for governor. After one of the bloodiest campaigns in Montana's history he was driven to defeat, losing by about 33,000 votes.

In 1922 Wheeler ran for the Senate. In that mid-term election which showed the potential strength of the Progressive movement and cast fear into the Republican ranks as well as dents into the Republican Congress, he was elected. At once he made himself seen, heard, and disliked. The Yankee from bloody Butte startled the Senate with his brash disregard for the sanctity of seniority. Three months after his appearance on the national scene he instigated his brilliant, daring exposure of Attorney General Daugherty. With Walsh dredging up the oil scandals and

Wheeler smoking out corruption in the Department of Justice, driving some of the privileged characters to suicide and others to the penitentiary, what might have been the death of the Republican Party seemed in the making. But Warren Harding died before the nails were driven home and became the beloved and martyred President, the victim of the wild persecutions of the radicals from the West.

The Progressives turned logically to Wheeler for second place. For one thing, his youth was in his favor: a Democratic crusader with great oratorical gifts, he could cover ground and take the message of Progressivism across the land. His meteoric rise to prominence, the publicity attendant upon his prosecution of Daugherty, his well-known espousal of the miners against the operators, were all in his favor. His bold break with his party clinched the matter. With the aging Fighting Bob La Follette at his side the young prosecutor from Butte set out to help slay the Dragon of Privilege in the summer of 1924.

CHAPTER TWENTY-TWO

Lost in the Silence

AND so, for twenty-eight and one-half million Americans who would exercise their electoral franchise in November 1924, there were three candidates and three platforms for which they could pay their money and from which they could take their choice.

Calvin Coolidge's most apologetic biographer has said that the 1924 campaign was "unimportant, uninteresting, and unexciting." From almost the beginning, he adds, the results were not in doubt. He cites the *Literary Digest* polls to show that there never was a week when Coolidge was not far out in front. This probably was the case for, when the votes were counted, Calvin Coolidge had received the largest plurality ever accorded a Republican candidate. But there were many moments when the Republican high command was not so sure that the nearly four and a half million dollars that it was distributing with such lavish generosity across the land was going to buy the victory so dearly sought.[1]

Calvin Coolidge never for a moment believed that Divine Providence, of which he claimed to be "one chosen instrument," was

[1] The sworn sums spent by each national organization are as follows:

Republican Party

Collected	$4,360,478.82
Spent	4,270,469.01
Returned	573,559.20

Democratic Party

Collected	$ 821,037.05
Spent	903,908.21

La Follette-Wheeler
National Headquarters

Collected	$ 221,837.21
Spent	221,977.58

These were the amounts officially reported. There is good evidence available that the Republicans spent much more than was reported. (The above figures are from *Campaign Expenditures*, Senate Report No. 1100, Sixty-eighth Congress, Second Session.)

going to let him down. He wholeheartedly subscribed to the sentiment invented by good old George Harvey, who gave the Republicans their most effective campaign slogan, "Coolidge or Chaos." Behind these alliterative words lay the Republican strategy — din it into the people often enough that only Coolidge could save America from revolution (but minimize the revolution so that the people wouldn't get the idea that there might be some good reason for having it), and the people would rally around the silent man in the White House to save the American way of life. Ignore the Democratic rival as much as possible, play up the radical threat of the dangerous demagogue La Follette (for perhaps he really was dangerous with his attacks on the *status quo*), and all the while Keep Cool with Coolidge — such was the Republican plan.

The President himself had one outstanding virtue. He knew the tremendous value of saying nothing. That he had nothing to say did not matter. He could sit on the steps of the old house at Plymouth, or he could shut himself up in his White House study and pretend to be busy, and, thus wrapped in the dignity of office, he need not open his mouth. To Plymouth would come such distinguished Americans as Harvey Firestone and Thomas A. Edison to sit with him in smiling silence as he handed that great connoisseur, Henry Ford, a rickety old sap bucket with this endearing if not enduring remark: "My father had it, I used it, now you've got it!" The cameras clicked, the reporters scribbled, and what could an attack upon corruption in high places or a discussion of the evils of monopoly do against such unrehearsed and unspoiled rustic simplicity as that?

Time and again Coolidge was attacked by his opponents in a vain effort to draw him out on the issues, but just as often as he was attacked — for his indifference to the fascistic evils of the Ku Klux Klan, for instance — he said exactly nothing. As Labor Day approached he delivered a carefully prepared speech (which said nothing) on "The High Place of Labor." At the dedication of a monument to General Lafayette he delivered a carefully prepared speech (which said very little) on "Ordered Liberty and World Peace." [2] Upon other occasions of a strictly nonpolitical

---

[2] It did say this, however: "If we want France paid, we can best work towards that end by assisting in the restoration of the German people, now shorn of militarism, to their full place in the family of mankind."

nature — for, as his biographer has said, he did not care "to prostitute his high office in order to gain votes"! — he discussed such momentous topics, striking right at the very heart of the issues, as "Religion and the Republic," "The Genius of America" (this before a group of foreign-born visitors to the White House), or "The First Continental Congress." And two weeks before the election he left the White House to appear at his favorite forum, the United States Chamber of Commerce, where such thoughts as he had fell upon understanding ears. "This is a business country," he said. "It wants a business government." The net effect of these tactics was to present Calvin Coolidge as a man too immersed in his nation's affairs to have time for partisan politics. He thus forced both Davis and La Follette to assume the burden of proof that the Republicans were unfit for leadership.

But while Coolidge played his role as the strong silent man with aplomb, "Hell and Maria" Dawes also wrote a part into the script for himself that gave him full opportunity to display his talents. When he first saw the La Follette-Wheeler platform he spotted the plank calling for the right of Congress to override decisions of the Supreme Court. Dawes astutely recognized this as an issue handmade for the party of law and order. Chairman Butler thought that the Republicans should stick to the economy issue, but Dawes was persistent and went over his head directly to Coolidge, who told him to go ahead. He first denounced it in his acceptance speech and later, as he traveled some 15,000 miles delivering 108 speeches, he really warmed up to the subject.

It was through the Supreme Court issue that the Republicans found their best chance to pin the label of radical on La Follette. Dawes, well known as a superpatriot, made so much noise about it that there were times during the campaign when it seemed as if he, and not Calvin Coolidge, were the Republican candidate. He was not alone, of course, in driving home, with a passion convincing to many good people, the fear that the entire Constitution was endangered by this attack upon the court's traditional supremacy over the American legislature. He set the pace, which never abated, when early in the campaign he cried out against the Progressives as "a heterogeneous collection of those opposed to the existing order of things, the greatest section of which, the Socialists, flies the Red flag!" Wherever he went Dawes could be counted upon to make another attack on radicalism. He clev erly beat at the Democrats with his frequent insinuations that their party was hopelessly smothered between La Follette's Red Radicalism on the left and the "progressive conservatism" of his own party on the right.

The emphasis upon the Supreme Court issue struck fear in the hearts of many people. The Irish looked to the court for protection of their liberties threatened by the Ku Klux Klan, which, in 1924, was at the height of its powers and undoubtedly controlled many legislatures. German Americans recalled that in some instances it had protected their civil rights during the wartime hysteria. Property owners, particularly in rural areas, looked at the court as their bulwark against encroachment. Many of the same arguments that were later to be raised when President Franklin D. Roosevelt sought to "pack" the court were shrilly used in 1924 as the Republican orators fumed against the radical threat.

More than they had in 1920 the Republicans used fear as a political weapon in the "unimportant, uninteresting" campaign of 1924. The presence of La Follette allowed them to stir up the specter of radicalism which they could not have done if they had had to fight only against John W. Davis of Broad and Wall Streets. La Follette's wartime pacifism was dragged out to frighten the people into believing that this man whom Theodore Roosevelt had once called "the worst enemy Democracy now has alive" would turn the country back to its enemies (whoever they were) if he were given the chance. But it was much more fearfully effective, in this period of increasing disillusionment with war and increasing faith in the effectiveness of disarmament, to raise the Red bogey, which the Republicans did with a vengeance. And, as La Follette's latest historian points out, a campaign against Russian Bolshevism and world revolution "would serve to discredit La Follette and, at the same time, frighten rich Republicans into contributing to what might otherwise be a lethargic campaign. The party leaders must have had in mind Oscar Ameringer's remark that it is the business of the old party politician to get campaign contributions from the rich and votes from the poor on the grounds that he will protect one from the other."[8]

The good old charge of "Moscow gold" was freely tossed around, mainly by asking, but not answering, such questions as "How much money has been sent here by Soviet Russia to win

[8] MacKay, *op. cit.*

this fight?" Newspaper advertisements appeared with such phrases as "I like Silence and Success better than Socialism and Sovietism." Wide publicity was given in the press — of which an estimated 80 per cent, including several powerful Democratic organs like the *Boston Post*, was supporting Coolidge — to terrified statements by great industrialists. Former Senator Coleman du Pont saw the Constitution being "torn down" if Coolidge was not elected.

Cyrus H. K. Curtis turned his New York and Philadelphia newspapers and his powerful magazines, especially the *Saturday Evening Post*, over to a blatant campaign to instill a fear of impending revolution into the hearts of the great army of Babbitts whose Bibles his publications were. President Harding's old supporter, General Atterbury of the Pennsylvania Railroad, distributed 30,000 copies daily of a violent *Country Gentleman* editorial by printing it on the back of dining-car menus. Samuel Blythe, who was Curtis's chief propagandist for Republicanism (although he disguised himself as a distinguished journalist), thought up such things as calling La Follette the candidate of "the Reds, the Pinks, the Blues and the Yellows." Thus it was dinned into the American ear that America was on the verge of being taken over by the Bolsheviks, its Constitution torn in shreds, its Supreme Court slaughtered, its railroads turned over to the politicians,[4] its colleges turned into laboratories "for mad experiments," its industry and business wrecked by foreigners, and its labor perverted by strangers within the gates.

Not content with this, or perhaps because they thought they should get more for their four and a half million dollars, the Republican high command thought up another scheme with which to frighten the people. They had built up La Follette and Wheeler as menaces to the continued prosperity of America. Of course, in doing this, they had to admit that there was at least an outside chance these dreadful demagogues would win. Their explanation of how this might happen was ingenious. To the fear of an emasculated Supreme Court and to the fear of Bolshevism was now added the fear of a Deadlocked Electoral College.

[4] Although an Italian politician, having taken over the railroads, was making them run on time, much to the delight of many a Republican, including Ambassador Richard Washburn Child, whose ecstasies over Mussolini did much to popularize him among the better people.

Article XII of the United States Constitution is explicit in its instructions as to what must be done in the extreme event of enough votes being cast for a third party candidate to make the choice of a President by the Electoral College impossible. Should the College become deadlocked the Constitution provides for throwing the election into the House of Representatives. There a majority is necessary for election. The Republicans were realists enough to know that the Democrats, in coalition with the insurgents and Progressives, might well be able to prevent either Coolidge or Davis from receiving this essential majority vote. The Constitution is also clear about what happens in this case. It says that "if the House . . . shall not choose a President . . . before the fourth day of March . . . then the Vice-President shall act as President, as in the case of the death or other constitutional disability of the President." The choice of the Vice-President under such circumstances is left to the Senate.

At the time this dire possibility arose most of the straw votes being taken in this "unimportant" campaign indicated that La Follette had enough strength to deadlock the College and throw the election into the House. At that time, when the new administration did not take over until March 4, the Lame Duck Congress would be the one to choose the Chief Executive. And, as we have seen, this Congress was controlled by the Democrats and insurgents. Was it not possible, even probable, that the Senate would choose the Democratic nominee, Charles W. Bryan, whose very name was anathema to all "right-thinking people," as Vice-President?

Constitutional though such a happening might be, it would lead to nothing but chaos. And the opposite of chaos in 1924 was Coolidge. Harlan F. Stone, then Attorney General but soon to become an Associate Justice of the Supreme Court, lent the weight of his legal opinion to the correctness of this prophecy of what might come to pass. Now it was Bryan, not La Follette, who was the great threat. Stone, and John W. Weeks, the Secretary of War, and a host of others, including some of New York's most prominent bankers, were so disturbed about this potential perversion of the electoral tradition that Secretary Weeks took to the expensive air waves to spread this new fear about. (It was not considered good strategy to suggest that, if La Follette was elected and was able to carry out his plan for the direct election of the President, such a mix-up could never again occur!)

Early in October the *Literary Digest*, then the not discredited taker of national election polls, published an advertisement more calculated to stir the pocketbooks of Republicans than to sell magazines. In bold type it shouted: *La Follette Cutting Down Coolidge Lead.* A poll by the Hearst newspapers (once favorable to La Follette but soon to announce themselves reservedly for Coolidge) made a similar report. The reactionaries took fright. Calvin Coolidge's secretary, Bascom Slemp, worked to get the National Committee to aid Congressmen whose elections looked close, but who would vote for Coolidge in case the election was held in the House. At about this time reports of violence, vote buying, intimidation, obstruction of La Follette meetings and rallies, greatly increased. The files of the Civil Liberties Union were jammed with complaints. Workmen were told they would be out of jobs if Coolidge lost. The employees of many corporations were forced to contribute to the Coolidge cause. Vigilantism replaced quiet persuasion. Conservative Democrats as well as Republicans in offices, shops, and factories were told that they had better vote for Coolidge or else. . . . The press, in the post-election words of Mr. Hearst's favorite newspaper, the *New York American*, succeeded in drawing "millions" of votes from La Follette to Coolidge "because La Follette's program was *successfully misrepresented.*"

Whether La Follette ever had sufficient strength to win, or even to bring the Electoral College to a deadlock, it is impossible even now to determine. His campaign was woefully unorganized; it had hardly enough money to function; it had virtually no press support, except in some farm papers, in *Labor*, and in the newspaper chain of E. W. Scripps. It lacked experienced political workers and had no "machine" support except from the Socialists and the La Follette organization in Wisconsin. Furthermore election laws kept La Follette's name off, or made it almost impossible for it to appear on, the ballots in many states. The campaign had to fight the $4,000,000 Republican war chest — which did not include payment for advertisements like those in the Curtis papers or those published by the *Literary Digest*.[5]

[5] It has been calculated that the Republicans spent at least $15,000,000 — and Senator Borah, chairman of the Senate Investigating Committee put the

The La Follette committee had to depend for funds mainly on the activities of one William T. Rawleigh, a Freeport, Illinois, patent medicine manufacturer who had an abiding hatred of high tariffs. He was treasurer for the campaign and threw in at least $30,000 in $10,000 chunks. Wisconsin-born, Rawleigh worshiped La Follette personally and apparently wanted nothing more than to see him succeed. So poor were the La Follette committees that they had only $50 to spend in New York on election day. In moral support they were not much better off. That great dissident, William Borah, supported Coolidge; George Norris was not active in La Follette's behalf. And the backing of the American Federation of Labor was given in such a halfhearted manner that it impressed no one.

One lucky factor aided the Republican sweep. Farm prices began to rise rapidly in October, hogs jumping to $11, the highest price in two years and $4 over what they had been quoted at in July. Wheat reached its highest peak since 1921. Other grains rose. Bad crops abroad were responsible for a rapidly expanding foreign demand. This jump in prices was felt throughout the Middle West and in the Northwest. On October 11, the *Chicago Tribune's* political observer predicted with deadly accuracy that

---

figure at $30,000,000; more than a dollar for every vote cast! — to make Coolidge President in 1924. Even if this was exaggerated, the unreported contributions, the sums spent on advertising and propaganda, but not attributed to the party, raised the expenditures far above the $4,270,469.01 the party admittedly spent. Frank Walsh, a legal representative of La Follette, estimated 92 per cent of the contributions made to the Republicans came from large industrial concerns and banks and that 71.4 per cent came from contributions of $1000 or more. (See MacKay, *op. cit.*, p. 186, and *New York Times*, November 2, 1924.) Samuel Untermeyer, in a private memorandum, said that of contributions totaling $2,101,400.80, more than $682,000 came in the form of contributions of $5000 or more. Among the contributors who gave more than $10,000 each were William Wrigley, Jr., James A. Patten of Evanston, Illinois, Payne Whitney, Arthur Curtiss James, the railroad magnate, and J. B. Duke, the tobacco tycoon. (MacKay, *op. cit.*, p. 187.)

A large part of the Democratic fund also came from big industrialists and bankers. John D. Ryan of New York gave $55,000; Thomas L. Chadbourne gave $20,000; and Jesse Jones of Houston and Washington (during the New Deal) came across with $25,000. Evidently the more conservative Democratic fund givers were as scared at the specter of a Bryan in the White House as were the Republicans. Contributions lagged sadly towards the end of the campaign and the Democrats had to borrow $120,000 from the New York Trust Company and ended the campaign deeply in the hole. (See MacKay, *op. cit.*, pp. 187–188, and Senate Document No. 1100.)

the rising prices meant the difference between victory and defeat for Coolidge.

While Coolidge sat smugly in the White House and Dawes ranted about the country, while La Follette toured the East and Middle West in vain attempt to stir an apathetic public to the evils of bigness, John W. Davis did the best he could in his unhappy position between the two extremes. He was subjected to as many attacks from the Left as from the Right. He was never allowed to forget that he was a Wall Street lawyer. He was called a "false liberal" because he once was the director of a railroad that had resorted to an injunction during a strike. He was assailed for having kept silent during A. Mitchell Palmer's dreadful Red hunts. And his recent assertion to the American Bar Association, which he headed, that "human rights" and "rights of property" were of equal importance was used to belabor him.

To such attacks he made no answers, but preserved his energy in a fruitless appeal to liberals and Progressives not to throw away their votes by giving them to La Follette. This, he said, would only help the Republican Party. How right he was! He did not attack La Follette's own past program, even if he did not approve of government ownership or the crippling of the court's final powers. Most of his fire was directed at the "corruption in high places, favoritism in legislation, impotence in government, and a hot struggle for profit and advantage which has burdened us at home and humiliated us abroad," and for which he blamed the Republican Party. He traveled thousands of miles, crisscrossing the entire country. He sailed into the Harding regime, but he carefully refrained from hurling "charges against the honesty and integrity of the present occupant of the White House." He tackled issues and showed a fine understanding of public affairs.

But one thing was wrong, very wrong. The Republicans would not pay any attention to him. Coolidge kept mum, Dawes chased the Red bugaboo up and down the land. "Thus," said Irving Stone, "Davis was forced to shadow-box! He got in some telling blows at his side-stepping opponents, but each time he struck hard the Republicans would murmur, 'Go away, we're not fighting you. We're fighting La Follette. You're not important in this election. You're the third party that has no chance! By remaining quiet you can help us defeat the Reds.'"

To the slogan, "Keep Cool with Coolidge," Davis replied in

one of his most effective speeches. "There are gentlemen in this country," he said, "who believe that the greatest duty a public servant can perform is to keep cool! No one can deny that the chief characteristic of the present administration is silence. If scandals break out in the government, the way to treat them is silence. If petted industries make extortionate profits under an extortionate tariff, the answer is — silence. If the League of Nations or foreign powers invite us into a conference on questions of world-wide importance, the answer is — silence! The Republican campaign is a vast, pervading and mysterious silence, broken only by Dawes warning the American people that under every bedstead lurks a Bolshevik ready to destroy them."

And it was in that very silence that John W. Davis, Democratic candidate for President, was swallowed up. He might tear into documented tatters Andrew W. Mellon's scandalous association with the Aluminum Trust, or Charles G. Dawes's unpleasant association with a Chicago bank scandal, or a score of damning instances of special privilege, but his words were lost — in silence. The path he dreamed might lead him to the Presidency was bringing him to political oblivion instead. For you might lead Coolidge to an issue, but you could not make him discuss it.

When the votes were all counted Calvin Coolidge had received 15,725,000 popular votes; Davis 8,386,500; La Follette, 4,822,000. There was no question now of the Electoral College being cheated of its rightful privilege. Coolidge had 382 electoral votes, Davis had 136, and La Follette — in spite of all the Republican fears or perhaps because of all the Republican dollars — had 13.

But the popular vote of 1924 is not a particularly satisfactory indication of the strength of the candidates. The most amazing thing about 1924, the year of the great indifference, was that only 52 per cent of the qualified voters went to the polls. In South Carolina only 8 per cent cast ballots. In Georgia and Mississippi only 10 per cent went to the polls. What price the Solid South in 1924? In six other "solidly Democratic" states less than 20 per cent of the men and women qualified to vote were sufficiently stirred, even by the Bolshevik bogey, to do so. La Follette's 13 electoral votes came from his own state of Wisconsin, although he received four times as many votes as Davis in California (where Hiram Johnson supported La Follette) and twice as many in 17 trans-Mississippi states. Calvin Coolidge's vote failed to exceed the combined vote for his two rivals only in nine states. At the same time the Republicans won back Congress with a majority of 12 in the Senate and 60 in the House.

The era of Coolidge Prosperity had begun. The stock market started its dizzy climb, experiencing in November and December the greatest boom on record up to then. The Republican Party — Calvin Coolidge's Republican Party and not that of the Old Guard — was in the saddle. There were few in November 1924 to recall and interpret correctly what Woodrow Wilson had meant when, in his First Inaugural address, he had said:

"The success of a party means little except when the nation is using that party for a large and definite purpose."

CHAPTER TWENTY-THREE

A President Abdicates

THERE have been Inaugural Addresses which by their very force and majesty have gone down in history not only as great state papers but as literature. The inaugural address which Calvin Coolidge delivered on March 4, 1925, is not one of them. It does, however, have one claim to historic mention: it was the first inaugural address ever broadcast over the radio. More people probably listened to it than had ever listened to a broadcast speech before. There is every reason to believe that the vast majority of those who heard the dry, twangy voice were eminently satisfied with what the President of the United States said. For, as Calvin Coolidge so keenly observed, the people of America had at long last achieved "a state of contentment seldom before seen."

Although it was officially an Inaugural Address, in reality Calvin Coolidge's message to the people of the United States was an announcement of his abdication. Under his cautious, and sometimes even cowardly guidance, the Presidency was to be stripped more completely of its powers of leadership, both political and moral, than it had ever been before. Although corruption of the Fall-Daugherty kind was not to plague his administration, and the hangers-on like Jess Smith and the blatant grafters like Colonel Forbes were gone from Washington, an even more destructive corruption was to overhang the National Capital for the next four years: the corruption born of inaction, indifference, intolerance; the corruption of the democratic spirit, which led the people to a senseless participation in what John W. Davis called the "hot struggle for profit and advantage" that was to burden us even more heavily at home and humiliate us even more deeply abroad before this incredible era had run its course.

Completely devoid of intellectual content, the message lulled the people and brought renewed hope to those who were the vested leaders of this materialistic age. For Calvin Coolidge made it very plain that he knew the "wise and correct course to follow." There would be no interference by his administration with things as they are. There would be no radical or idealistic attempts at regulation of the business, the industry, the economic setup of the country. In the most emphatic portion of his address he made it clear indeed that he understood the mandate of the election — "economy in public expenditure with reduction and reform of taxation." Neither he nor the government would make any move that would "destroy those who have secured success." Instead he would seek to "create conditions under which everyone will have a better chance." The temple was open to the money changers.

"We are not without problems," he admitted, "but our most important problem is not to secure new advantages but to maintain those we already possess." There was nothing wrong with the world. There was no need for visionary men. For was it not a fact, obvious to anyone with eyes to read the stock market table, that prosperity had arrived and that even "under the helpful influences of restrictive immigration and a protective tariff, employment was plentiful, the rate of pay high"? Shut out the world and trust in self-sufficiency. Perhaps also we should take membership in the World Court, but only if every inch of American sovereignty were secure and our safe position of "political detachment and independence" were maintained.

"America seeks no earthly empire built on blood and force," Coolidge declared. "No ambition, no temptation, lures her to the thought of foreign dominions. The legions which she sends forth are armed, not with the sword, but with the cross. The higher state to which she seeks the allegiance of all mankind is not of human but divine origin. She cherishes no purpose save to merit favor in the eyes of God."

Coolidge would have been a little happier over the enthusiastic reception of this speech if it had not been for the antics of the Vice-President. Apparently Dawes had not quite recovered from the exuberance of his campaigning for he chose the hour that should have been solemnly dedicated to the inauguration of the President to deliver one of his more bombastic outbursts. When President Coolidge arrived for the ceremonies he found the eyes of everyone turned, not upon himself, but upon Dawes, who was delivering a blistering attack upon the Senate, over which he was to preside, for its lack of application, accomplishment, and seriousness. The headlines that should have been Coolidge's became Dawes's, but there is no record that the Senate changed its ways.

Done with his pious platitudes, President Coolidge turned to those problems he grudgingly admitted he knew we were not without. His cabinet was to be somewhat different from that "association of great minds" with which he had sat down during his first years in Washington. Frank B. Kellogg, now Ambassador to Great Britain, would soon replace Charles Evans Hughes as Secretary of State. Henry Wallace of the brave heart had died in November and had been replaced by William M. Jardine, the head of the Kansas State Agricultural College and a vigorous opponent of McNary-Haugenism in any form. In the Navy Department was Curtis D. Wilbur as replacement for the unhappy Denby. Dwight F. Davis had taken over the War Department where former Senator Weeks had left it. Otherwise there were no changes. Mr. Mellon was still emulating Alexander Hamilton; Mr. New was still Postmaster General, "Puddler Jim" Davis still rumbled on at the Labor Department, as did Hubert Work in Interior, where he had gone after the disgrace of Fall. And Mr. Hoover, of course, still ran the Department of Commerce with his firm hand.

Immediately after the inauguration, the Sixty-eighth Congress convened for its second session. One of its first tasks was the confirmation of an Attorney General. At once President Coolidge learned that victory at the polls did not mean he would have unquestioned control over Congress. The Senate made this clear to him when he sent the name of Charles B. Warren as his choice for this cabinet post. Warren had long been active in Republican politics. He was attorney for the Michigan Sugar Company and was known around the Capitol as a "fixer" for the sugar trust. That he had been chairman of the platform committee at Cleveland made no difference. His reputation was such that the Senate could not conscientiously place him in an office that might well be asked someday to investigate and even prosecute the powerful sugar monopoly. The Progressives and the insurgents, remembering how the Senate had accepted Fall without question, jumped on him. President Coolidge broke his silence long enough to repudiate their attacks, but, for the first time in more than fifty years, the Senate refused to approve a cabinet appointment.

It was a narrow victory for Warren's opponents, and it was all Dawes's fault. Had this eminent critic of the Senate's lack of application not been taking an afternoon off to nap in his hotel room he could have saved the day for Coolidge and Warren. The President was so angry at the humiliating defeat that he snapped the name of the sugar attorney right back at the Senate. This time, Dawes was present and wide-awake, but Warren's name was rejected by a vote of 46 to 39. President Coolidge then dipped into his Vermont memories and called upon a Ludlow, Vermont, attorney named John Garibaldi Sargent to take the post. Since the Senate knew nothing about the old gentleman they unanimously confirmed him. Chief Justice Taft said he made a very good Attorney General.

President Coolidge, incidentally, had only one chance to insure judicial backing of his expressed belief that "business should be unhampered and free" by adding to the Supreme Court during his Presidency. And when this chance did come he made a slight mistake in judgment. The retirement of Associate Justice McKenna produced the last change in the Taft court. Coolidge appointed Harlan Fiske Stone to the vacancy, apparently in the belief that Stone was a conservative, since he had been a successful corporation lawyer prior to his becoming a professor of law at Columbia. Senator Norris, already incensed by the way Coolidge was filling high office with men imbued "with the viewpoint of special interests and corporations," sought to persuade the Senate that Stone was another of these. He said the lawyer had "spent all his life in the atmosphere of big business" and the "viewpoint of the individual is part of the man, is part of the judge." But Norris lost his fight, and sixteen years later, when President Roosevelt elevated Stone to the Chief Justiceship, he made a handsome public apology for his earlier error. Not only Norris but Coolidge himself was surprised to find Justice Stone immediately aligning himself with Oliver Wendell Holmes, Jr., and Louis D. Brandeis, thus splitting the court 6 to 3 in favor of what Taft called "progressive conservatism."

Not only in the Warren incident but in almost every crisis during his regime Calvin Coolidge failed to show marked ability in exercising leadership over Congress. He did not want such leadership. In his unwillingness to create or guide legislation he was even more unaware of the purposes of his office than Warren G. Harding had been. In his *Autobiography*, Coolidge offered this apology for his stand. After admitting that he thought the President, "as the party leader," should do his best to see that the party's platform was translated into legislative and administrative action, he added: "I have never felt it was my duty to attempt to coerce Senators or Representatives, or make reprisals. The people sent them to Washington. I felt I had done my duty when I had done the best I could with them. In this way I avoided almost entirely a personal opposition, which I think was of more value to the country than to attempt to prevail through arousing personal fear."

William Allen White better expressed this dislike for a fight for principle, this distaste for entanglement with the legislature, when he said that Calvin Coolidge felt that "public administrators would get along better if they would restrain the impulse to butt in or be dragged into trouble. They should remain silent until an issue is reduced to its lowest terms, until it boils down to something like a moral issue." As the *New York Times* put it in 1926, Coolidge believed the Congress was successful when its members "assumed their own responsibility and undertook to function as an independent branch of the government without too much subservience to the executive." The fact is, Calvin Coolidge had a profound distaste for legislation. He thought there were too many laws. He felt the salvation lay in quiet administration and not in brash expansion of regulations.

So deeply did Coolidge believe in the separation of the two branches of government that Congress often found it difficult, even impossible, to discover the President's views. During his administration he had to face no domestic problem more important or more pressing than that of agriculture. But only once, in advance of legislation, did he make his views known. Congress had to read his veto messages to find out what he did *not* want. "Apparently," says Professor W. E. Binkley, "he wanted to attend to his constitutional functions, recommend legislation, and then usually let the matter alone. He would not busy himself with Congressmen, getting the measure passed. If Congress rejected his recommendations they could bear the odium while he reaped the credit for proposing them."

Occasionally President Coolidge would appeal to the public for support, usually by the method of issuing statements through the press. But he very seldom directly approached the people. He made little or no use of the radio. Perhaps he felt it beneath the dignity of his office; at any rate, as he said, he believed that the President "cannot, with success, constantly appeal to the country. After a while he will get no response." (It is a good thing for Coolidge's peace of mind that he did not live to know the power of the Fireside Chat!) Coolidge's innate mistrust of the people — the people who sent not only Congress but himself to Washington — was one of the gravest defects in his character.

Even less than during the Harding regime was there any organic connection between the White House and the Capitol. That arch Republican, McKinley, had realized the necessity for a close relationship and so had Teddy Roosevelt, who had a special telephone installed so that he could always be in touch with his agent in the Senate, Senator Lodge. But Coolidge cultivated no intimate and trusted deputy in either House except the ineffectual Senator Butler, whom he could depend upon to try to impose his wishes upon Congress.[1]

Coolidge's tremendous popular victory at the polls had brought him great prestige, but in spite of his training in Massachusetts, he seemed to lack sufficient sense of the political realities to translate his popularity into legislative leadership. Of course, he had no definite program to put across. The negative qualities of Republicanism in 1924 did not call for dynamic leadership. If they had the party would have looked beyond the Massachusetts State House for its man.

So little did Congressmen look to Coolidge for guidance that

[1] William M. Butler, the national chairman, was appointed by Governor Channing Harris Cox of Massachusetts to fill out the unexpired term of Senator Lodge, who had died. Butler, who was not too well liked by many Republican Senators and who had the disadvantage of being a newcomer to the Senate, acted as Coolidge's personal spokesman on the Senate floor. This gave him a certain prestige, but was not always conducive to maintaining harmony between the White House and the Senate. In 1926 Senator Butler, in spite of Coolidge's support, was defeated for election to the Senate by David I. Walsh, Democrat, who won by more than 50,000 votes. Butler was a dictatorial sort of person, a bumptious Babbitt. He offended many people and made many enemies within his own party. A typical businessman in politics, he belonged definitely to the Coolidge era when business was the business of America.

there came a time when that most faithful of all Republicans, the dictatorial Speaker Longworth, would leave his chair to take the floor of the House to rebuke the President. A naval appropriations bill was under discussion. It was an administrative measure. But the Republican speaker, who should have been the legislative guide for the Republican President, spoke out in defiance of Coolidge, the Bureau of the Budget, and party policy to remind all that Congress was, in the final analysis, responsible to the people. Coolidge's few attempts to influence the Senate through intimate White House conferences with its leaders were so unsuccessful that Mark Sullivan was led to write a critical article entitled "Coolidge Versus the Senate."

The record of his first year in the Presidency, with a hostile Congress, was far from happy: Congress passed the soldiers' bonus over his head; they tacked Japanese exclusion onto the immigration bill over his protests; they ignored his plea for adhesion to the World Court; they slashed his and Mellon's tax measure.

After his election this same Congress in lame-duck session acted as if he had not been returned to the White House by a record-breaking popular vote. In the face of his pleas for economy they raised their own pay. They contemptuously tossed aside his vague recommendations with respect to agriculture. And they sneered at his economy program by passing a postal salary bill, which he vetoed and which was saved from the final enactment only by the drastic efforts of Senator Curtis, the new Republican leader, who had taken over following the death of Henry Cabot Lodge in the week following Calvin Coolidge's election.

Although the Republicans had a majority of six in the Senate when the Sixty-ninth Congress met in December 1925,[2] this preponderance meant little. The insurgents were still in business. The administration could hardly depend upon such unpredictable gentlemen as Senators Borah, Norris, Brookhart, Frazier, Nye, Norbeck, or McMaster. The sudden and tragic death of old Fighting Bob La Follette had not taken that hated name from the roster of those who so often joined with the Democrats to embarrass the administration. Young Bob La Follette, Jr., had been sent to Washington by the saddened people of Wisconsin to sit in his

[2] The Sixty-eighth dissolved on March 4 and there was no session of Congress until the Sixty-ninth convened on December 7, 1925, to stay in continuous session until November 10, 1926.

father's seat. In the House there was also a nucleus of insurgents. A dozen of them had felt the whiplash of "Boss" Longworth when they had voted against him in his race with Finis J. Garrett of Tennessee for the speakership, their punishment being removal from important committees to minor assignments.

Calvin Coolidge's message to the Sixty-ninth Congress was a dull paper, even for him. He high-lighted it with a lecture to Congress, telling that body that the "functions which the Congress are to perform are not those of local government. The greatest solicitude should be exercised to prevent any encroachments upon the rights of the States or their various political subdivisions. Local self-government is one of our most precious possessions. It is the greatest contributing factor to the stability, strength, liberty and progress of the nation. It ought not to be infringed by assault or undermined by purchase. It ought not to abdicate power through weakness or resign its authority through favor. It does not at all follow that because abuses exist it is the concern of the federal government to attempt their reform."

Many Republicans, listening to this seemingly old-fashioned and slightly Democratic-tinged espousal of States' rights, were as shocked as they ever allowed themselves to be shocked by anything Calvin Coolidge said or did. It seemed to them to be a reversal of a historic party principle. But it was quite in keeping with the Republican policy of nonintervention in the affairs of business by government. The more cynical realized that Coolidge was saying in a sort of political double-talk that the federal government should let regulation and control be the affair of the more easily manipulated state legislatures. Stability, strength, liberty, and progress — for Business — could best be secured if the United States government kept its hands off.

As to the rest of the message, it was a safe-and-sane document mildly espousing adherence to the World Court and the upholding of the "spirit" of the Prohibition laws.

A few weeks before Congress convened, Andrew Mellon had announced the glad tidings that his examination of the nation's financial structure revealed that the Treasury could afford to accept a cut in federal taxes amounting to $300,000,000. The Congress, which only a short time before had slapped Coolidge with the rejection of Warren, put up hardly any opposition to Secretary Mellon's perennial request for income tax reduction. The minimum surtax on incomes was cut from 40 per cent on $500,000 to 20 per cent on incomes of $150,000 — which meant that America's growing family of millionaires paid in 1926 less than one third the income tax they had paid the year before. For example, Andrew W. Mellon saved more than $800,000 that year.

One phenomenon which politicians of either party had long feared became a subject for investigation by this Congress. Everyone was realizing by now that Prohibition was getting out of hand. No one had the courage to come right out and say it was corrupting American life and ought to be repealed. But Senator James Reed of Missouri did hale Wayne B. Wheeler of the Anti-Saloon League, probably the most powerful lobby then active in Washington, before a committee. He subjected Wheeler to a grueling examination which revealed, among other things, a close alliance between the League and what, for want of a better term, was called the Bootleggers' Lobby. But, as so often happens to Congressional investigations, nothing but flaming headlines resulted. Congress took no action.

In the lame-duck session of the Sixty-eighth Congress which had so belabored the President, there had arisen a phrase that struck terror to the hearts of the Republican Party and haunted it even after Mr. Coolidge chose not to run. This dread phrase was — McNary-Haugenism.

There were to be several McNary-Haugen bills offered in Congress to aid the farm industry in the years that led to the New Deal and its Agricultural Adjustment Acts. This first such measure was the product of the fertile mind of George Nelson Peek, the president of the Moline Plow Company, whose general counsel was General Hugh Johnson, later to become the vitriolic director of President Roosevelt's National Recovery Act and creator of its unforgotten symbol, the Blue Eagle. Peek has been best described by Russell Lord: "An industrial agrarian of magnificent stubbornness and simplicity, he plowed just one furrow — 'Equality for Agriculture' — and plowed it straight." He had made a fortune in the plow business but before 1920 had realized his ambition to "come back and live in the country the way I wanted to live." He was doing that in 1920 when, as he put it, "the rest of the country started putting the screws on agriculture again. Then I got mad and came out of my hold to fight." In conversation with General Johnson one day he coined the phrase that was at the bottom of his long fight for parity prices: "You can't sell a plow to a busted customer."

Stripped of its complexities, the bill he authored and which Senator Charles L. McNary and Representative Gilbert N. Haugen, of Oregon and Iowa respectively, fathered in Congress was an act to restore the purchasing power of farm commodities to a prewar level by segregating exports from domestic supplies and dumping them at a surplus-disposal price abroad. In private industry this was a familiar practice. The dumping of surpluses at lower prices abroad to sustain the domestic price of the same plow or automobile, or refrigerator or shoehorn, at a desired level was an old trick. Peek was the first to suggest transferring it to farm products. But in private industry such a plan would be arrived at by a board of directors or even by a meeting of sales managers. In order to put it over for such a diverse, unorganized, and individualistic industry as agriculture, Peek proposed to substitute the government for the board of directors, an administrator for the sales manager.

When the bill reached Congress, it provided for machinery to raise domestic prices on raw materials by segregating the exportable surplus so that the domestic market would not be affected by world price, compensating the government for losses incidental to the scheme by a small "equalization fee" to be levied upon the farmers selling the raw materials.

This first attempt at artificial price raising by government fiat rather than by the private agreement of private entrepreneurs was defeated in the House in June 1924, by a vote of 223 to 153. It was again presented, endorsed by more than 200 farm, labor, and other organizations, among them the Farm Bureau Federation and the National Grange, which supported it through their strong Washington lobbies. The Sixty-ninth Congress looked at it with different eyes than had its predecessors. The bill passed the House, although many Representatives found it prudent to refrain from voting. In the Senate it failed of passage by the narrow margin of six votes. But when the second session of the Sixty-ninth met in December 1926, it was back in the legislative hopper awaiting action.

The McNary-Haugen measure would have aided the big farmers of the nation and to a lesser extent the more prosperous middle-class agriculturalists. It would have been of little help to the small farmers — those who raised rocks, a little corn, and a few potatoes on the hillsides near Plymouth, Vermont. It was not a widespread measure of relief. It would hardly have wrecked the Treasury nor would it have been a dire threat to the power of industrial and finance capitalism. Nevertheless the big industrialists fought it with all the power at their control.

The arguments they assembled against it were many: It would encourage expanded production and thus menace prices even more. The dumping would have unfavorable repercussions on the industries doing business abroad. Countries raising the same products as American farmers would not stand idly by while American products flooded their markets. The Wall Street financiers and industrialists trembled at the thought of foreign competitors resorting to reprisals in the form of tariffs set up to limit the imports to foreign countries of American manufactured goods.

The debate over this issue was long and bitter and filled columns of newspaper space that probably were read by a minimum of the nation's newspaper readers, who were more interested in the rescue of Floyd Collins from a cave, or the affair of Peaches and Daddy Browning, or such issues as short skirts, bobbed hair, or the petting-and-flask problem, with which the press helped to dull the American mind and keep it from worrying over such matters as agriculture.

Mr. Mellon issued a stern warning that the McNary-Haugen bill was economically unsound. Its enactment, he said, would raise the cost of living and lower the purchasing power of wages by increasing production and decreasing consumption. In spite of this the bill at last passed the House, 214 to 178, and the Senate by a vote of 47 to 39. The vote cut squarely across the party lines.

Calvin Coolidge let the bill lie on his desk a week and then sent it back with a veto message that Chief Justice Taft called a "sockdolager." The President objected to the bill because he was unalterably opposed to governmental intervention in business and because he thought the equalization fee was a tax for the benefit of special groups. And anyway, he added chillingly, it wouldn't help the farmer while it would create an enormous bureaucracy. In the right circles Coolidge was highly praised for his courage in vetoing the bill. And many a Congressman, it was said, who had voted for the measure purely for politically expedient reasons was glad he did. But Coolidge was not yet done with McNary-Haugenism.

Slightly modified, the bill popped up again in 1928 before the Seventieth Congress, and once again it passed both Houses. And once again President Coolidge — who had already chosen not to seek re-election — dipped his pen in icy ink to veto it. A valiant attempt to override the veto failed, as it had before. By this time Secretary Hoover had become well involved in McNary-Haugenism, which he looked upon with a particularly jaundiced eye. Its backers — "the fellows who," in George Wickersham's words, "are fabricating bogus gifts for the farmers" — were equally angry at both Coolidge and Hoover. That summer Coolidge thought it politically wise to spend his vacation in the Black Hills of Dakota, right in the heart of the enemy's country, and other bigwigs of the party felt it would do no harm to take trips out that way too. When Hoover became President an attempt to incorporate some McNary-Haugen features in the Agricultural Marketing Act met his vigorous, and successful, opposition. McNary-Haugenism, one of the most bitterly fought issues of the entire Coolidge era, became a dead issue after Coolidge's second veto, insofar as a chance for enactment went. But it was still alive during the 1928 political campaign.[3]

There was one other threat to Coolidge complacency that enlivened the years of his silent reign. This was Muscle Shoals.

"The early Twenties," George Norris wrote in his autobiography, "brought the American people to their knees in worship at the shrine of private business and industry. It was said, and accepted without question by millions of Americans, that private enterprise could do no wrong."

It was Norris's privilege, as much as anyone's during these years, to prove this wrong. He did this most effectively and lastingly in the course of a fight to which he came reluctantly but to which he stuck with courage and tenacity until he had won.

His tremendous, and often singlehanded, struggle for the crea-

[3] "Practically all the powers ever written into the Norris and then the McNary-Haugen bills, together with the powers under the Grange-backed McKinley-Atkins bill of 1926, not to mention the Dickinson bill of the same year, and others, were written as rather minor parts of the Farm Act of 1933 — once the supreme point of crisis, demanding almost any kind of rough-shod action, had come." (Russell Lord, *The Wallaces of Iowa*, pp. 272–273.) This was the A.A.A. found unconstitutional by the Supreme Court, 6–3. Justice Stone, Coolidge's only Court appointee, wrote the dissenting opinion for himself, Cardozo, and Brandeis!

tion of the Tennessee Valley Authority, one of the greatest land-marks along the march of democracy, was in direct opposition to the economic philosophy of Calvin Coolidge, his predecessor and his successor.

Perhaps nothing was more basic to the clash of interests of the 1920's than the fight over Muscle Shoals which lasted throughout twelve years of Republican rule.[4]

The struggle started during the war when the desperate government, in need of nitrates for explosives, sought to obtain them by extracting nitrogen from the air. The process then in use required a huge amount of electricity.

Under the authority of the National Defense Act of 1916, two nitrate plants were built at Muscle Shoals on the Tennessee River in Alabama. Work also was started on a 100-foot dam, later known as Wilson Dam, as the nucleus of a vast power project. It was confidently thought that after the war the nitrate plants could be turned over to the making of fertilizer. This was before the hard-pressed Germans, their supply of South American nitrates cut off by the blockade, perfected a cheaper and more efficient process.

At the war's end, work on the Wilson Dam stopped. A Congressional committee recommended that the entire project at Muscle Shoals be abandoned, and the House, where all appropriations originate, cut off funds. The first bill for the completion of Wilson Dam, after a lengthy debate, was thrown in the lap of Senator Norris, chairman of the Committee on Agriculture of the Senate. With the thoroughness and tenacity with which he approached all legislation he went to work, making a complete study of the entire problem. For the next twelve years he led the offensive for TVA.

The two plants and the unfinished dam had cost the government $150,000,000. In 1921 Secretary of War Weeks set out to lease Muscle Shoals for private development and operation. Several private interests made bids, but the one which Congress took most seriously and which captured the imagination of the public was the bid made by Henry Ford in July 1921.

[4] It is interesting to notice that the two best-known popular historians of this period, Frederick Lewis Allen and Mark Sullivan, ignore it. Sullivan gives it one paragraph on page 618 of *The Twenties*, while the more liberal Mr. Allen surprisingly enough omits it entirely.

Many hearings were held and several bids other than Ford's were incorporated in measures introduced in the House. One such bill was the so-called Underwood bill, an administration measure, which would have had the effect of turning the resources of the entire Tennessee Valley over to private corporations for private exploitation.

In the public imagination none of the nation's industrial heroes was more heroic than Henry Ford. His "Peace Ship" exploit was forgotten and he had not yet shocked American sensibilities with his cruelly senseless anti-Semitic campaign. Henry Ford was the symbol of success, of rugged individualism, of 100 per cent business Americanism. The people joked at his automobiles, bought them by the millions, and worshiped the man.

Against the bids of Ford and others Norris stood almost alone. In spite of his efforts it began to look as if the huge developments on one of the nation's greatest public resources were going to slip from the people's grasp. The public was apathetic to the fight, lulled by the clever propaganda of the vast hydroelectric empire that was then coming into being and which Wendell Willkie, a few years later, would arise to defend against the New Deal.

The expectation that Ford, or one of his rivals, would soon have the whole of the Tennessee Valley under his rule brought about one of the most amazing spectacles of an amazing time. The valley became a minor Florida,[5] the site of real estate speculation seldom paralleled in history. There is no evidence that Ford sponsored this, but he must have been aware of it. Thousands of people were hoodwinked in the belief that, as Norris said, they were "getting in on the ground floor of a new American wonderland," a Fordian utopia.

During the height of the boom a town was incorporated near Muscle Shoals, and plots were laid out. In the leading cities of the country, including Washington, offices were set up for the sale of the real estate that was to be at the center of this fair new land of private enterprise.

"Special trains were run from New York City to Muscle Shoals," Norris recalled, "filled with prospective land purchasers. People were taken up in airplanes to view the wonderful sweep of country where a city, rivaling even New York, was to rise

[5] The Florida real estate boom is a fascinating story of the 1920's that unfortunately does not belong in this book.

when this great power development had been turned over to Mr. Ford and his genius for ultimate development. In that boom thousands of lots were sold to people living in scattered sections of the U. S. so that every purchaser became a committee of one to help Mr. Ford gain possession of Muscle Shoals. . . . Thousands and thousands of dollars were siphoned out of the pockets of poor people, principally laborers, by the installment method of selling lots in this great Muscle Shoals area. . . . Men told me they expected a city there which would outstrip New York in population. Men of wealth and power shared this belief. . . ."

Norris, whose other name was Integrity, was convinced that thousands were being duped, and equally convinced that only under government ownership could the valley be developed for the whole people. He stood squarely and in lonely splendor against the onslaught. For his stand he was once burned in effigy. When he visited Muscle Shoals he had to be accompanied by an armed guard.

This was, as Norris says with magnificent understatement, "a period of great confusion and uncertainty in Congress." It was not until February 1924 that Congress could agree on what to do with Muscle Shoals. In the meantime the government was selling its power to the Alabama Power Company. The nitrate plants were idle. Now both House and Senate passed measures which, if they could have reached a joint agreement, would have turned Muscle Shoals over to Henry Ford. But fortunately it was during the lame-duck session and the joint conferees did not make their report until six days before adjournment. Thus, with the expiration of the Sixty-eighth Congress, Muscle Shoals was left pretty much where it had been since the end of the war.

Senator Norris had no intention of letting it stay there. Through investigations which he continued with unabated tenacity he marshaled an array of facts and figures that conclusively proved that public-owned hydro plants in Canada were furnishing power to consumers at less than half the average price paid by Americans. In 1926 he introduced a resolution to provide for the operation of the dams on the Tennessee, and for the incorporation of the Federal Power Corporation. This died in committee.

But late in 1927 the indomitable Norris was back with another resolution, not quite so wide in scope. It asked only for the completion of Wilson Dam and the unfinished plant for the manufacture and distribution of fertilizer. It also allowed for the sale of surplus power. This time, because of the agricultural features, the measure received support from the South and the West. On May 25, 1928, this bill was adopted by both houses. President Coolidge was silent. Congress adjourned four days later. Without opening his mouth or picking up a pen President Coolidge killed it with the pocket veto.

Even now the fight was not over. After Herbert Hoover became President, Norris again introduced a resolution providing for the building of another dam on the Tennessee, the construction of transmission lines, and the manufacture and sale of both power and fertilizer by the government. This, too, passed both houses of Congress. But instead of being coldly silent, as his former chief had been, President Hoover was violent in his veto message.

> . . . The remedy for abuses in the conduct of [the power] industry lies in regulation and not by the Federal Government entering upon the business itself. . . . I hesitate to contemplate the future of our institutions, of our country, if the preoccupation of its officials is to be no longer the promotion of justice and equal opportunity but is to be devoted to barter in the markets. . . . Muscle Shoals can only be administered by the people upon the ground, responsible to their own communities and not for purposes of pursuit of social theories or national politics.

Four years later Herbert Hoover and his philosophy were to be repudiated by a rudely awakened people as no other man or philosophy had been repudiated before in our history. And under Franklin Delano Roosevelt the Tennessee Valley Authority came into being.

CHAPTER TWENTY-FOUR

Imperialism and Isolation

IF Calvin Coolidge had his troubles with the Sixty-ninth Congress his lot was not to be made much easier by the Seventieth, which came into being as a result of the inevitable mid-term elections. Unfortunately for the progress of liberal action this turned out to be a pretty apathetic contest. In 1926 the Democrats were still groggy from 1924. No national leader, who by personality or program could salve the party's wounds, had shown up.[1] The party was still badly split. There was no one outstanding issue to bring it together, save the irreproachable one of Prosperity, to which the Republicans had prior claim. Prohibition had not yet become an overwhelming national issue.

With La Follette dead and the conference for Progressive Political Action all but in the grave with him; with the Socialists once again badly bewildered, the Communists split, and the Farmer-Labor groups all but dissolved (except in a strictly local sense), there was, once again, no place for the liberal to go. The illusion of prosperity made the workers and the middle class generally suspicious of suggestions of needed reform. Business appreciated this and found no reason, in 1926, even to raise the bogey of Radicalism. But the 1926 election was no personal victory for Coolidge, or even a tribute to his leadership. In one of the dullest elections on record the Republicans lost their Senate majority. In the House there was an appreciable lessening of Republican power, although the party still claimed a majority and Nicholas Longworth stayed

---

[1] William Allen White wrote a friend in July 1926 that ". . . the nation has not yet been shocked out of its materialism. And of course Coolidge is a tremendous shock absorber. His emotionless attitude is an anaesthetic. . . ." White saw no one on the horizon "who is going to shock us into the realization of our national lethargy" at that time. (*Selected Letters of William Allen White*, p. 261.)

on as Speaker. Senator Butler's defeat by David I. Walsh, a Democrat, in Coolidge's own state, was widely interpreted as a victory for labor and liberalism and a rebuke to Coolidge. Throughout the West the gains made by Progressives were hardly worth boasting about. But in New York Al Smith won his fourth term as governor, and the Democrats won in Maryland, Ohio, and South Dakota. On the whole, however, the election reflected the utter indifference of the people to their own political fate. And this indifference left Business in practical charge of the government, with Mr. Hoover protecting the interests of Industry and Mr. Mellon protecting the interests of Finance and Mr. Coolidge watching in silent benevolence over both.

The apathy of the people to their own long-range welfare on the domestic front was exceeded only by their apathy as to what went on in the rest of the world. With such affairs, commonly called the foreign policy of the United States, Coolidge was quite content to let matters take the easiest course. He himself was an isolationist. Furthermore, he knew no foreign language, he had visited no foreign lands, and he had an almost pathological fear of "furriners," as his attitude towards the Lawrence strikers earlier in his career had shown. In Charles Evans Hughes, whom he inherited, and in Frank B. Kellogg, whom he transferred from London to the ranking position in the State Department, he had two men whom he could trust to lift the onerous duty of formulating policy from his narrow shoulders.

In the course of abdicating his powers Coolidge failed miserably to accomplish one of his avowed aims, adherence of the United States to the World Court. After the death of Henry Cabot Lodge, the chairmanship of the Senate Foreign Relations Committee had fallen to Senator Borah, who was as ardently isolationist but far from as blatantly imperialistic as his predecessor. Under his leadership, and in the face of a House resolution favoring adherence, which had passed in March 1925 by a vote of 303 to 28, the wish of both parties, as expressed in their platforms, was thwarted.

Senator Borah had learned a valuable lesson from Lodge. The committee which he headed now tacked five reservations onto the House resolution. These were ostensibly designed to safeguard American sovereignty from the League. It was the same old trick to keep America out of the League that had been used to such evil advantage under the generalship of the aging Lodge.[2]

Once these reservations were laid before the Senate that body voted, 76 to 17, to join the Court — if the League would accept the reservations as written. There was the hitch, tied in there by Borah's committee, that committee whose pride of opinion, as Homer Cummings put it, was more important to them than the peace of the world. Just as the committee had hoped and expected, the League membership was willing to accept all the reservations — except the one dealing with advisory opinions. Senator Borah was exultant. President Coolidge was not one to put up a fight for an idea. He did not do so now. He interpreted the League's attitude as rejection, and was all for letting the matter drop. His Secretary of Commerce, Mr. Hoover, might call our joining the Court the "minimum possible step in eliminating the causes of war," and further declare that there could "be no confidence in the continuity of our civilization unless preventive safeguards can be established," but President Coolidge was unmoved. As far as he was concerned, the Senate had set the final terms of the United States — so let the forty-eight nations who made up the Court accept them or reject them.

Never was the small-mindedness of Calvin Coolidge more clearly expressed than in his Armistice Day speech in which he rejected the request of those twenty-one members of the Court who had informed him that they wished to discuss further the onerous 5th Reservation which gave the United States alone veto power over the opinions of the World Court.

"We are the creditor nation," he said. "We are more prosperous than some others. This means that our interests have come within the European circle where the distrust and suspicion, if nothing more, have been altogether too common. To turn such attention to us indicates at least that we are not ignored." Realizing that these nations had their own trials and sufferings, Coolidge, with

---

[2] These reservations sought to give the United States, although not a member of the League under whose 14th Article the Permanent Court of International Government was established, a share in filling vacancies on the Court, recognition of our financial obligation to the Court, and permission to withdraw from the Court at any time. The most important was the 5th, which was designed to safeguard the Monroe Doctrine and American immigration policies, and which forbade the Court to render advisory opinions on any subject of interest to the United States.

moral fervor, offered "our patience, our sympathy, and such help as we believe will enable them to be restored to a sound and prosperous condition." He then continued:

"While the nations involved cannot yet be said to have made a final determination . . . many have indicated that they are unwilling to concur in the conditions adopted by the Senate. While no final determination can be made by our government until final answers are received, the situation has been sufficiently developed *that I do not intend to ask the Senate to modify its position.* I do not think the Senate would take favorable action on any such proposal, and unless the requirements of the Senate resolution are met by the other interested nations I can see no prospect of adhering to this Court."

Thus with these puny words did Calvin Coolidge end our second effort to substitute world government for world war. The President and the Senate had been forced by public opinion, which would not die merely because Warren Harding had said the League was dead, to take a step towards providing a possible alternative to war. Now, when the other nations concerned asked further discussion of one of five controversial conditions, Calvin Coolidge withdrew. With his ultimatum of "take it or leave it" the United States fell even farther from that high and expectant level of world leadership to which Woodrow Wilson had brought it in 1919. Then the people in every land had turned to America as the one nation, so they believed, owning the vision and the strength to plan and bring to success an organization for the pacification of the world. Now — seven short years later — they listened to a President of the United States who could only say, "At least we are not ignored"! With those defeatist words we had reached true isolation at last.

Along with isolation went a curious kind of Coolidge Imperialism. It stretched into Mexico, Nicaragua, and to the Philippines.

Woodrow Wilson had long refused to interfere in the rights of the Mexican people to live under a government of their own choosing. His defense of a democratic government south of the border had laid a firm basis for a solution of the "Mexican problem" which still existed when President Coolidge took office. The delicate situation between the two nations was centered in the Mexican Constitution of 1917 which nationalized all oil and mineral resources. Under President Obregón an agreement was reached in 1923 whereby American rights acquired prior to 1917 were to be recognized and American claims growing out of the revolutionary period before 1920 were to be satisfied. But in 1924, Calles became President and he sought to pacify the agrarian and anticlerical elements, whose candidate he was, by seeking to make the constitutional provisions retroactive. Thus laws were passed substituting fifty-year concessions for existing titles.

Great was the anger of the Standard Oil Company, the Sinclair-Doheny petroleum group, and other American corporations with Mexican interests, over that nation's strange insistence upon retaining control over its own oil reserves. Secretary Kellogg violently protested the laws and arrogantly insisted that they be repealed. In note after note he told Mexico just what she could or could not do. The United States, he made it clear, "expects the Mexican government not to take any action under the laws in question . . . which would operate either directly or indirectly, to deprive American citizens of their . . . property and property rights." For three years Kellogg put the pressure on Mexico, sometimes rising even to hysterical heights in his campaign against that nation's sovereignty. As was to be expected he raised the specter of Communism and invoked the protection of the Catholic Church. The Hearst press joined in with gusto — until a Senate committee proved to be forgeries the "documents" which Mr. Hearst's papers had printed "proving" that certain Senators had been bribed (ostensibly with Moscow gold) to oppose the Coolidge-Kellogg imperialism.

Each legalistic, arrogant note Kellogg addressed to Mexico made the situation worse. But this policy was consistent with Coolidge's assertion that "towards the governments of countries which we have recognized this side of the Panama Canal, we feel a moral responsibility that does not attach to other nations. . . . The person and the property of a citizen are a part of the general domain of the nation even when abroad." This shocking perversion of the Monroe Doctrine, which had been established to keep reactionary European nations out of American political affairs, came with pretty ill grace from a nation which would not join the World Court unless every shred of its own sovereignty were preserved. Coolidge was roundly criticized, even by those generally favorable to his policies. He was deeply hurt by the criticism, and eventually was forced to save face by sending his old friend Dwight Morrow to Mexico as ambassador. Morrow was able to secure modifications, favorable to American interests, of the petroleum law. Through Morrow's skill as a diplomat better relations than had existed for a decade were established between the two nations. The soft-spoken Morgan partner succeeded where the arrogant Kellogg failed, and Wall Street was happy.

President Coolidge inherited a bad situation in the Philippines and left it only little better than he had found it. President Harding had postponed the independence promised the people of the islands by the Jones Act of 1916 and had sent Major General Leonard Wood and W. Cameron Forbes to the Philippines to look into conditions there. General Wood, a Republican still bitten by the Presidential bug, sought to use his assignment to restore his prestige at home. He started out violently opposed to Philippine independence and the report he sent back was so clearly biased that the Philippine legislature promptly sent a committee to Washington to register protest. In spite of his unpopularity Wood was kept in the Philippines by Harding and Coolidge. During his Governor Generalship the Council of State was abolished and private interests were allowed to take over many government enterprises. At last hostility to Wood became so great that Coolidge was forced to do something. He sent one Carmi Thompson, who had been one of Harding's financial backers in the 1920 campaign, to investigate. Thompson's report, advising postponement of independence "for some time to come," was a political compromise which resulted in Wood's being replaced by Henry L. Stimson. This estimable diplomat did correct some of Wood's grievous mistakes. Congress refused to tamper with the Jones Act, thus ending the hopes of certain industrial interests that the Philippines would be turned over to them for exploitation. But the dream of independence on the part of the people of the Philippines was still a long way from realization.

The Coolidge policy of interfering in the internal affairs of other nations, especially in nations where, as in Nicaragua, American interests had millions of dollars invested, caused the President unhappy moments trying to find a connection between his moral law and his imperialism. Coolidge's moral law well served such large interests as the United Fruit Company, the Guggenheim copper interests, the sugar trusts, the Rockefeller, Morgan, and other banking firms, whose holdings in Chile, Guatemala, Costa

Rica, Colombia, and Bolivia were extensive. Coolidge kept some 5000 marines in Nicaragua, much against a strong public opinion at home, and they forcibly ran an election there, harried its liberal, anti-imperialist leader, and otherwise acted in a hardheaded and highhanded manner. Coolidge's policy of Caribbean imperialism probably made him more enemies among democratic thinking Americans than any of his domestic mistakes. His use of the sword did not sit well with peace-loving Americans.

It was with a gasp of relief that President Coolidge and his State Department received the announcement of Foreign Minister Briand of France in April 1927 that France was prepared to enter into a treaty with the United States that would outlaw war.

Senator Borah took the lead in urging the administration to widen the scope of the suggested pact. Thus it was that, after some negotiations, Secretary Kellogg invited fourteen other nations to join in. On August 27, 1928, the Pact of Paris, usually called the Kellogg-Briand treaty, was signed. Among the fifteen signatories were the United States, Great Britain, France, Germany, Italy, and Japan. These "high contracting parties" all "solemnly declared" that they "condemn recourse to war for the solution of international controversies, and renounce it as an instrument of national policy in their relation with one another." It added other high-sounding phrases, such as "the settlement or solution of all disputes or conflicts . . . which may rise among [these nations] shall never be sought except by pacific means."

Everybody cheered. This was a great victory for all peace-loving people. The only fault in the great document was that it contained no provision for its own enforcement. It left international relationships resting solely upon the moral law. Its fate is history.

CHAPTER TWENTY-FIVE

I Do Not Choose to Run

THE age of commercialism and science was at its zenith when the election year of 1928 dawned. The record for Prosperity, set in 1926 when new heights of production and profits had been scaled, promised to topple before the year had ended. Everyone surely seemed to be in a state of contentment. Strikes were few. The worker was happy, maybe because he had read Department of Commerce reports telling him that the purchasing power of his wage was twice that of his British cousin, four times that of his cousins in Brussels, Rome, or Madrid.

Shortly before Christmas Calvin Coolidge had told the people: "The great wealth created by our enterprise and industry, and saved by our economy, has had the widest distribution among our own people, and has gone out in a steady stream to serve the charity and business of the world." That this bit of Christmas cheer did not quite jibe with published government statistics which showed that 90 per cent of the nation's wealth was held by 13 per cent of the people was too rude a matter to mention.

Under the guidance of Mr. Coolidge's moral law a strangely unmoral wave of gambling, almost amounting to a mania, had somehow swept the land. Everyone almost at once wanted to be just as rich as Mr. Mellon. They all wanted to buy their way into such fine examples of American private enterprise as United States Steel, Allied Chemical and Dye, the Radio Corporation of America, Auburn Auto, General Motors, Continental Can, Montgomery Ward, and many, many other corporations which they had been taught to reverence in this Golden Age of Normalcy.

It is quite probable that not much more than 1 per cent of the population, as John T. Flynn once estimated, threw its money to the bright young boys from Yale and Princeton who had "gone into investment banking," in the hope that it would soon multiply to astronomical proportions. But this 1 per cent set the pace for the rest of the nation, or at least so it seemed. The gambling fever, which had caught multitudes in the high tides of the Florida coast in 1925 and 1926, went uncontrolled. Fortunes were made. Bootblacks scanned the stock reports before the baseball results. And nobody was particularly shocked when Black Starr and Frost, jewelers on Fifth Avenue for 118 years, as well as at Palm Beach and Paris, took two pages of the *New Yorker* to advertise a "perfectly, exquisitely matched" necklace for only $685,000. Westbrook Pegler with some justification called this "the era of wonderful nonsense."

A few of the more conservative members of the banking fraternity felt, as 1928 opened, that common stocks were, as Claude M. Fuess puts it, "altogether too high in relation to their earnings, both actual and potential, and that the outlook for business was not bright." Here and there a crusty old maverick said investors ought to be more prudent. But the lowering of the rediscount rate by the Federal Reserve Board from 4 to 3½ per cent in August 1927 had stimulated speculation and there was no prudence in the land.

Shortly after New Year's Day Calvin Coolidge held a press conference. Among the questions submitted was one concerning brokers' loans. Unable to answer it, Coolidge had set it aside and later given it to a secretary to prepare an answer. He may also have consulted Secretary Mellon. At any rate, a few days later he allowed himself to be quoted directly to the effect that, in his opinion, brokers' loans were not too high, in spite of the fact that they then stood at nearly $4,000,000,000. Coolidge attributed the sharp rise in brokers' loans to larger bank deposits and to the fact that there were more securities listed than heretofore on the Stock Exchange!

"It was the one important occasion when Coolidge did not keep his mouth shut," wrote Fuess, "and his untimely utterance proved to be the most unfortunate blunder he ever made."

This Presidential reassurance, coming from the apostle of thrift, sent the market booming. By its issuance Coolidge had helped encourage the ridiculous inflation that was making paper profits of millions daily. By March stocks started their mad climb to those stratospheric heights they eventually reached in the fateful October of 1929.

President Coolidge's January statement was not, of course, the only optimistic remark the President had made. Even before this the *New York Times* had said that his several statements had "the effect of converting an aimless, colorless stock market into a lively buoyant affair." It certainly became so! As a result of these statements certain recent reports of curtailed industrial and commercial activity (which had brought an increase of about 600,000 in the unemployment statistic) were dispelled. If Coolidge endorsed speculation it must be sound. Investment brokers talked about "the confidence that exists in high places" and, in the argot of the day, went out and bought another yacht.

The day after Coolidge's reckless statement the *Times* explained that the President believed "the increase represents a natural expansion of business in the securities market and sees nothing unfavorable in it." But later, in private conversation, Coolidge said that personally he thought "any loan made for gambling in stocks was 'an excessive loan.' " When his guest asked him why he had not said so publicly, he replied:

"Well, I regard myself as the representative of the government and not as an individual. When technical matters come up I feel called upon to refer them to the proper department of the government which has some information about them and then, unless there is some good reason, I use this information as a basis for whatever I have to say; but that does not prevent me from thinking what I please as an individual."

The Federal Reserve Board did act to quiet the market by raising the rediscount rate in February back to 4 per cent, and in May it put the rate at 4½, and in June, when the conventions were being held, to 5 per cent. This had a momentary effect but, after Hoover's election in November, the volume of trading on the floor of the New York Stock Exchange reached 7,000,000 shares in a day and a seat on the Exchange cost only $105,000 less than Black Starr and Frost's string of pearls. Radio common jumped to 400 a share and, although it dropped 72 points in a single December day, that was only a strange interlude and recovery was quick. The year closed with prices higher than ever. Six months after Coolidge left office Radio was listed at 505!

Coolidge's public endorsement of speculation caused widespread comment; but the stir it made was nothing compared to that occasioned by another statement which he had made in the summer of 1927. At a moment when it was universally believed he would seek re-election to the Presidency in 1928 he said: "I do not choose to run for President in 1928."

Posterity was to remember Calvin Coolidge more for that utterance than for any other thing he said or did in his entire career. No act or statement he made during all his years in public life caused quite the commotion that simple sentence created when he had it typed out on thin strips of paper and passed it among the correspondents who had been yawning their way through the dullness of the President's vacation in the Black Hills of South Dakota.

The campaign to re-elect Coolidge had begun almost at the time of his inauguration in March 1925. The echoes of his inaugural speech had hardly died down when Mark Sullivan printed an article in *World's Work* entitled "A Third Term for Coolidge," the gist of which was that the third-term bogey had long passed from the American political scene. This really started the ball rolling. Coolidge did not publicly acknowledge the situation, but in his private letters there were indications that he was not averse to the idea. He undoubtedly did not consider the period between Harding's death and his own election as a "first term" in office. Arthur Brisbane, chief editorial writer of the Hearst newspapers, did not think it was either, and dedicated himself to furthering the campaign for Coolidge's re-election in 1928.

There were some astute observers, like Albert Cummins of Iowa, who thought Coolidge would have had enough of the White House by 1928 and would be glad to be out of it, but the consensus was of a different nature. The political soothsayers generally agreed that if Prosperity continued unabated he could have the nomination and be elected. They thought perhaps he might have to be prodded before he would consent to become the candidate, but they did not think he would have to be pushed very hard.

One thing spoiled the bright picture. The fight over farm relief threatened to split the Republican Party. It was generally believed that if this happened Coolidge might refuse the nomination. But this was pure speculation. The one man who could clarify the situation kept silent.

Throughout the winter and spring there raged a wordy debate over the third term. While editorial and feature writers had a field day over the academic aspects of the unusual situation, Coolidge was placed under a great deal of pressure in an effort to force him to reveal his own attitude. Endorsers of the candidacy ranged from George Harvey to Chauncey M. Depew and, of course, Henry Ford reiterated his faith in the man in the White House. Coolidge's continued silence was annoying. It raised the impression that he wanted a third term, but that he wanted it handed to him without even the suggestion of any opposition within the party. Washington correspondents, noting an increasingly large number of party regulars being entertained at the White House, drew from this the interpretation that Coolidge was quietly getting the machine politicians lined up on his side. The correspondents thought he was being very coy.

Nicholas Murray Butler, who perhaps still entertained the illusion that he someday might be the party's choice, sought to read him out as a possible candidate. His efforts failed, as did all others to get Coolidge even to hint what he wanted. As the debate over the third term's constitutionality waxed, three resolutions against a third term were offered in Congress. One was introduced by young Bob La Follette and, although it was couched in nonpartisan terms, its purpose obviously was to draw a statement from the silent President. He did not fall for the bait. Every visitor to the White House was certain of newspaper publicity on the issue and most of them, whether they discussed the matter or not, took advantage of their visits to get into print. All they had to say was they were sure he would run in 1928, or they didn't think so, to make the front pages.

Senator Borah said Coolidge could have the nomination if he wanted it, but Senator Norris warned against his seeking it. The Nebraskan looked at a possible third term as "a long step toward monarchical form of government." The term "dictator" had not come into fashion then. Within the party, especially among the remnants of the Old Guard — which in either party neither dies nor surrenders — there was a distinct coolness towards Coolidge, not because his popularity was doubted or his vote-getting ability discounted, but because they saw an opportunity to regain lost power if they could name his successor. But his cold veto of the McNary-Haugen bill greatly lessened the opposition, although it sealed his doom as far as the Farm Bloc was concerned.

When Senator Peter Norbeck invited President Coolidge to spend his summer vacation in the Black Hills this was widely and correctly interpreted as the beginning of a campaign to win back the Western deserters. His acceptance of the invitation seemed to be a political way of his saying that he was very much in the running. Most observers agreed that he wanted to be drafted and that he was heading for the Black Hills in a bid to regain support in the important Western regions.

At his Black Hills retreat Coolidge went fishing, shocking the orthodox by using worms for trout. The great American press printed reams of some of the silliest stories ever written, all about Coolidge fishing and saying nothing, building him up for 1928. Most newspapers publishers agreed he was a great man and ought to stay in the White House. He posed for some very funny pictures, dressed up in Indian clothes, looking the most uncomfortable man in America. Coolidge's thin Vermont face under a ten-gallon hat, part of the costume he once donned when some cowboys came over from Wyoming to greet him, was something to behold.

Speculation as to Coolidge's intentions was at its height as the midsummer heat settled over the country. Most visitors to Rapid City were certain the President was a candidate for the nomination and several years later "Ike" Hoover, in his *Forty-two Years in the White House*, presented persuasive evidence that Coolidge's whole vacation trip was planned "with every intention of making political capital out of the stay." It at least offered an opportunity to those who opposed him to form their lines.

On Tuesday, August 2, the fourth anniversary of Coolidge's accession to office, he rode thirty miles down the valley from the lodge where he was staying to the shack that was used as an office in Rapid City. His purpose was to attend his semiweekly press conference. He met the press at nine o'clock and, as the newsless reporters were leaving, casually remarked: "If you will return at twelve o'clock there will be an additional statement." In midmorning he called in his secretary and asked him to type out on legal-size paper several copies of a statement ten words long which he had neatly written out. When this was done Coolidge took a pair of shears and cut them into neat slips each about two inches wide. When the reporters assembled at noon he lined them up and handed one of the slips to each of them. As soon as the reporters could dash for the wires the world knew that Calvin Coolidge had said:

"I do not choose to run for President in 1928."

At once editorial offices and political headquarters across the land were thrown into a turmoil. What did Coolidge mean? Translation of the laconic Coolidge message became the national pastime. Its ambiguity set politicians and pundits alike to pondering its potential meaning. Those who did not want Coolidge to run again took it to mean that he had irrevocably withdrawn himself from the race. Those who did want him to be the Republican candidate took it to mean that, although he himself did not "choose" to run, if he were the party's "choice" he would do so.

Coolidge, in later years, explained the choice of the word "choose" and gave his reasons for not wanting to remain in the White House after 1928. He said he had selected the words of his statement with care because he had "never wished to run in 1928 and had determined to make a public announcement . . . so that the party would have ample time to choose some one else." In his Yankee argot he meant what he thought he said and his reasons for saying it were simple. Item, he did not think the people would longer have confidence in him if he seemed to be grasping for office. Item, he knew a President could effect "little in the way of constructive accomplishment" in the latter part of his term in office. Item, if re-elected he would have to spend ten years in the White House, too long a time, he thought, for any man. Item, he didn't think Mrs. Coolidge could stand the strain of four more years as the First Lady of the Land. Item, there were plenty of others in the party as capable and as worthy as he. Item, "My election seemed assured. Nevertheless, I felt it was not best for the country that I should succeed myself. A new impulse is more likely to be beneficial."

Although the announcement was quite unexpected it apparently was not made on the spur of the moment. Four years later, in a magazine article, Coolidge said his decision "had been made a long time" and added cryptically that his action "was based on the belief that it was best for the country." At about this time he said to Hubert Work:

"I know how to save money. All my training has been in that direction. The country is in a sound financial position. Perhaps the time has come when we ought to spend money. I do not feel that I am qualified to do it."

To Senator Jim Watson of Indiana he said:

"I think I know myself very well. . . . Immediately following the terrible turmoil of that great conflict [the World War] the people wanted rest, and that is what I was naturally adapted to give them, and did give them. They have prospered under those conditions, because the times demanded them. But a different condition now confronts us. From this time on, there must be something constructive applied to the affairs of government, and it will not be sufficient to say, 'Let business take care of itself.' . . . And so something affirmative must be suggested, and I do not feel I am the man to fill that sort of position or undertake to meet the demand occasioned by that situation. Somebody can do it, but I do not want to undertake it."

Did Calvin Coolidge, with shrewd Yankee intuition, foresee the coming debacle? It is unlikely that he saw all the way into the future, but his remarks to Work and Watson amply indicate that he feared the result of the policies of his and Harding's administrations, that he suspected the bubble would burst. And he wanted no part of the disaster.

If Coolidge kept silent about himself, he also said nothing to indicate his choice as his successor. He still rankled over the way Dawes had stolen the spotlight at his inauguration and how he had slept through the vote on Warren; he would not favor Dawes. But Dawes, who was openly antilabor, demagogic, and fascistic in his tendencies, did not loom very large on the political horizon. There the overshadowing figure was Herbert Hoover, for whom Calvin Coolidge had never shown any great love. Others who had their hats ready to toss in the ring were Senator Charles Curtis of Kansas, the majority floor leader; the aging Frank Lowden, the almost also-ran of 1920; Senator Borah; President Butler (who later withdrew in favor of Lowden); Senator Frank B. Wills, that year's favorite son from Ohio; Indiana's 1928 favorite son, Jim Watson, and West Virginia's, Senator Guy Goff.

The campaign in behalf of Herbert Hoover was well organized and the start of 1928 saw the movement expanding rapidly. He had long had the backing of the *Chicago Tribune*, the most powerful paper in the Midwest. In January the Scripps-Howard chain of newspapers, having translated Coolidge's August statement as meaning the President would not seek re-election, declared for him in preference to Dawes or Lowden. Nothing aided his open ambition to become President more than Calvin Coolidge's silence. There was a popular demand for Hoover, who was still considered a liberal among Republicans. Almost every discussion of the political situation placed him at the top of the heap — unless Coolidge should at the last moment "choose" to run. Coolidge's marked antipathy towards him was tempered by the fact that Hoover was definitely on the President's side against McNary-Haugenism. Since Dawes and Lowden were not, Coolidge's silence hurt their campaigns as much as it aided Hoover's. There was one barrier Hoover had to hurdle, however, and that was the animosity of Charles D. Hilles, the New York National Committeeman, who would not let the "Back to Coolidge" movement die down. His zeal for Coolidge spread to other states and there was a concerted movement afoot to send uninstructed delegates to Kansas City, where the 1928 convention was to be held, who would be ready to swing to Coolidge if the proper moment arrived.

On February 12 Herbert Hoover "allowed" his name to be placed in the Ohio primaries. Shrewdly he declared, "If the greatest trust which can be given by our people should come to me, I should consider it my duty to carry forward the principles of the Republican Party and the great objective of President Coolidge's policies — all of which have brought to our country such a high degree of happiness, progress and security." This followed shortly the passage by the Senate of a resolution which said any departure from the two-term tradition would be "unwise, unpatriotic, and fraught with peril to our free institutions." This had received such impressive Republican backing that it was generally interpreted to mean that a majority of the party leaders were opposed to another candidacy for Coolidge. Other candidates quickly announced their intentions. Hoover-for-President Clubs were started and the Hoover boom began.

In April Coolidge refused to allow his name to go on the Massachusetts primary but this did not dampen what seemed to be a genuine demand to draft him. Hilles and others were ready to throw large blocks of votes his way when the convention opened, thus causing a stampede in his behalf. But many believed that Coolidge himself would stop this by definitely refusing the nomination on the eve of the convention. He kept silent, as usual, even to Senator Butler, who left the White House in May convinced that Coolidge expected either a stampede in his behalf or a deadlock out of which would come his nomination. But Chief Justice Taft and other observers were certain he would yield to no "sweep of enthusiasm."

Calvin Coolidge had a wry, even sadistic, sense of humor and must have enjoyed all the hubbub he was creating. He announced that he would spend his vacation at Cedar Island Lodge on a lake near Brule, Wisconsin, and he planned to entrain the night before the convention opened. By thus isolating himself on a train for seventy-two hours, it appeared as if certainly he hoped to step off the train to find himself the nominee, without having openly done anything to bring it about. But Mrs. Coolidge was ill and he did not get away from the White House until after the convention was well under way.

The Republican National Convention assembled on Tuesday, June 12, at Kansas City. The Coolidge supporters were still hopeful, but the well-organized Hooverites were even more sanguine of quick success. No final word had yet come from Coolidge, and William Butler had spent the night before scurrying around urging his followers to take no stand until they heard from him. The draft-Coolidge plan was simple. His name was not to be placed in nomination. But when the balloting started it was agreed that Connecticut, in the palm of J. Henry Roraback's capable hand, would cast its seventeen votes for Coolidge. An irresistible avalanche of Coolidge votes was expected to follow.

But there was Hoover. And Hoover had been planning to become President since 1920. He had cast his lot that year with the Republicans, thus purging himself of any connection with the party of Woodrow Wilson, who had found him in relative obscurity and helped bring him to fame. He had worked incessantly as Secretary of Commerce under Harding and Coolidge to enhance his own national reputation. In that post he had built a wide organization, presumably commercial in intent, but obviously political in ultimate purpose. When the Mississippi burst its banks in 1927 President Coolidge had placed him in charge of the government's relief program. Overnight he rescued his forgotten reputation as administrator, engineer, and great humanitarian. But the old stock-promoter well knew that humanitarianism alone was not enough to bring him the nomination. He thereupon seized every opportunity to remind the people of his Iowa childhood, which he seemingly spent picking potato bugs and helping till the soil. He also let it be widely known that he had a sound and thorough grasp of economics — that, indeed, the prosperity of the past four years had been born in the Department of Commerce.

Calvin Coolidge did not like Hoover. He thought he was too bossy. Around the White House he was known as "Secretary of Commerce and Undersecretary of All Other Departments" and once Coolidge had snapped, "That man has offered me unsolicited advice for six years, all of it bad!" If Coolidge had wanted Hoover as his successor he could have aided him, in one way, by offering an administration farm relief program, thus relieving Hoover of having to think up a program of his own.

Then William S. Vare, the boss of the Pennsylvania machine, which Mellon was supposed to control, decided to get on the Hoover bandwagon. On the eve of the convention he astounded Mellon, Butler, and Hilles, the reputed party leaders, by declaring for Hoover. Many another shrewd party chieftain saw the wisdom of his act and followed along. Mellon came out in Hoover's favor and then Senator Butler announced that Massachusetts would cast its votes for Herbert Hoover, too.

With Mellon, Butler, and Vare on Hoover's side, Lowden's attempt to storm the convention as the choice of the farmers came to nothing. Rumors that an invasion of farmers was about to descend upon the convention demanding a realistic farm program (which would have damaged Hoover, who had backed Coolidge's vetoes) did not materialize.[1] The favorite sons knew they had no place to go.

A listless and apathetic atmosphere hung over Kansas City. Simeon Fess delivered a keynote address that is remembered only for its dreariness. The leadership of the old Senate soviet of 1920 was gone; the Coolidge machine of 1924 had fallen apart. The party bosses wanted to take no strong stand on any issue. The heat was oppressive. There were only two matters in which the people manifested much interest: farm relief and Prohibition. The platform did its best to avoid commitment on them both. There was to be nothing in it that would disturb Prosperity.

The platform did not mention the McNary-Haugen bills or Coolidge's vetoes of them. It blamed the farm dislocation on the

[1] Three hundred did show up but they were ignored.

war. It said time heals everything. It boasted about credits offered farmers through the Federal Farm Loan system and said that the Republicans had done the most for the farmer anyone had done — when it raised the tariff on farm products away back in 1922. It said the main objective was to avoid "putting the government into business," but it went on record as favoring some kind of federal farm marketing system, leaving the organization of this system, whatever it was to be, to the incoming administration, which, of course, would be Republican. So vague were the farm proposals that Lowden temporarily withdrew his name as a candidate in ineffectual protest.

On Prohibition, which by now had slugged and shot its way to a point where it was a matter of national concern, the platform was equally evasive. It did not praise the Eighteenth Amendment and it promised to support the law of the land. As to the rest of the platform, it praised honest government and conscientiously deplored the fact that "any official has ever fallen" from the path of righteousness; it praised Calvin Coolidge; it spoke of the "high wages" labor was getting for its hire; it called the American standard of living the highest ever attained anywhere; it promised to reduce taxes, seek greater governmental economy, and maintain that "fundamental and essential principle of the economic life of this nation" — the tariff; it backed Coolidgean imperialism in Latin America; and it promised not to cancel the war debts.

On Thursday, June 14, Herbert Hoover was nominated on the first ballot with 837 votes. There was a scramble for second place, but Senator Charles Curtis had things all sewed up. On the first ballot he received 1052 votes. For the first time in the nation's history both candidates came from states west of the Mississippi. Against the loud protests of Wisconsin, whose delegates remained faithful to George Norris to the end, as they had twice before remained faithful to La Follette, the nominations were declared unanimous.

CHAPTER TWENTY-SIX

The Governor and the Engineer

WHEN Al Smith's scheme to wrest the nomination from William Gibbs McAdoo failed in 1924 his political doom was far from sealed. He went out and ran for governor again. Although John W. Davis lost the state by almost 1,000,000 votes, Al Smith carried it by more than 100,000 and became the first man in nearly a century to be thrice elected governor of New York. Two years later he thought he would retire but when Ogden L. Mills, who later was to achieve fame as the greatest Secretary of the Treasury since Andrew Mellon, became the Republican candidate he changed his mind. For years Mills had opposed the progressive program which Smith had greatly broadened in his third term, and the Governor was determined to save it from Republican wreckage at Mills's hands. He did, defeating Mills by the overwhelming majority of a quarter of a million votes.

There was no question now as to where the Democratic Party could turn for leadership. Out of the East Side of New York and the Executive Mansion at Albany had emerged a national figure of tremendous power. Al Smith had shown, as had no man since Woodrow Wilson, an understanding of the purposes of government. Not from books, but from practical experience, he had learned how to use the power of democracy for the general welfare. He had applied modern methods to government and made them work. In doing so he had done nothing to disturb economic stability or make inoperative the capitalist system.

Within a year after his defeat of Ogden Mills the demand for Smith's nomination in 1928 had become national in its scope. From almost every corner of the land letters poured into Albany and visitors crowded the trains up the Hudson to see and sound out the man with the cigar and the brown derby. Special correspondents made the most of his background, his habits, his way of speech, his achievements. Millions of Americans soon knew all about the East Side, the Fulton Fish Market, and the man with his heart in the right place who had come out of them to a place of greatness.

Months before Calvin Coolidge chose not to run it was universally assumed that Al Smith would be the party's candidate in 1928. It was also universally assumed that as a candidate he could surmount the difficulties of being an avowed Wet and a sachem of Tammany Hall. These were national political liabilities, but by careful management they could be outweighed by his liberal record. His street-urchin accent, his jovial manner, and his appearance of being sincerely "for the people" could be made into definite assets. The fact that he was a devout Roman Catholic was another matter.

There had never been a Catholic President in the country's history; nor had a Catholic ever been nominated for that greatest of honors. For more than a hundred years the United States had been a Protestant nation, as far as its Chief Executive was concerned. Across wide stretches of territory the Church of Rome was feared. Catholicism was an anathema to millions of honest people who knew nothing about it. In the rural sections of New England, deep down through the Bible Belt, across the land to the temples of Los Angeles, anti-Catholicism lay deep. Often, as the Ku Klux Klan had shown, it arose violently to the surface. There was no use denying its existence. It was traditional. In these bigoted sections it was only necessary to whisper that a man was a Catholic to damn him in the eyes of millions. Politicians of both parties had raised the Catholic issue in almost every national campaign for one hundred years, secretly and scurrilously accusing candidates of being a Catholic in order to alienate the anti-Catholic vote.

Well aware of this historic situation, and also well aware of its importance politically in 1928, a New York lawyer whose hobby had long been canon law undertook to seek out the answers to the problem brought about by Al Smith's religion. Towards the end of March, 1927, Charles C. Marshall wrote a "letter" to the *Atlantic Monthly*, then edited by Ellery Sedgwick, in which he studiously and conscientiously raised the question of the desirability of having a Roman Catholic for President. In this article, which was prefaced with praise for Smith's record and the probity of his character, Marshall, from his own knowledge of canon law, posed certain questions which he knew were troubling many people.

Was it not true, he asked, that the Church relegated to itself all power not assumed by the state, thus depriving other religions of the right to take part in the religious or moral affairs of the state? Did not the Church believe itself the only true religion and granted no tolerance to other religions? Did not the Church believe that in conflicts between the civil and the secular power the jurisdiction of the Church prevails? Did not the Church believe the "power of the Pope" was superior to the sovereignty of the state? Did not the Church intend to control marriage and education, and thus bring all other religions within its control? Had not the Church, in the past, used armed intervention to enforce its demands upon the state?

Whether true or not, millions of Protestants believed that these questions were answerable only in the affirmative. The *Atlantic* released Marshall's letter to the press and — for the first time since the shameful days of Know-Nothingism nearly one hundred years before — the issue of Catholicism versus the Presidency was brought out into the open as a part of a Presidential campaign. It was, however, brought out on a high level and, although he was no deep student of church law, Governor Smith responded to the challenge on an equally high plane.[1]

Smith's closing paragraph was unquestionably one of the finest statements of politico-religious faith ever penned by an American statesman:

> I believe that no tribunal of any church has any power to make any decree in the law of the land, other than to establish the status of its own communicants within its own church. I believe in the support of the public school as one of the cornerstones of American liberty. I recognize no power in the institution of my church to interfere with the operation of the Constitution of the United States or the enforcement of the law of the land. I believe in absolute freedom of conscience for all men, and in equality of all churches, all sects before the law as a matter of right.

Smith's ringing divorcement of church and state should have put an end to the religious controversy then and there. In its

---

[1] Smith sent his answer to the *Atlantic* without a title. Sedgwick recognized its high qualities and happily called it "Governor Smith, Catholic and Patriot, Replies."

pages he had shown that as Governor of New York he had never allowed the Church in any way to dictate to him as to policy or choice of associates. Frank Kent asked the question, "Would the Catholic Church influence Smith as President?" and answered it, "No more than the Baptist or Methodist Church would." But in spite of his brave and positive declaration Al Smith was to lose the Presidency mainly because he was a member of the Roman Catholic Church.

As the Democrats headed to Houston, Texas, for their National Convention, Al Smith was far out in the lead. The Democratic Party had recovered from the earthquake of 1920 and the eruption of 1924. It had once again become an organic party; at least, it showed a semblance of being whole once more. The Klan had been exposed and more or less laughed out of existence. A great deal of work had gone into pulling the parts together and the party entered Houston with an air of confidence and an appearance of solidarity that had too long been missing.

Although Al Smith had shown up extremely well in the primaries there were others who might just as well have led the Democratic Party to victory. There was Thomas Walsh of Montana, who had relentlessly uncovered the oil scandals of the Harding administration in the course of a political career as liberal as that of any man in the Democratic Party. He had led the fight against seating Truman Newberry, the free-spending Senator-elect from Michigan, and it was Walsh, as much as anyone, who had forced a recalcitrant Senate to accept the nomination of Justice Brandeis to the Supreme Court. His investigation of the propaganda activities of the public utilities was a magnificent, useful, and daring achievement. He had fought for the child labor amendment and woman's suffrage; he had helped draft the Federal Reserve Act; he was against the use of the injunction in labor disputes. But he, too, was Catholic (although also a Dry) from the politically unimportant state of Montana.

Like Al Smith, Governor Albert C. Ritchie had been a liberal, competent, and effective chief executive. His record in many respects — schools, the budget, civil service, prison reform — paralleled that of the New Yorker. To Ritchie States' rights were the most important rights guaranteed by the Constitution and for them he fought untiringly. He believed in States' rights with such old-fashioned Jeffersonian fervor that he opposed the federal child labor amendment, federal inheritance taxes, Prohibition, and other encroachments upon what he believed were the fundamental concern of the individual states. It was his hatred of federal interference that had led him to become one of the most effectively outspoken enemies of Prohibition in the country. He was known as a liberal, a belief enforced by his refusal as governor to take part in a Preparedness Day sponsored by President Coolidge, and furthered by his refusal to use state troops to suppress strikes.

One other governor was in the running, Vic Donahey of Ohio, who had the advantage of being from a pivotal state, where he had the support of labor, the Methodist Church and the Anti-Saloon League, and the hatred of the Ku Klux Klan. But his background paled before that of Al Smith, who outshone all the rest even before the Democrats gathered in Sam Houston Hall on June 26.

The Houston Convention was to be no repetition of the unseemly public disrobing of Democrats that had taken place four years before in Madison Square Garden. The mood of the delegates, as they listened enthusiastically to the oracular Claude G. Bowers evoke the spirit of his beloved Thomas Jefferson in the keynote speech, was one of confidence. Gone was the outward manifestation of bitter factionalism; in its place was a belief that the man they nominated would be the next President. So general was the acceptance of Governor Smith as that man that the expected booms for Ritchie, Walsh, or Donahey failed to materialize. When Franklin D. Roosevelt once again placed Smith's name in nomination as the Happy Warrior the enthusiasm was general. All but seven states joined in the unrestrained display and Alfred E. Smith was nominated on the first ballot.[2]

The contest over the Vice-Presidential nominee took shape almost as soon as the convention opened. Senator Joseph T. Robinson, of Arkansas, had the edge over Senator Barkley of Kentucky, since the Democratic floor leader had Smith's backing. Barkley had strong backing from the farm, labor, and Prohibition blocs,

[2] On the first roll call Smith received the necessary two thirds after Ohio had changed its vote and given him the votes it had first cast for favorite son Atlee Pomerene. The runners-up were three "favorite sons," Senator George of Georgia, Senator Reed of Missouri, and Representative Cordell Hull of Tennessee. Ritchie, Walsh, and Donahey were not placed in nomination, although prior to the convention they had loomed large as the men most available if Smith had not been so far ahead.

but he could not stand against Robinson's conservative appeal. Robinson's backers took the stand that while their candidate was progressive he was not radical and there was nothing in his record which big business could criticize. Barkley was known as one of the sponsors of the Railway Labor Board bill. Robinson met some opposition from the Deep South, where the Klan still exerted some power under the name of the Knights of the Great Forest. Nevertheless, Robinson received the nomination with the landslide vote of 1035⅙ out of 1100 possible votes.

Out of the Houston convention came a platform that was superior to that conjured up by the witch doctors at Kansas City; but even so it hardly ranked with the masterly summary of the issues that the Progressives had wrought with blessed brevity in 1924. In fact, it was not a liberal document, in spite of its attacks upon Republican rule which, it said, had left the country with "industry depressed, agriculture prostrate, American shipping destroyed, workmen without employment," and in spite of its attacks upon the Republican tariff. It offered nothing towards a program which would alleviate the Republican-created distress. Its pledge to effect duties that would "permit effective competition . . . and at the same time produce a fair revenue for the support of government" and assure "actual difference between the cost of production at home and abroad" was a warning that the Democratic Party had no honest intention of tampering with the Fordney-McCumber tariff of 1922.

The Democratic leaders were not anxious to create controversy. They did their best to appease both Wets and Drys on the Prohibition issue, which was to loom larger this year than ever before. Prior to Smith's nomination the Drys threatened to bolt the convention, and the fight over the Prohibition plank was finally brought to the floor. After much wrangling a compromise plank was agreed upon which Smith interpreted, in a telegram to the convention, as giving him leeway to advocate modification of the Volstead Act. He then declared his intention of supporting a change in the law, thus forcing the issue into the main political stream.

The Democrats endorsed the equalization fee principle of McNary-Haugenism in the plank on the farm problem, and advocated legislation which would allow the Farm Board to loan money to farmers at the same low rate of interest charged by the Shipping Board. Otherwise it had little to offer. In spite of eloquent pleas by Newton D. Baker and Carter Glass for re-adoption of its 1924 League of Nations plank, that issue was coldly dropped. Collective bargaining by labor was endorsed and labor injunctions opposed. Demand was made for the enforcement of the Antitrust Acts.

Neither here nor in the Republican platform was there any grappling with the tremendous problems facing a nation fast in the grip of a disastrous stock-market inflation which went higher and higher day by day as the unemployment figures crept up to nearly 4,000,000 and hunger and privation increased alarmingly under the cloak of Prosperity.

There was no organized third party movement of protest or rebellion in 1928. The coalition which had made up the Progressive movement of four short years before had been dissolved. The Socialists, however, had not withdrawn from the political arena. They came forward with a candidate who was to appeal particularly to intellectuals, college students, and some small business-men. Norman Mattoon Thomas, an Ohio-born Presbyterian minister, had founded the magazine *World Tomorrow* and had been an editor of the *Nation*. He may have been a Socialist but he was no Marxist. He seemed already to have dedicated his life to running unsuccessfully for public office, a career which gave him an opportunity at least to inject some consideration of vital issues into campaigns which otherwise would have been conducted solely along orthodox political lines. He had run for governor of New York in 1924 against Smith and Mills, and for mayor of New York City in 1925. A fine speaker, who infused high thoughts on such topics as industrial democracy (of which there was much talk in the 1920's) with a sort of evangelical eloquence, Thomas failed to attract the working class. Such votes as he was to garner came almost entirely from people who would probably otherwise have voted for Al Smith, although he also had a mild appeal to some who were still under the illusion that Herbert Hoover was a liberal. The Communist Party managed to get its candidate, William Z. Foster, on the ballot in thirty-two states, eighteen more than it had been able to manage in 1924.

It was, of course, Al Smith who furnished the excitement of the almost indescribable campaign. Herbert Hoover and Charles Curtis found themselves in a position where they did not have to say much of anything. In the final analysis Al Smith did not say very much either, although it sounded as if he did and what he said was, in many respects, soundly superior to Hoover's promises of a Republican Utopia, with a car in every garage and a chicken in every pot. Neither candidate dug into the real issues confronting the nation. Except for Norman Thomas, who had neither funds nor organization and very little else except his liberal mind, no one discussed the really chaotic condition into which the United States had already plunged more than a year before the Wall Street crash.

There was no full debate on conditions in the coal industry, the wasteful competitive warfare of the oil industry, the disastrous effect on the railroads of speculation and banker control. There was no frank discussion of Muscle Shoals. Such an important domestic problem as flood control was ignored. Conservation of national resources was not discussed. The confused international debt situation was passed by as if it did not exist.

What did seem to be important was Mrs. Al Smith's lack of social grace, her husband's lack of grammatical finesse. How he pronounced "radio" engendered far more acrimonious debate than his animadversions on the evils of the power trust. Al Smith and his personal and political family were subjected to an almost unbelievably vicious whispering campaign that spread to every corner of the land. The religious issue was distorted beyond anything that had ever before happened in a Presidential campaign. He was accused of building a tunnel to the White House so the Pope could secretly visit him from the Vatican — and millions believed it! The Pope would have his own office in the White House! The Roman Catholic Church would rule the country and no free, white, Protestant American could hold office! Parochial schools would supplant public schools! A priestocracy would rule even in the states! And Al Smith would throw out the old Democratic Party and in its place set up a Catholic party!

From unknown sources a flood of virulent propaganda against Smith and the Church to which he belonged, filled with vicious lies and innuendoes, such as America had not known in all its history, covered the nation. In one state alone at least $500,000 worth of the vile pamphlets were circulated. Al Smith, as temperate a man as there was in public life, was portrayed as a drunkard, and caricatured as a whisky-soaked, tobacco-chewing, ill-mannered ruffian, worse than any Tammany villain of Boss Tweed's hey-day. He was painted as a creature who would disgrace his country in the eyes of the rest of the world, an ignoramus not fit for the White House, too ill-bred to mingle with ambassadors from foreign lands.

The Republican Party made the most of the slanders. Herbert Hoover repudiated the vilification of his opponent, for the record, but made no real effort to control the assaults on Smith's character. The violence of the assaults drew some support to Smith, mainly in protest at the un-American spirit of unfairness inherent in the methods used to discredit the candidate. Those who admired Smith, for his courage and for his daring in hitting out at Prohibitionists, Klansmen, and other such groups, idolized him as deeply as, a few years later, millions of common people were to idolize Franklin Roosevelt. A group of distinguished Harvard University professors came to his defense with a fine statement: "We support Governor Smith because of his power to reverse the present trend toward political apathy and arouse in the citizens of the United States an active, intelligent interest and participation in their government."

The major criticism of Smith, aside from his religious affiliation, was his possession of a "New York mind," his "lack of a national viewpoint," and his "inexperience in international affairs." This criticism came mainly from the very same sources which had supported Calvin Coolidge four years before. Granted Smith's regionalism and inexperience, he at least had the integrity, which Coolidge lacked, of admitting it. And he owned — as he had shown as governor — the kind of ripe mind that sought information from the right sources, assimilated it readily, and put it to good use. He turned to Midwest farm experts before he made his major speech on farm relief, and what he said made as much sense as anything Herbert Hoover deigned to reveal on the subject. When asked what kind of President he thought he would make his disarming reply was, "The same kind as I made a governor."

Smith went about the country pointing out to the people that their national structure, the one the Republicans so honestly claimed as their own, was in imminent danger of collapse. He decried inefficiency in government and pleaded for reform along progressive lines. He recalled the scandals and pointed out the errors of eight years of Republican control. His was a voice calling, not in a wilderness, but in the rank meadows of Prosperity where it likewise fell on deaf ears.

At a time when Mussolini had marched to power in Italy and Hitler was raising his blatant voice in the beer halls of Germany, rallying his National Socialist Party to its attack on civilization, and fascism was not far beneath the surface in the United States, the American people had to choose between Herbert Hoover and Alfred E. Smith. Where lay the difference? Cynically, the *Wall Street Journal* explained:

> Never before, here or anywhere else, has a Government been so completely fused with business. There can be no doubt that Hoover as President would be a dynamic business President. He would be the first business, as distinguished from political, president the country has ever had.
>
> Al Smith's record in politics is the best possible pledge that he will make a successful administrator of the biggest business of all, that of managing the political business organization of the United States.
>
> Hoover would serve the public by serving business; Smith would serve business by serving the public.

That Al Smith, for all his fine liberalism in 1928 — a liberalism that was to be drowned in a pool of bitter jealousy a few years later — was no radical, no advocate of a change in the system, was apparent in his choice of a campaign manager. For this position the man from the sidewalks of New York selected John J. Raskob of General Motors. Raskob, the familiar of millionaires and backer of the open shop, had made a fortune in wartime profits. His speculations in the Coolidge boom were notoriously successful.

Taking a look at the record, as Al Smith so often asked the people to do, we find Raskob's friend silent on many things. Al Smith spoke not on the matter of income taxes, he made no mention of the League of Nations, he said nothing about the recognition of Russia, whose bitter enemy his opponent Hoover had been for a decade. There was no deep fear of Al Smith in the canyons of Wall Street. His bravest stand was on Prohibition. An election ahead of his time, he bravely advocated modification of the Volstead Act in such a way that control over "light wines and beer" would be returned to the individual states.

Labor took no decisive stand in 1928. The American Federation of Labor had retired to its shell and an abortive attempt of Progressives to push George Norris to the front as La Follette's successor had come to nothing. Norris distrusted the effectuality of any third party, but he at least had the courage to bolt the Republicans with a ringing denunciation of Herbert Hoover. The party's other great liberal, Borah, campaigned for Hoover with great vigor.

The campaign in reality was one between two individuals. The one was mildly liberal Democrat; the other an experimental Republican. The former was a Wet who also spoke in soft denunciation of monopoly. The latter was a Dry who defended, in colorless words, the established order of things. Hoover represented *laissez faire* and industrial efficiency. Smith represented social responsibility in government. Thus, in a minor way, were the people given a choice between two men whose political philosophy was more contrasting than had been the case in 1920 and 1924. But "two cars in every garage and a chicken in every pot" was a far more palatable slogan than Al Smith's invitation to look at the record of misrule.

Herbert Hoover won the election in another Republican landslide. At least, that is the way it looked when the election returns were in. Hoover carried forty states, five in the traditionally Democratic Solid South,[3] and his popular vote was 21,000,000 to 15,000,000 for Smith. These were so divided that Hoover won 444 electoral votes to Smith's 87.

"But never," says D. L. Dumond, "were statistics more deceiving."[4] Smith received 6,000,000 more votes than any candidate of the Democratic Party had ever received. This was 40 per cent of the total vote cast.[5] In 1920 Cox had received but 34 per cent and Davis only 30 per cent in 1924. In Arizona, Minnesota, Nebraska, North Dakota, Washington, and Wisconsin the results of the election "were pregnant with meaning because in all of those states independent progressives who openly opposed the Republican candidates and policies were elected by tremendous majorities while Smith was being repudiated." Henrik Shipstead, the Farmer-Laborite, carried Minnesota, for example, against a Republican candidate by 400,000 votes, while Smith lost it by only

[3] Texas, Tennessee, Florida, North Carolina, and Virginia.
[4] *America in Our Time* by Dwight Lowell Dumond, pp. 430–431.
[5] Nor must it be forgotten that in 1928 nearly 7,000,000 more voters went to the polls than had gone in 1924. The political apathy of 1920 and 1924 was definitely on the wane.

100,000. Looking back at 1928 it becomes even more certain that the handwriting was on the wall and it is even possible to believe that Alfred E. Smith might well have won over Herbert Hoover had he not been a victim of his own religion and the deep-seated intolerance of Americans which, as we have seen, comes strangely forward every four years.

Perhaps the bitterest pill which Al Smith had to swallow was his loss of New York State. The state which four times had sent him to Albany as its chief executive turned him down for the Presidency by 103,481 votes. As he had responded to John W. Davis four years before and run for governor at a time when he felt he could not afford to do so — and won by a vast majority — so had his close friend Franklin Delano Roosevelt run for governor this year at Smith's own desperate request. Roosevelt's victory was far less impressive than Smith's had been. Roosevelt carried the state by the small plurality of 25,564. But the event was of profounder significance than the return indicated, as the next four eventful years were to prove.

Calvin Coolidge rounded out the rest of his term in glum silence. There had been a slight recession on the stock market following the Hoover victory, but soon an increasingly hysterical public, by its wild and uncontrolled speculation, was pushing the market to unheard-of heights. Coolidge addressed his "farewell message" to the lame-duck session of the Seventieth Congress. It was a typical message. "No Congress . . . ever assembled," he said, "on surveying the state of the nation, has met with a more pleasing prospect than that which appears at the present time." His policies of thrift in government and of noninterference with business, he said, was responsible; if the direction of government were not altered, all would continue to be well. He then asked Congress to ratify the Kellogg-Briand pact; to set up a farm board for the promotion of orderly marketing; to lease Muscle Shoals to private industry; to build Boulder Dam on the Colorado River (but in such a way as to "leave the electrical field open to private enterprise"); and to build up the Navy. Congress was in a tractable mood. It approved the Kellogg-Briand pact in almost the same breath with which it authorized the construction of fifteen new cruisers for the Navy. It appropriated money to control the Mississippi; but, thanks to George Norris, the bill authorizing the building of the Boulder Dam left the way open for public operation. It made the Prohibition laws even more restrictive. It did nothing about farm relief, the railroad situation, the re-apportionment of Congress, or about Senator Norris's resolution for the abolition of lame-duck sessions.

While the nation, and Congress, waited for the incoming administration to take over and solve all problems in March 1929, the President-elect, traveling in a battleship provided by the administration, toured South America, drumming up trade for American industry. Hoover's pilgrimage of friendship and good will was supposed to alleviate somewhat the criticism leveled against the imperialist policy of intervention the Republicans had long endorsed. The *Magazine of Wall Street* was greatly impressed by Hoover's bold bid "in opening channels for American goods the world over." American business was all set for a vast surge of even greater prosperity than it had already experienced when Herbert Clark Hoover entered the White House on March 4, 1929, and Calvin Coolidge retired to private life.

CHAPTER TWENTY-SEVEN

Capitalism Triumphant

"ONE of the oldest and perhaps the noblest of human aspirations has been abolition of poverty. By poverty I mean the grinding by undernourishment, cold and ignorance, and fear of old age of those who have the will to work. We in America today are nearer to the final triumph over poverty than ever before in the history of any land. The poorhouse is vanishing from among us. . . ."

Thus spake Herbert Hoover on August 11, 1928, as he accepted the nomination of the Republican Party.

"There is," he added, as he promised to go forward with the policies of the past eight years, "no guaranty against poverty equal to a job for every man."

Now in March 1929, facing the great crowd gathered in Washington to see him inaugurated as President of the United States, Herbert Hoover amplified the philosophy that had won for him the reputation of the Great Humanitarian.

"In the field which is more largely social," he said, "our first obligation should be the protection of the health, the assurance of the education and training of every child in our land. In the field which is more largely economic our first objective must be to provide security from poverty and want. We want security in living for every home. We want to see a nation built of home owners and farm owners. We want to see their savings protected. We want to see them in steady jobs. We want to see more and more of them insured against death and accident, unemployment and old age. We want them all secure."

Not for a long time had a leader of the Republican Party spoken in this wise with words so bravely challenging and hopeful. They seemed to have sprung from the heart and they filled their hearers with an unaccustomed feeling of expectancy. There appeared to be about them some of that same fine spirit of brave challenge and hope that later was to cling to the words of Franklin Delano Roosevelt. But there was a vast difference. They stemmed from an entirely different philosophy. Herbert Hoover believed that society should take care of its own, its old, its sick, its jobless, and its homeless. But . . .

Herbert Hoover never confused government with society. He did not believe that government should interfere with the process. This should be, he thought, wholly the duty of private enterprise. The federal government might investigate, propose, and even direct — but it must never control. He believed that rugged individualism was all-important. Private enterprise and individual initiative were the wellsprings of his philosophy. "You cannot," he said with finality, "extend the mastery of government over the daily working life of the people without at the same time making it the master of the people's souls and thoughts."

It is significant that Herbert Hoover thought of federal aid as *mastery*, rather than as a part of the democratic function of a government of the people, by the people, and for the people. Because of this flaw in his political philosophy — a flaw that had also long been evident in traditional Republican policies — Herbert Hoover failed as President of the United States more completely and more abjectly than any other man who found himself President at a time of great crisis. There were other reasons why Hoover was to go down in history as the Great Failure, but this was at the bottom of them all.

No man had been elected to the White House since Grant's inauguration in 1869 with less genuine political experience than Herbert Hoover. As Belgian Relief Commissioner and as wartime Food Administrator his work had been wholly administrative. The Presidency, of course, is the chief administrative office in the government, but it calls for a far wider play of talents than almost any other administrative or executive post in the world. The President's major function is to mediate between the technician, the public, and the Congress, which is a political body. To do this calls for a special kind of understanding and experience which was altogether lacking from Hoover's background. His one close association with the actual workings of government had been as a member of Harding's and Coolidge's cabinet, but there he had occupied the least political of all posts, the secretaryship of the Department of Commerce.

Hoover had sold himself to the public to a great extent on the grounds that he was an engineer, a businessman, and an executive — not a "politician." This had seemed a happy combination and those who had put their trust in it expected great things to come of it, especially a type of leadership which would bring a new sense of direction to government. No longer, they thought, need Congress flounder along as it had been doing under Coolidge. It was not as well known then as it became later that Hoover was a Whig at heart, who did not believe in a "strong" executive but who owned to the belief prevalent among business interests that a strong executive is apt to be a champion of the masses and not the servant of monopoly.

Although born in the farming state of Iowa and educated at Leland Stanford University in California, Herbert Hoover had spent very little of his life in the United States. Although trained as an engineer, he had spent very little time at his profession. Most of his years had been spent in England and the Orient, and his energies in organizing and promoting mining and other stock companies for the exploitation of the resources of undeveloped territories. From this he had wrested a large personal fortune. His methods in Manchuria, Mongolia, and China were such that once an English court had soundly rebuked Hoover for his ways of conducting business. He had, however, presumably left all this behind when he repatriated himself in 1917.

Prior to the decade of his Americanization he had known little about his native land, its conditions economically, culturally, or politically. During this decade he had held no elective office and his personal associations, as well as those made through his appointive offices, were strictly with businessmen. He had no background or training in economic theory. As a relief administrator he had used part of the funds at his disposal to help overthrow the Béla Kun government in Hungary and to finance the White Guard invasion of Soviet Russia.

Because he had been an appointee of Woodrow Wilson and because, as a founder of the Child Health Association in 1921, he had supported the constitutional amendment to permit the abolition of child labor, he had acquired a reputation as a liberal. In the conservative circles of society which he frequented he was. But as Secretary of Commerce he had served faithfully the two most reactionary administrations the country had ever known.

He had spoken bravely for the League of Nations — but had not raised his voice when Harding pronounced it dead. He had supported the World Court — but had not fought for it by word or deed when the Senate put it aside. He had been on the side of most of the reactionary legislation enacted under Harding or Coolidge. He had interfered with the coal and railroad strikes, and stood on the side of Daugherty and Harding in their use of the vicious injunction. Not once had he raised his voice against the scandals of the administration in whose cabinet he sat. On taxation he was with Mellon, and on farm relief he was with Coolidge. On most other matters he kept a discreet silence. He was vain, autocratic in his dealings with his underlings, and tremendously ambitious.

William Allen White once called him an "adding machine." He liked to collect, at great pains and great expense, all sorts of scientific data, but he did not seem to do very much with them. After he became President he appointed many commissions to investigate matters of vital importance. Most of them failed to report until the crisis had passed and their need was gone. He said nothing and did nothing that would interfere in any way with *status quo*.

To help him Hoover had asked Andrew Mellon to remain in his cabinet as Secretary of the Treasury, but he had made some other changes. The most notable appointment was that of Henry L. Stimson as Secretary of State. James W. Good became Secretary of War, William D. Mitchell was named Attorney General; and the others were Walter F. Brown, Postmaster General; Charles Francis Adams, Secretary of the Navy; Ray Lyman Wilbur, Interior; Arthur M. Hyde, Agriculture; Robert P. Lamont, Commerce; and James J. Davis, Labor. No more conservative group of advisers could be imagined.

With these men to back him up, Herbert Hoover was determined as he took office to prove the truth of his observation made at the opening of the campaign: "With impressive proof on all sides of magnificent progress, no one can rightly deny the fundamental correctness of our economic system."

There were two matters of concern to this perfect system which called for immediate legislative action — farm relief and the tariff. Hoover would have let them wait until the regular session of the Seventy-First Congress met in December. But in answer to de-

266

mands that he redeem his pledges given in the campaign, he reluctantly called Congress into extraordinary session in April. Awaiting Congress were two magical measures designed to increase the prosperity of the manufacturer and at the same time to diminish the destitution of the farmer. These called for the upward revision of the tariff and the industrializing of agriculture through encouragement of co-operatives and the establishment of a governmental board to control surpluses.

Almost from the start Hoover was to have his troubles with Congress. He sent a long, windy message in which he asserted that he had long held that the causes of the "agricultural depression" could only be met "by the creation of a great instrumentality clothed with sufficient authority and resources" but which must be surrounded by "certain safeguards" that would not "undermine the freedom of our farmers and our people." Congress took the first part seriously, but did not see eye to eye with him on the latter.

The administration-backed Agricultural Marketing Act, which in some respects anticipated the New Deal's farm program, passed the House by the record vote of 366 to 35. It created a Federal Farm Board of eight members, to be appointed by the President with the consent of the Senate, with power to make loans to co-operatives from a revolving fund of $500,000,000 and to purchase surpluses for the maintenance of prices. Of this Hoover approved, but the Senate, in the face of his hostility, added the hated export debenture. The House seemed more than disposed to back up this addition. Hoover was indignant. He denounced the proposal as a direct subsidy to "special interests" and said it would stimulate overproduction by attempting to keep domestic prices higher than world prices through treasury appropriations. After several weeks of wrangling the House rejected the Senate proposal and the Agricultural Marketing Act became law on June 15, substantially in the form originally advocated by Hoover.

The Federal Farm Board soon established a number of national co-operatives, notably to deal in grain, cotton, and livestock, to which it loaned $165,000,000 for marketing purposes. It created a grain and cotton stabilization corporation — which lost $239,-000,000 buying and selling on the wheat and cotton markets. Wheat was depressed in 1929 because of the large crop the previous year and prospects of a still larger one at the next harvest.

The board carried on extensive, but futile, propaganda for the voluntary reduction of acreage. Straight down the line the board did exactly what Herbert Hoover said no governmental agency should do — "engage in buying and selling and price-fixing of products."

The Farm Marketing Act of 1929 cost the taxpayers millions of dollars, but it did not in the slightest check overproduction or stabilize prices. Neither did it aid the small farmer whose farms were mortgaged and who had no further security to put up. Dispossession of farmers increased drastically in the ensuing months. A drought added to their woes. In February 1931, Congress — against the resistance of Hoover — was forced to take more direct action. It appropriated $67,000,000 for direct loans to be used for seed, fertilizer, feed, food, medical supplies, and voluntary crop reduction. A year later, in setting up the Reconstruction Finance Corporation, Congress provided additional credit to the Farm Land Banks, but even then it was too late to bring succor to thousands. Throughout the entire Hoover administration no definite action was taken to restore foreign markets. Instead, they were further restricted by the administration's tariff policies and by the refusal of the administration to cancel the European war debts. It later tried to correct this when it declared a moratorium on debt payments, but most of the damage was already done. Under Hoover's Presidency, what Dwight L. Dumond once aptly called "a narrow program of economic isolation" went hand-in-hand with a refusal to bring about a reduction of agricultural production to meet the needs of the domestic market.

In his message to Congress Hoover had asked for a limited revision of tariff duties as an aid to agriculture. But when Chairman Willis C. Hawley of the House Ways and Means Committee reported the tariff bill early in May, duties had been raised to the highest level ever known in American history. The bill had Secretary Mellon's full approval. It took the House exactly three short weeks to conclude its consideration of the bill, which it passed by a vote of 264 to 147. In the Senate it was quickly guided through the Finance Committee by Senator Smoot.

Senator Borah had made an honest effort to save the day for agriculture by introducing a resolution which would have confined tariff revisions to agricultural products. But his resolution, which was offered in behalf of the administration, lost by one vote.

The way was opened for the worst spectacle of lobbying and logrolling that Washington had seen since the days of the infamous Payne-Aldrich tariff in 1909. More than one historian has called Hoover's inaction a major failure of his career, pointing to it as a typical example of his unwillingness to exert a constructive leadership over Congress. At a time when the greatest collapse in world economy of modern times was already under way, Hoover allowed the legislature to run hog-wild without a word from him.

This lack of leadership was equally apparent when the bill came to the floor of the Senate. Inquiries as to the President's wishes resulted merely in Senator Smoot's bland assertion, "I know the President is in favor of protection." It was not until late in the proceedings, when it had become obvious that the special session would end with tariff revision unfinished, that Hoover broke his silence. In a White House press release he said:

> The President has declined to interfere or express an opinion on the details of rates or any compromise thereof, as it is obvious that, if for no other reason, he could not pretend to have the necessary information in respect to many thousands of commodities which such determination requires.

Certain that President Hoover really desired moderate rates, a small coalition of Progressive Republicans and Democrats followed Senator Borah's lead in trying to stem the avaricious, profit-seeking lobbyists. As Senator Reed said, when this coalition began showing its strength, they had made up their mind to "knock out every increase in industrial rates and we might as well go ahead and be done with it." But did Hoover take the hint and come to the coalitionists' aid? On the contrary. Instead, he accused Borah and his bloc of refusing to afford industry adequate protection! The logrolling continued. The special session ended with the House, which unlike the Senate was under administration control, refusing to accept most of the 1253 amendments to the act adopted by the Senate, and it was not until the following spring that the Smoot-Hawley bill passed and was ready for Hoover's signature.

In the meantime many things were happening in the United States and in the world. While the Congress debated the tariff the administration was forced to look beyond our borders. Harding and Coolidge may have been able to avoid deep concern with foreign affairs. Herbert Hoover was not to escape as easily.

Toward the end of the year the Chinese Nationalist Government, then as now headed by Chiang Kai-shek, became embroiled with Soviet Russia over the Chinese Eastern Railway. Open hostilities broke out without a formal declaration of war. Henry L. Stimson, who had resigned as Governor General of the Philippines to become Secretary of State, was of the opinion that Russia had violated the Kellogg-Briand Pact, to which both she and China were signatories. Secretary Stimson had little more love for Communist Russia than had his chief, Herbert Hoover. He was, however, a forthright man with no sympathy for isolation. He sent identical notes to both countries, reminding them of their obligations under the treaty.

Russia resented this intervention on two reasonable grounds: (1) that negotiations were already under way to settle the dispute and that the United States was bringing "unjustifiable pressure" on these negotiations; and (2) that we had no right to give our unasked "advice and counsel" to a nation with which, by our own will, we had no official diplomatic relations. In this country there was considerable criticism of Stimson's act and he was forced to withdraw. But he had, by his notes, which had Herbert Hoover's full approval, laid the foundation for a strong Far Eastern policy that was consistently followed until the outbreak of World War II.

Secretary Stimson extended this policy two years later when Japan invaded Manchuria. He called Japan's attention to her open violation of the Kellogg-Briand pact, but without result. He then turned, again without success, to the League of Nations, and when this failed stated in unequivocal tones that the United States would never recognize "any situation, treaty, or agreement" that was in violation of the pact.

Neither Great Britain nor France would support Stimson's principle of nonaggression, and Japan, well aware that democratic America alone would not try to force the issue, ignored the protest. Thus when Japan invaded Shanghai in 1932, there was little Stimson could do but make another protest. He and others wished to go further and impose an economic boycott, but President Hoover, his ear ever attuned to the business interests, resisted this on the ground that it would lead to war. When Great Britain later refused to co-operate in invoking the Nine-Power Treaty of 1922 Stimson announced that the United States henceforth would refuse to recognize any new order established by force in the Far East. Thus, while the country domestically pursued a blind policy of economic isolation, under Stimson's leadership and with Hoover's approval, it began negating the soft and frightened foreign policies pursued under Calvin Coolidge.

CHAPTER TWENTY-EIGHT

The October Revolution

THURSDAY, October 24, 1929!

That was the day of the great panic on Wall Street. That was the day that marked the beginning of the end of Normalcy which had been heralded in almost nine years before when the Republican earthquake landed Warren Gamaliel Harding in the White House. That was the day that marked the beginning of the end of the Prosperity Calvin Coolidge had nursed so tenderly and Herbert Hoover had promised would never end. It came almost without warning; almost, but not quite. There had been black clouds in the skies throughout September. There had been storm warnings — for those who could read. But from the Gulf to Eastport no official red flag of danger had been ordered up. The government did not believe in scaring the people. Perhaps the storm would blow away.

On September 3 the market had begun to slip. Within a month the big stocks like American Can, Radio, General Electric, had dropped from 20 to 50 points below their highest levels. But this did not cause speculators big or little to scurry to cover. The declines of June and December, 1928, and of March and May, 1929, had been followed by recovery. So, thought the wiseacres, would this decline. Instead of getting out they rushed in to buy more and more at what they thought were bargain prices. Early in October it seemed that they were right. Prices went up. And then, for no apparent reason, they began going down again.

A few cautious advisers during these unsettled weeks predicted not disaster — for none had the courage to speak everything that was privately in their minds — but "further liquidations" and "trends towards lower levels." Others explained the situation as "another period of readjustment" or "an intermediate movement and not the precursor of a business depression." Charles E.

Mitchell, chairman of the National City Bank of New York, a man obviously to be listened to, helped disperse such clouds of gloom as dotted the sky when he said: "The industrial situation of the United States is absolutely sound and our credit situation is in no way critical. . . . The interest given brokers' loans is always exaggerated. Altogether too much attention is paid to it." And, while he admitted that "in some cases" speculation had "gone too far," he was not worried. The "shaking down" of prices had done "an immense amount of good."

But the expected recovery did not appear. On Tuesday, October 22, gains made during the day were almost all lost in the last hour of trading. On Wednesday liquidation increased, setting the tape back 104 hours during a 6,000,000 share day. And on Thursday the heavens burst. . . .

More than a billion dollars' worth of paper values were wiped out. There was a frenzied, panic-stricken rush to get liquid, but each transaction drove the market down and down and down.

What had caused the debacle that so quickly extended from a stock market crash into a world-wide era of poverty, starvation, and despair?

There were a variety of answers to that question. Fundamentally it was blamable upon an unbalanced world economy which had put all Europe under a staggering burden of debts and taxes. The terrific expenses of conducting the World War; the loans for that war not yet paid off; the world-wide fever of speculation; and the dread fear that Europe was heading for another war. These were leading factors. The gold needed for trade had been siphoned off to the United States and the American high tariff walls kept it from going back through normal channels of trade.

In this country the abnormal postwar business conditions had led to a frenzied boom in speculation which had pushed prices, and particularly prices of corporate stocks, high above true values. Vast amounts of bank loans had been thrown, not into legitimate businesses, but into the speculative markets, until banks were loaded with securities, bonds, and mortgages whose worth was based on inflated valuations.

Add to these reasons the policy of both the government and Big Business, which had approached the economic situation from the viewpoint of production and had neglected the problem of distribution and consumption. This was most apparent in agriculture. There surpluses had piled up, but farm prices had declined; and at last the farmer could no longer find any money with which to purchase the goods of American factories.

Along with this blindness had gone the myopia of the Federal Reserve Board, which had done little to check inflation, which had stubbornly refused to impose major restraints which might have kept inflation from getting out of control. It had taken a realistic attitude towards none of the problems that were its concern — agriculture, world trade, or labor.

Meanwhile unemployment, mainly technological in nature, had increased distressingly. Even at the time Herbert Hoover was being elected and saying there was no need for social legislation in a country whose ultimate goal was a car in every garage and a chicken in every pot, there were some 4,000,000 jobless men and women in the United States.

The years of normalcy had also seen bigger and bigger amounts of money moving from consumers' trade channels into the pockets of the rich. Under the benevolent Presidencies of Harding, Coolidge, and Hoover the immensely wealthy families and their managements had been building up their great concentration of economic power. By the end of this era the du Ponts, the Mellons, and the Rockefellers alone controlled 15 per cent of the 200 largest corporations, and 13 other family groups controlled a score of other giants. In this era of maldistribution of the returns from machine production, the Ford, McCormick, Harkness, Duke, Pew, Clark, Kress, and Pitcairn families had reached their zenith of wealth and power. Capitalism had so worked out that the "take" of the few was too great; while the rest suffered from an inability to consume the goods they made.

All this Herbert Hoover, if he were the great economist he pretended to be, must have known. But he went even further astray when he said: "The fundamental business of this country, that is, production and distribution of commodities, is on a sound and prosperous basis."

Hoover could make a good case for the productive capacity of the United States, but to say also that the distribution of commodities was on a sound basis was to speak nonsense. The breakdown of the processes of distribution was one of the major economic calamities of the Age of Normalcy, and if Hoover had been half the economist he pretended to be he would have known it.

In spite of Hoover's reassuring words the prosperity which, he soon was claiming, lurked "just around the corner" failed miserably to appear. Perhaps there was little that Herbert Hoover, or any one man, could do to stop the dreadful decline; and certainly there was nothing Hoover could do as long as he clung to the outworn political and economic philosophies of the Republican Party. As long as he continued to accept without question (as he did) the views of the reactionary servants of monopoly, who advised that there was no connection between the stock-market crash and a debased world economy, there was nothing he could do. As long as he believed in the myth of prosperity and as long as he continued to propagandize its obvious errors, there was nothing he could do. But the sad thing is that once events had shown that prosperity was a myth, that the stock-market crash was a symptom of deep-seated economic disorder, that the policies followed for nine years were fallacious — he continued to do nothing fundamental.

Lacking a clear understanding of the economic realities, Herbert Hoover, who subscribed to Wesley Mitchell's theory of the inevitability of cyclical depressions, felt that the depression would be of short duration. Since he was convinced this was the case he was unconvinced of any necessity for decisive federal intervention. His whole political philosophy was built upon the Whiggish belief that government should not interfere. Therefore he tried to persuade.

Convinced, with most big business leaders, that the deflation that had now set in must run its course, Hoover tried to soften the decline rather than to stop it by emergency measures. As the basic industries laid off workers by the thousands, President Hoover repeatedly urged that wage cuts and discharges of employees be "prevented" by industry. His pleas went unheeded and in three years wages dropped 60 per cent. Hoover called a series of Washington conferences where he urged that profits should be cut, not wages, and that there should be no wage reductions at all in most instances. But industry refused to act.

Although it was obvious that recovery depended upon the restoration of the purchasing power, which lessened with every wage cut and with every dismissal, Herbert Hoover and his advisers did not believe in spending federal funds to help restore this vanished power.

Herbert Hoover did believe that industry itself must be helped. He believed in starting at the top and letting relief filter downward. He thought that if the big corporations and the industries were put on their feet, then they would call people back to work and all would be well. Give business a free hand, he said, and all would work out in the end.

Each time there was an upward flurry on the stock market the White House would issue a reassuring bulletin. Almost inevitably stocks declined again. In March 1930, President Hoover predicted that "the worst effect of the crash on unemployment will have been passed during the next sixty days." And sixty days later he said that he was "convinced we have now passed the worst and with continued unity of effort we shall rapidly recover."

As he spoke the bread lines lengthened in the big cities and the sheriffs closed in on the farms.

But there remained a hope. The Republicans had always maintained that the high protective tariff was the basis of all American prosperity. If it worked in good times, they argued, why should it not also work in bad? In its final form, of the 3218 dutiable items in the Smoot-Hawley tariff schedule 887 had been increased and only 235 reduced; the others, already high, remained unchanged. The largest increases were on such products as cereals, meats, dairy products, cotton, sugar, and leather. Plate glass, aluminum, and automobiles led the list of those decreased. In general terms the Smoot-Hawley Act increased tariffs 7 per cent over the vicious Fordney-McCumber Act of 1922.

An avalanche of protests hit the White House. A manifesto was signed by more than 1000 leading economists who pointed out that the act would increase prices, restrict imports, lead to retaliations in foreign lands, and that it would not help the farmers. Nearly every foreign nation protested on similar grounds. But President Hoover — who privately called the act "vicious, extortionate and obnoxious" — was adamant in his refusal to listen to the warnings. He signed the bill.[1]

Quickly the foreign countries retaliated by increasing their own tariffs and the tariff war added immeasurably to the world de-

[1] June 17, 1930. In the campaign of 1932, when the forecasts of the economists had been proved right, he defended his action and failed to protest to the National Republican Committee which had smeared the right-seeing economists as "communists, socialists, and radicals."

pression. Among those to raise their rates was Canada. Between 1929 and 1933 exports to that country dropped $738,795,000. The foreign trade of the United States was very nearly destroyed by act of Congress in 1930.

Six months after the October crash Mr. Hoover's government counted the nation's unemployed at 3,187,000, although the figure probably was even higher. A year after the crash the figure was set at 4,000,000, although labor leaders and many economists said that figure was much too low. Herbert Hoover still stood firmly against furnishing direct federal relief to the jobless. He said:

> This is not an issue as to whether people shall go hungry or cold in the United States. It is solely a question of the best method by which hunger and cold shall be prevented. It is a question as to whether the American people on the one hand will maintain the spirit of charity and mutual self-help through voluntary giving and the responsibility of local government as distinguished on the other hand from the appropriations out of the Federal Treasury for such purposes. My own conviction is strongly that if we break down this sense of responsibility of individual generosity to individual and mutual self-help in the country in times of national difficulty and if we start appropriations of this character we have not only impaired something infinitely valuable in the life of the American people but have struck at the roots of self-government.

No wonder there began to well through America a hatred for this cold, impersonal man in the White House, who could talk that way when millions walked the streets looking in vain for work, who could speak such callous words in the face of starving people.

President Hoover did not bat an eye at handing out millions to corporations through the Reconstruction Finance Corporation, but he set himself in angry rigidity against the La Follette-Costigan measure to spend $750,000,000 among the states for public works and to feed the people. He spent millions to succor bankrupt corporations, while men sold apples on street corners until they could be rehired profitably by business. But he would do no more.

While President Hoover prattled about charity and mutual self-help, the people began to awaken from the deep sleep of Republican normalcy in an effort to help themselves. The American Federation of Labor, long nearly moribund, set out to organize the Southern textile workers. At Gastonia, North Carolina, their efforts were met with guns and the strike for recognition of their union ended in bloodshed. Other efforts were beaten down by the authorities in Tennessee and Virginia. Although these strikes "failed" they awakened the workers and they frightened the employers. The brutality of the latter brought sympathy to the workers, and made the work of the Communists easier.

Unemployed councils and hunger marches, inspired by the Communists, found ready volunteers. President Hoover was not the only one who feared that these hungry, aroused people might well lead the way to revolution. He, however, was in a position to do something about the rabble, and he did. When 20,000 unemployed veterans "marched" on Washington and encamped on government property it was at his orders that they were driven out by machine guns, tanks, and mounted troops. Two were shot dead. One thousand men — and their women and children — were tear gassed. The country was shocked by this callous abuse of power, this blundering, inept, and fascistic exhibition of fear in high places. Hoover's fate was doomed on that awful July day in 1932.

But before the dark, disastrous events led to bloodshed in the National Capital under the shadow of the Capitol itself, many other surrenders had been made in the White House.

Herbert Hoover tried to impose on the Supreme Court a reactionary judge named John J. Parker, upholder of the hated "yellow-dog contracts." The Senate refused to accept him. But its righteous indignation at this perverse act by President Hoover did not last long enough to keep them from confirming Charles Evans Hughes, who had traveled a long way from liberalism, as Chief Justice to replace William Howard Taft.

On this occasion Senator Borah, who had long since seen the error of his ways in supporting Hoover, had this to say:

"Bear in mind that at the present time coal and iron, oil and gas and power, light, transportation, and transmission have all practically gone into the hands of a very few people. The great problem is, How shall the people . . . be permitted to enjoy these natural resources and these means of transportation, free from extortion and oppression? I can conceive of no more vital question than this, which has long divided our Supreme Court. It has divided the Court not because one group of justices is less conscientious in their views, but because of a wide divergence in viewpoint. I am deeply imbued with the wisdom and justice of the minority. I do not want to strengthen the viewpoint of the majority." He spoke wisely, but in vain.

Hoover had his way when Congress tried to spend money for public works to decrease unemployment. No, said the great engineer; for to "increase taxes for the purposes of construction work defeats its own purpose, as such taxes directly diminish employment in private industry." The people who had trudged from closed factory to closed factory, from empty office to empty office, groaned and swore revenge on Hoover.

As usual they pinned their hopes on the mid-term elections, praying that the new Congress would be able to put a stop to the misgovernment of the Hoover administration. An aroused people went to the polls, and when they finished voting the Seventy-second Congress was to have a Democratic House by 219 to 214; close enough, to be sure, but Democratic nevertheless; and an all but Democratic Senate, by 46 to 47. In each house was one Farmer-Labor member. The political tide had turned.

One of his commissions had by now reported. The so-called Wickersham commission had been assigned to investigate law enforcement throughout the nation. Its long report painted a woeful picture of crime and how the various agencies fought it. It was an excellent report. But its really good features, such as the exposure of the wide use of the third degree and other police brutalities, was lost in the interest shown in its section on Prohibition. The report admitted that enforcement of the Eighteenth Amendment was a failure, but it was against repeal, or even modification, of the Volstead Act. It was widely believed that President Hoover himself had dictated this part of the report, which was in variance with the views expressed throughout the rest of the paper by the majority of the commissioners.

The mid-term vote was clearly a censure of President Hoover and his do-nothing policies. But it did not seem to affect him at all. He continued to set himself sullenly against all attempts at reform. When insurgents in Congress pleaded for increased aid for relief he accused them of "playing politics at the expense of human misery" and told the people: "Prosperity cannot be restored by raids on the public treasury." And when Senator La Follette replied, "The relief of human suffering in this emergency should take precedence over the consideration of the wealthy income-tax payer," Hoover could only call that remark "demagogy."

But soon thereafter, realizing that there was a Presidential election coming up in 1932, he began to change his approach. In his public utterances he started to take the depression seriously, to admit that it existed. "We have passed through no less than fifteen major depressions in the last century," he said. "We have come out of each depression into a period of prosperity greater than ever before. We shall do so again." He had convinced himself that the depression was mainly psychological and he tried to tell the hungry people the same. But he had to admit it existed, and he had to find something besides Republican policies to blame. So he blamed the war and the evil deeds on Europe.

"Without the war we should have had no such depression. We can and will make a large measure of recovery irrespective of the rest of the world. We did so with even worse foreign conditions in 1921." And he added, "We are suffering more today from frozen confidence than from frozen securities." But remember, "Nothing can be gained in recovery and employment by detouring capital away from industry and commerce into the Treasury of the United States, either by taxes or loans, on the assumption that the Government can create more employment by use of these funds than can industry and commerce itself."

He was aiming his shafts at unemployment insurance and relief. To his mind they were the most awful dangers facing America. They would ruin America, for "the moment the Government enters into this field it invariably degenerates into the dole."

Herbert Hoover was hitting at America's pride. He was hitting at the traditional fear and disgrace of the poorhouse. He was calling a democratic use of the government to help the people when there was no help elsewhere by the hated European word, the "dole." It was a clever maneuver, but pride does not always abide an empty stomach or the sight of starving children. He had outspoken himself. He had aroused the people's anger and the name Hoover began to be despised throughout the land.

CHAPTER TWENTY-NINE

Into the Lower Depths

RELUCTANTLY President Hoover came to the conclusion that the system of free enterprise which he had believed so perfect and had defended so ardently was proving inadequate to extirpate the depression as quickly as he had said it would. Belatedly he took it upon himself to exercise the leadership that belonged to his office, but of which he had refused to make good use during his first two years in the White House. The Seventy-second Congress was to be well aware of his presence in Washington. Unfortunately for his place in history, as well as for the immediate welfare of the people of the United States, he had waited too long to make his decision.

By nature an autocrat, by training an executive whose word was final, and by economic circumstances a firm believer in the Hamiltonian theory of the elect, Herbert Hoover possessed none of that understanding of democracy that would have fitted him for leadership. He was cold and distant, and terribly dull. He lacked political grace. He had been in office hardly a year when an experienced Washington correspondent wrote in the *New Republic:* "Mr. Hoover is most poisonously unpopular in Washington. Never have I seen the time when there was meaner talk about the occupant of the White House than there is today." He was distinctly disliked by the representatives of the press in the Capital. Much as his theories may have been endorsed on the editorial pages and approved in publishers' meetings, the working press quickly lost confidence in him and his patently dishonest press releases. Long before Charles Michelson began his so-called "smear Hoover" campaign for the Democratic National Committee, Herbert Hoover had won the hearty dislike of the Washington press corps, and their dislike and distrust crept into what they wrote.

An extremely sensitive and absolutely humorless man, by his own stuffed-shirt attitude Herbert Hoover built up a picture of himself as a most unlikable man. As Lindsay Rogers once wrote in the *New York Times*, "The country got few impressions of Mr. Hoover as a human being. Almost the only self-revealing incident was the letter to President Thompson of Ohio State University, suggesting that by way of reminder of sin and trouble Presidents were forced to wear 'hair shirts.'" Whereas the human, if often ridiculous, Calvin Coolidge was almost wholly a newspaper creation, Herbert Hoover never came to life in print. Mrs. Hoover, too, was without the graciousness which had endeared Grace Coolidge to the public. Her aristocratic manners, her lofty attitude towards people she obviously considered her inferiors, did nothing to endear the First Family to the people.

Added to his distant personality from which radiated no warmth was an almost incredible inability to make himself understood. He had an impressive talent for verbal obscurity. Beside his chilly speeches Warren Harding's "pompous phrases moving over the landscape in search of an idea" were models of lucidity. For all the fact that his press agents boasted that he could translate Latin from the original and otherwise was a widely cultured man, his speeches read as if he had been brought up on a steady diet of corporation reports as printed in *The Times* of London. Barrows Dunham recalls his speeches of the 1932 campaign. "No ray could disclose," he wrote, "no key unlock the secret of those sentences. Across a vast and slumbrous gulf of sound, one heard dim struggles with unutterable thoughts."

President Hoover's message to Congress contained nothing he had not said before. His suggestion that Congress remain in session over the Christmas holidays, coming, as it did, after months of refusal to call a special session to cope with the increasing emergency, did not help his cause. After a brief skirmish by the insurgents to unseat Senator George H. Moses as president *pro tempore*, in retaliation for his having called them "Sons of the Wild Jackass" in the previous session, the Senate rolled up its sleeves to tackle two measures designed to lift the country out of the depression. These were the bills creating the Reconstruction Finance Corporation and the administration-backed Glass-Steagall bill, a hastily devised measure liberalizing the terms on which banks might obtain loans from the Federal Reserve System necessitated by the increasing number of bank failures throughout the country.

The Seventy-second Congress was one of the least effective Congresses in many years. Much of the blame for its failure to cope with the crisis rests at the door of the administration. But not all. The Democrats, more even than the insurgents, played politics with distress. Their main objective was to make the Hoover administration so intolerable that there would be no question of a Democratic victory in 1932. Neither Speaker John Nance Garner of Texas nor Senator Joseph Robinson of Arkansas, the topmost Democratic leaders, was noted for his liberalism. With their tongues they lashed at Herbert Hoover, but by their acts they supported his futile program. Like the President, in spite of their Democratic affiliation, the Southern Bourbons who still dominated the party were not opposed to the fundamentally reactionary Hoover policies. It was Speaker Garner who tried to foist the undemocratic and Hearst-inspired national sales tax upon an already overburdened people. He might have succeeded had it not been for the magnificent fight against it waged in the Senate by Senator Norris and especially in the House by Representative Fiorello La Guardia.

Although the Congress was predominantly Democratic it made no effort to rescind the outrageous tariff schedules set by its predecessor, but left them standing at the same high levels, although it did transfer the flexibility power from the President to Congress. It asked President Hoover to call a world-wide conference for the reduction of tariffs, but this mild effort to get the United States out of the tariff war which the United States had started was purely a political gesture meant to embarrass the Republicans. President Hoover vetoed it, as he was expected to do.

Early in 1932 the country was startled when Wright Patman arose in the House and solemnly spoke these words:

"Mr. Speaker, I rise to a question of constitutional privilege. On my own responsibility as a member of this House I impeach Andrew William Mellon, Secretary of the Treasury, for his high crimes and misdemeanors."

The bold young man based his brash action on a statute of 1789 which forbade any person "directly or indirectly . . . concerned with or interested in carrying on the business of trade or commerce" from holding the office of Secretary of the Treasury.

What actual evidence he had to back up his impeachment was never revealed. Secretary Mellon resigned before the House Judiciary Committee investigated the case of the greatest Secretary of the Treasury since Alexander Hamilton. He was at once appointed Ambassador to the Court of St. James's. In London he was no longer to be an embarrassment to the administration. His impeccable reputation had been punctured long before Patman's impeachment and he had been revealed as just another banker helpless before the depressing events he had neither forecast nor found the means to avoid.

In Mellon's place Herbert Hoover appointed Ogden L. Mills, who had been a director of half a dozen large corporations before President Coolidge had made him Undersecretary of the Treasury in 1927. He believed with his chief that the depression was about to run its course. To help it on its way he had conceived the Reconstruction Finance Corporation, which was established by act of Congress in January 1932. The RFC was a corporation capitalized at $500,000,000 which was authorized to sell a maximum of $1,500,000,000 worth of five-year notes or bonds to the public or to the Treasury of the United States. Loans were to be made through regional offices directly to banks and railroads, to agriculture (through the Department of Agriculture) and to industry. Limited to $100,000,000 for a five-year limit, these loans were to be kept secret even from Congress. Small businessmen and bankrupt farmers were ineligible for such loans. They went almost entirely to the large banks, roads, and corporations, although at a later date some funds were allocated to local relief agencies. Former Vice-President Dawes headed the RFC until he withdrew in order to borrow $90,000,000 of its funds for his Chicago bank.

While the administration aided Big Business as best it could, this money did not do what Hoover had said it should do. Unemployment increased because most of the money failed to filter down to the lower levels. In this situation the President suggested a "Share the Work" program — whereby government employees, at Congressional edict, were required to take a month's furlough without pay. Thus the government broke its own pledge, made earlier, to "protect the standard of wages." President Hoover voluntarily cut his salary, and the salaries of cabinet members were also reduced in this surface effort to enforce governmental economy. Senator Borah's move to reduce Congressional salaries never got out of committee.

Millions of jobless persons regarded Hoover's salary-cutting act as a cynical gesture and the resentment against him grew. Perhaps nothing indicated the cynicism of the administration more completely than the so-called "block plan" of relief. Endorsed by President Hoover and sanctioned by J. Pierpont Morgan, this was an outrageously paternalistic plan whereby each person was supposed to pledge help to the more needy in his own neighborhood. It failed to help many people, for in most city blocks there were more people needing help than were able to give it.

Soon it was obvious to all but the most callous that the government, as not only the Communists took every occasion to assert, had "deserted the people" in their time of dire need. Actual starvation was not uncommon in the large cities. Homeless men tramped the streets, abject and pitiable. "Hoovervilles" sprang up around the dumps and railroad yards of almost every city and many smaller localities. "The dignity of poverty that Hoover considered so splendid for the nation's morale," one left-wing historian of the period wrote, "was hardly discernible in the gaunt faces of men and women who had sold their blankets for food, who slept on floors of homes denuded of everything that could be bartered or pawned, who had neither fuel to heat their dwellings nor clothing for their children, and who had not the least idea where they could find something to eat next day." Exaggerated? Not one bit. Stark poverty was abroad in the land of prosperity in the closing days of Normalcy.

Although there were at least 10,000,000 unemployed in the country there is no evidence in the record of Herbert Hoover that he yet felt that ultimate responsibility for their relief rested with the federal government. There were, in Congress, some who did. Among them was "a Republican by antecedents with Democratic propensities," as he put it, named Edward P. Costigan, Senator from Colorado; also young Bob La Follette, and able Senator Robert Wagner of New York. Throughout the session they worked for the passage of several relief bills. In the end they were all gathered together by Speaker Garner, who was already bitten with the Presidential bug, into an omnibus Public Works Bill. This provided for a Treasury bond issue of about $1,200,000,000 for public works, as well as for an additional amount for loans through the RFC for "any person," whether state, corporate, or individual.

Ten minutes after this bill reached President Hoover's desk he vetoed it with cold remarks about its being a "pork barrel" measure in the mask of relief. Instead of passing it over his veto, Congress adopted a compromise measure providing $300,000,000 for direct relief through state loans, $322,000,000 for a "discretionary public works program" to be initiated by the Treasury when it saw fit, and $1,500,000 for "self-liquidating public works."

The utter dreariness of this session was relieved by the passage of two liberal and much needed measures. One was Senator Norris's constitutional amendment for the abolition of the lame-duck session of Congress; the other was the now famous Norris-La Guardia Act, outlawing the yellow-dog contract and limiting the use of the injunction in labor disputes. Only an obviously favorable public reaction kept President Hoover from vetoing them both. Nothing further was done for the farmer, although the government issued bulletins suggesting "subsistence" farming — at a time when more than 1,000,000 forced sales of farms in the West and Midwest were taking place.

While farmers could find no markets and workers were starving in the cities the atmosphere was right for the appearance of such demagogues as Huey Long, with his Share the Wealth movement; for Father Charles E. Coughlin, with his anti-Semitism and attacks upon the international bankers; for Howard Scott and his "scientific system of national industrial management" called Technocracy; and for Dr. Townsend with his Old Age Pensions plan. Communism came up openly from underground at the same time that Gerard Swope of General Electric evolved his scheme for national planning against depressions. It was not long before a new Red scare was being manufactured by Representative Hamilton Fish, who, as head of a Congressional investigating committee, was asking that all Communists be jailed or deported.

Although President Hoover had started out to assert his leadership with the Seventy-second Congress and had kept that body posted upon his views by no less than sixty-three messages, he had failed to achieve his aim. Twice he asserted himself as leader — in the matter of taxation and in his rejection of the first relief bill. But even the most partisan observer could not credit him with victory. On the whole his party and his policies had proved desperately inadequate to meet the crisis of his time. The fundamentals of Republicanism had been challenged and found wanting. Herbert Hoover, the instrument of those policies, was no more a failure than that which he represented.

On the home front his vaunted Reconstruction Finance Corporation had failed miserably to restore confidence in the American banking system. Taxes, the bête noir of Republicanism, had risen to new heights. The budget, the cornerstone of Republican government, was unbalanced. The Farm Board had failed to stabilize prices. Party and policy had failed.

On the foreign front the administration's promises to stabilize world currency and extend foreign trade had not been kept.

In the spring of 1932 the United States was farther from "sight of the day when poverty will be banished from this nation" than it had ever been in its entire history. Or so it seemed to the hungry, jobless, homeless, frightened millions, and to millions of others who did not know when they too might face the loss of job or home or farm. They turned their fear and hatred upon one man — Herbert Hoover. And with great impatience they waited for that day in November when, in the exercise of their inalienable franchise, they could forever rid themselves of him and that for which he stood.

CHAPTER THIRTY

A New Day Dawns

ALL through the spring of 1932 Herbert Hoover, a glum and angry man, sat in the White House waiting in vain for the boom that he had said time and again always follows a breakdown. Long ago he had put his faith in the magical myth of cycles and he knew, if nobody else did, that prosperity must be just around the corner. He waited and trusted, alone.

The Republican Party was in a difficult position. On the eve of its quadrennial convention it had nothing to offer the people but Herbert Hoover. For eight years he had sat unchallenged in the cabinets of two Republican Presidents. For nearly four years he had been President and titular leader of the Republican Party. He had expressed and advocated and espoused Republican policies without a single serious deviation from the party line. To repudiate him now, to do anything but renominate him, would be to repudiate everything the party had stood for since the days of William McKinley. And such repudiation would mean the end of the party, for it could hardly withstand the shock of such disloyal action. There was nothing to do but support him to the bitter end. And that the end would be bitter, whatever the party might do, was obvious to all but the least realistic among them.

It was, therefore, a depressed and haunted gathering that met in Chicago on the fourteenth of June, 1932. Dominating the delegates was the Great Engineer, who was completely in control. Here for once he was to meet no opposition. What he said went, from the platform up and down. There were no other candidates, unless Senator Joseph I. France of Maryland, who was unable to command the delegation of his own state, could be called one.

To the platform committee was given the disheartening task of trying to prove that the Hoover Administration had been a howling success and that only by continuing it in office would the country be saved from disaster. As might be expected under the circumstances the document became a distressing example of face-saving. Its attacks upon the Democratic Party were almost hysterical. The entire blame for the depression was laid at the door of the House of Representatives that had been elected in 1930.

"The vagaries of the present Democratic House offer characteristic and appalling proof of the existing incapacity of that party for leadership in a national crisis," the platform read. "Individualism running amok has displaced party discipline and has trampled under foot party leadership. Goaded to desperation by their confessed failure, the party leaders have resorted to 'pork barrel' legislation to obtain a unity of action that could not otherwise be achieved."

A desperate platform committee had somewhere to find a scapegoat and this was the best they could do, forgetting, of course, that the depression had come months before the Democrats won control of the House.

Although the platform praised Hoover as a "leader wise, courageous, patient, understanding, and resourceful," its authors evidently were not callous enough to heap too many encomiums on his already overburdened shoulders. The best it could say, in the final analysis, was that without him the depression would have been far worse. It blamed the "stupidity" of the Democratic Party and events in Central Europe for the depression and pointed with pride to the Reconstruction Finance Corporation and the Federal Farm Board, which together had "saved" the national economy from complete collapse. It urged support of the World Court and, rather belatedly, close co-operation with the League of Nations, but it said nothing about reducing the Smoot-Hawley tariff.

The subject of Prohibition raised some arguments. But, as one member of the administration said later, "We did not go out there to Chicago to write a poem in English prose. We went out there to construct a net in which to catch votes. . . ." And so Senator Hiram Bingham of Connecticut, leader of the Republican Wets, had his say; and so did Herbert Hoover, leader of the Drys. In other words, the platform advocated, not repeal, but resubmission of the Eighteenth Amendment to the voters so that "gains already made" would be held and the states could "deal with the problem as their citizens may determine." It was a pretty straddle.

Herbert Hoover was nominated on the first ballot, receiving all but twenty-eight of the votes cast.

If there was only one man in the Republican Party the situation was far different in the ranks of Democracy. One did not need to be much of a realist to know that the Democratic Party could lose the election in 1932 only by some strange and wholly unlikely bungling. And so there was a long list of hopefuls on hand as the Democrats began to gather for their meeting, which was also held in Chicago. Long before the convention John Nance Garner and Governor Ritchie of Maryland had launched intensive campaigns. Governor William Murray, Oklahoma's own "Alfalfa Bill," hoped that agricultural discontent would swing the vote his way. Al Smith, nursing his growing grudge against Franklin Roosevelt, thought that he could yet turn his 1928 defeat into a 1932 victory. And Newton D. Baker, who had kept alive the torch of Woodrow Wilson's League in every convention since 1920, was available as a dark horse, if unpredictable events should bring about a deadlock.

But far above all the hopefuls loomed another candidate, Governor Roosevelt of New York. For two years Roosevelt had been carefully planning for the time that was now at hand. From the time he had gone to Warm Springs, Georgia, in his brave struggle to recover from infantile paralysis, he had been working to reanimate and reorganize the Democratic Party. At the same time he had been striving to forward his own political progress. His close friend and secretary, Louis McHenry Howe, had had the dream of his becoming President for a long time. James Farley had helped him in the practical planning necessary to corral the delegates he would need if the dream were ever to become reality. His nomination of Al Smith in 1924 and again in 1928 had brought him into the political limelight, and his election twice as governor of New York had made him a national political figure. His magic name was also an asset.

In 1932 Franklin D. Roosevelt had no definite plan for the alleviation of the national distress, or any economic panacea for the depression. But he had that which Herbert Hoover so definitely and woefully lacked — personality. He also had faith in the common man. His liberalism was little, if any, advanced over that which had animated his predecessor in Albany. He believed in States' rights, as behooved any governor. He was opposed to higher income taxes in all brackets. But he took a genuine interest in conservation, he thought public utilities should rigidly be controlled, and he had shown, in his gubernatorial exercises, that he believed the government should be used to help the underprivileged, the economically displaced persons who had nowhere else to turn.

Fundamentally he had little understanding of the underlying reasons for the economic distress of the world. He was well read in history, but as unread as most politicians in economic theory. He believed in reform and he had a deep understanding of the good uses of political power. He understood as well as any living person that politics was the agent of the people, something to be used and not mistrusted. By tradition and circumstances a Jeffersonian Democrat, he also had a Jacksonian viewpoint. Nothing he had done and little he had said placed him far to the Left. He had learned much under Woodrow Wilson — both the Wilson of the New Freedom and the wartime Wilson who had inspired him so greatly in 1920, when he had carried the fight for the League of Nations over thousands of American miles.

Franklin Roosevelt did not approach the Chicago convention as an amateur. He loved the game of politics deeply. He had carefully prepared himself for the fight. He had surrounded himself with able and practical men. He knew, by virtue of his second election as governor by an unprecedented majority, that he had the people with him. He had weathered the embarrassment of the impeachment of Mayor James J. Walker of New York. He was shrewd and at the same time intellectually honest. His smile was not superficial, his handshake not just that of the ordinary politician. Behind it was a teeming mind that had not yet clarified itself on all the issues, but that was driven by an almost humble desire to make himself a place in history on behalf of the people of whose party he dared to make himself the leader.

All was not clear sailing at the convention. James Farley's ill-advised but understandable attempt to challenge the historical two-thirds rule nearly lost him the nomination. Roosevelt had many enemies within the party and Farley's last-minute move almost brought about a disastrous desertion of delegates pledged to him. But Farley turned tail in time. Realizing his error, Farley had to fight doggedly to force the seating of delegations whose right to seats was held by many to be questionable. Among them were Huey Long's adherents, whose presence, when they jumped on the Roosevelt bandwagon, was embarrassing.

While the Roosevelt forces were jockeying, the platform committee was preparing a brief and forthright document, one of the few really great platforms ever presented at a national convention. Boldly it stated: "We favor the repeal of the Eighteenth Amendment." And it also advocated the "immediate modification of the Volstead Act to legalize the sale of beer. . . ." And then, in pithy sentences, it pledged a balanced budget, strict economy, sound currency, a competitive tariff for revenue, reciprocal tariff agreements with other nations, federal aid to the states for unemployment, advance planning of public works, and unemployment and old-age insurance. On agriculture it was less definite and its labor plank was somewhat vague as to how it would afford "better protection." It pledged strict enforcement of the antitrust laws and regulation of public utilities. Not forgetting the debacle of 1929, it pledged regulations for the control of the security exchanges. It favored America's entry into the World Court, although with reservations, and better relations with the Pan-American states, where Republican "imperialism" had long interfered. It promised independence to the Philippines. And it spoke of a foreign policy which would be based on peace and co-operation with other nations.

During the spring Franklin Roosevelt had made a speech that had struck Al Smith as a "demagogic appeal." In it he had asked for "plans like those of 1917 that build from the bottom up and not from the top down, that put their faith once more in the forgotten man at the bottom of the economic pyramid."

If the Democratic platform did not exactly furnish a blueprint to rescue the forgotten man it came much closer to it than did the document written by the Republicans at Mr. Hoover's direction. It was at least a platform on which a liberal could honestly run, even if he crossed his fingers and held some reservations.

Before it came time for the balloting the Roosevelt backers demanded that the votes be taken just as soon as the nominating and seconding speeches had droned their way to a close. Thus the voting began late at night. The weary delegates gave Roosevelt a clear majority on the first three ballots. Convinced that an old-fashioned Democratic deadlock was coming the favorite sons took heart. Al Smith's heart fluttered with expectation. He thought the lightning was about to strike for a second time.

But Roosevelt's managers were shrewd and practical men. Like Roosevelt himself they had been brought up in a hard school of politics and they knew how to make a deal when a deal was needed. One was needed now. And one was made. In return for the votes of the California and Texas delegates, enough to swing the tide to Roosevelt, a promise was made to make John Garner Vice-President. Garner's backers, William G. McAdoo, Samuel Rayburn, and William Randolph Hearst, being without any intimation that Roosevelt would ever become a "traitor to his class," agreed.

When the convention reassembled McAdoo arose and announced that California had come to Chicago to nominate a President, not to deadlock a convention or engage in another devastating contest like that of 1924. It was not without its touch of irony that the man who had gone to Madison Square Garden in 1924 with a majority should be the one now to shout:

"California, forty-four votes for Franklin D. Roosevelt."

That did the trick. It made no difference if Al Smith walked out of the convention with a bitterness in his heart that was to stay there until his dying day. State after state jumped on the bandwagon — except Massachusetts, which was faithful to Smith, and New York, still tight in Tammany's clutch. When Texas cast its forty-six votes for Roosevelt, the time had come for Franklin Roosevelt to board his waiting plane, his acceptance speech safe in his pocket.

The joint product of Roosevelt himself, Louis Howe, Raymond Moley, and others of Roosevelt's first Brain Trust, the speech captured the heart and mind of all America with its now famous words:

I pledge you, I pledge myself, to a new deal for the American people. Let us all here assembled constitute ourselves prophets of a new order of competence and of courage. This is more than a political campaign; it is a call to arms. Give me your help, not to win votes alone, but to win in this crusade to restore America to its own people.

That was it — the words that millions had waited in vain for two sad years to hear from someone with the capacity to speak them. Courage! Competence! A new deal! Restore America to its own people! With those words the Republican Party was defeated and Herbert Hoover retired to private life.

Once again the Socialists nominated Norman Thomas but this

was not a year for anyone but Roosevelt. There was no hint of third party action, even if the nomination of Hoover drove most progressive members and liberals out of the Republican ranks. If they were to remain true to their political philosophy they had to take their stand with Roosevelt, and they did. First to do so was Senator Norris, who was quickly followed by La Follette, Hiram Johnson, and Bronson Cutting of New Mexico. Hoover denounced them as radicals, but they and their followers were unmoved. These men were among the most intellectually honest in political life. They came from agricultural states, where, since the days of Lincoln, they and their people had voted Republican. But the party had let them down. It had deserted them for the mastery of the industrial and financial East; it was not they who had deserted it. In 1932 they did not become Democrats. But they, too, supported a "new deal."

It is painful to recall the bumbling words of Hoover as they came over the radio in the summer and early autumn of 1932. His voice seemed to engender hatred. Beside it the voice of Roosevelt was golden. The campaign was between two men as well as between two parties, but one of them never had a chance. There was something pitiful in Hoover's defense of the Smoot-Hawley tariff, his maunderings about the gold standard; and there was something almost indecent in his effrontery in declaring that the standard of the nation's health had been raised under Republican administrations, even during the depression. There was something sickening about Calvin Coolidge's praise of Hoover for having kept America off the "dole" — when millions were already subsisting on such relief as state or city could afford to give.

Three Republican administrations had proved too many for the people. Years of Prohibition, with its gang terrorism as well as its bad booze, had been too much, and millions flocked to the party that promised repeal. Vague though Roosevelt may have been as to his specific plans for recovery they were better than anything Hoover, or Ogden Mills, could offer. Election day told the story.

Roosevelt received 472 electoral votes to Hoover's 59.

Roosevelt received 22,809,000 popular votes to Hoover's 15,-758,000.

Hoover carried six states: Maine, New Hampshire, Vermont, Connecticut, Delaware, and Pennsylvania.

294

But it was more than an election that took place in November 1932. It was a veritable political revolution. Only eight Republican governors survived. Stalwarts like Smoot of Utah, Hiram Bingham, although a Wet, and George Moses, almost the last of the Old Guard, were snowed under. The House of Representatives went Democratic, almost three to one. The vote of 881,000 for Norman Thomas and 102,000 for William Z. Foster were but added evidence of the revolt against Republicanism. For the first time in seventy years the Democratic Party had become the party of complete power. The Republicans had paid the penalty for having claimed credit for Prosperity and, perhaps even more, for having been in power when the crash came.

Four months were to intervene between the election and the time for Hoover to move out to make room for the man who had won by a 7,000,000 plurality. During those months the nation sank to the lowest state economically and from a point of view of morale that it had known since the gloomiest days of the Civil War. Fully 15,000,000 people were out of work. At least 200 cities stared bankruptcy in the face. Since there was no legal way to reduce fixed charges on bonded indebtedness slashes were made in appropriations for schools, fire and police forces, garbage disposal, streets, the care of public buildings, playgrounds. A chill of despair crept into the very bones of the people as they awaited the promised New Deal. Farms were foreclosed and sheriffs driven away by angry, terrified farmers who refused to leave the land they had tended all their lives. Gangs of wild children roamed the streets. There was no question in many minds that the United States would be soon torn by an aimless revolution if things went on as they were. People were silent, struck dumb with fear. No one who lived through those months will ever forget them. The wind blew cold down every street in the winter of 1932–1933, whipping at the soul of man.

On March 4, 1933, Franklin D. Roosevelt became the thirty-second President of the United States. That day he said:

> This is the time to speak the truth, the whole truth, frankly and boldly. . . . So, first of all, let me assert my firm belief that the only thing we have to fear is fear itself — nameless, unreasoning, unjustified terror which paralyzes needed efforts to convert retreat into advance. In every dark hour of

our national life a leadership of frankness and vigor has met with that understanding and support of the people themselves which is essential to victory. . . .

Plenty is at our doorstep, but a generous use of it languishes in the very sight of the supply. Primarily this is because the rulers of the exchange of mankind's goods have failed through their own stubbornness and their own incompetence, have admitted their failure, and have abdicated. Practices of the unscrupulous money changers stand indicted in the court of public opinion, rejected by the hearts and minds of men. . . .

The money changers have fled from their high seats in the temple of our civilization. We may now restore the temple to ancient truths. . . .

I am prepared under my constitutional duty to recommend the measures that a stricken Nation in the midst of a stricken world may require. These measures, or such other measures as the Congress may build out of its experience and wisdom, I shall seek, within my constitutional authority, to bring to speedy adoption. But in the event that Congress shall fail . . . and in the event that the national emergency is still critical . . . I shall ask the Congress for the one remaining instrument to meet the crisis — broad Executive power to wage a war against the emergency, as great as the power that would be given me if we were in fact invaded by a foreign foe.

For the trust imposed in me I will return the courage and the devotion that befit the time. . . .

Franklin Delano Roosevelt thus read the obituary of Normalcy. The body buried, he and the people who had turned to him for salvation moved belatedly to the task of ministering to themselves and to their fellow men.

Acknowledgments

I am indebted to Charles Scribner's Sons for permission to quote from *Our Times*, by Mark Sullivan, and from *American Chronicle*, by Ray Stannard Baker; to Henry Holt & Company for permission to quote from *The Selected Letters of William Allen White*; to The Macmillan Company for permission to quote from *The Autobiography of William Allen White* and from *Fighting Liberal*, by George Norris; to Simon & Schuster for permission to quote from *Journey Through My Years*, by James M. Cox; to Alfred A. Knopf for permission to quote from *President and Congress*, by Wilfred E. Binkley, and from *Freedom and Responsibility in the American Way of Life* by Carl Becker; to Harper and Brothers for permission to quote from *Only Yesterday*, by Frederick Lewis Allen; to Houghton Mifflin Company for permission to quote from *The Incredible Era* by Samuel Hopkins Adams, and from *The Wallaces of Iowa*; and to Mrs. Grace G. Coolidge for permission to quote from *The Autobiography of Calvin Coolidge*.

As usual I owe a great debt to many writers who have preceded me in this field, but especially to Mr. Sullivan, Mr. Allen, Mr. Kenneth Campbell MacKay, author of *The Progressive Movement of 1924* (Columbia University Press, 1947), and Mr. Claude M. Fuess, author of *Calvin Coolidge, the Man from Vermont*. I should also like to thank the ever-patient Stanley Salmen, Miss Yole de Blasio and Miss Constance Rose, who helped me with the research, and of course my wife, Ruth Mansfield Schriftgiesser, for her indulgence. Finally I would like to pay tribute to the American Newspaper Guild, whose great efforts since 1933 have made it possible for the working journalist to find some of that leisure which makes for the good life.

Bibliography

Adamic, Louis, *Dinner at the White House*. New York, 1944.

Adams, Samuel Hopkins, *The Incredible Era*. Boston, 1939.

Agar, Herbert, *The Pursuit of Happiness*. Boston, 1938.

Alderfer, H. F., *The Personality and Politics of Warren G. Harding*. Manuscript filed at the New York Public Library.

Allen, Frederick Lewis, *I Remember Distinctly*. New York, 1947.

—— *Lords of Creation*. New York, 1935.

—— *Only Yesterday*. New York, 1931.

Allen, Robert S., *Why Hoover Faces Defeat*. New York, 1932.

Allen, Robert S., and Pearson, Drew, *More Merry-Go-Round*. New York, 1932.

—— *Washington Merry-Go-Round*. New York, 1931.

American Labor Year Book. New York, 1919–1933.

American Year Book. New York, 1919–1933.

Andrews, Wayne, *The Vanderbilt Legend*. New York, 1941.

Annals of the American Academy of Political and Social Sciences.

Bailey, Thomas A., *Woodrow Wilson and the Great Betrayal*. New York, 1945.

Baker, Ray Stannard, *An American Chronicle*. New York, 1945.

Barnes, Julius, et al., "Herbert Hoover's Priceless Work in Washington." *Industrial Management*, Vol. 71, 1926.

Bartlett, Ruhl J., *The League to Enforce Peace*. Chapel Hill, 1944.

—— *The Record of American Diplomacy*. New York, 1947.

Bates, Ernest Sutherland, *The Story of Congress*. New York, 1936.

Beard, Charles A., *American Foreign Policy in the Making*. New Haven, 1946.

Beard, Charles A., and Beard, Mary, *America in Mid-Passage*. New York, 1939.

—— *The Rise of American Civilization*. New York, 1927.

Becker, Carl L., *The United States, An Experiment in Democracy*. New York, 1920.

Bell, H. C. F., *Woodrow Wilson and the People*. Garden City, 1945.

Bemis, Samuel Flagg, *A Diplomatic History of the United States*. New York, 1942.

Bendiner, Robert, "Burton K. Wheeler." *Nation*, April 20, 1940.

Bent, Silas, *Strange Bedfellows*. New York, 1928.

Berle, Jr., A. A., and Means, G. C., *The Modern Corporation and Private Property*. New York, 1933.

Berman, Edward, *Labor Disputes and the President of the U. S.* New York, 1924.

Binkley, Wilfred E., *American Political Parties*. New York, 1943.

—— *President and Congress*. New York, 1947.

Black, John D., *Agricultural Reform in the U. S.* New York, 1929.

Blythe, Samuel G., *A Calm View of a Calm Man*. New York, 1923.

Bowers, Claude G., *Beveridge and the Progressive Era*. Boston, 1932.

Bradford, Gamaliel, "The Genius of the Average: Calvin Coolidge." *Atlantic Monthly*, Vol. CXLV.

—— *The Quick and the Dead*. Boston, 1931.

Brown, George Rothwell, *The Leadership of Congress*. Indianapolis, 1922.

Bryn-Jones, David, *Frank B. Kellogg*. New York, 1937.

Buell, R. L., *The Washington Conference*. New York, 1922.

Butler, Nicholas Murray, *Across the Busy Years*. New York, 1939.

Capper, Arthur, *The Agricultural Bloc*. New York, 1922.

Carver, Thomas N., *The Present Economic Revolution in the U. S.* Boston, 1925.

Chase, Stuart, *A New Deal*. New York, 1932.

—— *Men and Machines*. New York, 1929.

—— *Prosperity: Fact and Myth*. New York, 1929.

Cochran, Thomas C., and Miller, William, *The Age of Enterprise*. New York, 1942.

Colcord, Samuel, *The Great Deception*. New York, 1924.

Coleman, McAlister, *Eugene V. Debs, A Man Unafraid*. New York, 1930.

Committee on Recent Economic Changes, *Recent Economic Changes in the U. S.* 2 vols., New York, 1929.

Congressional Record, 66th to 72nd Congress. Washington, 1919–1933.

Cook, Sherwin Lawrence, *Torchlight Parade*. New York, 1931.

Coolidge, John Calvin, *The Autobiography of Calvin Coolidge*. New York, 1931.

—— *Foundations of the Republic*. New York, 1926.

—— *Have Faith in Massachusetts*. Boston, 1919.

—— *The Price of Freedom*. New York, 1924.

Corey, Herbert, *The Truth About Hoover*. Boston, 1932.

Corey, Lewis, *The Decline of American Capitalism*. New York, 1934.

Corwin, E. S., *The President: Office and Powers*. New York, 1941.

Cox, James Middleton, *Journey Through My Years*. New York, 1946.

Cranston, Alan, *The Killing of the Peace*. New York, 1945.

Cranston, Ruth, *The Story of Woodrow Wilson*. New York, 1945.

Crowther, Samuel, *The Presidency versus Hoover*. Garden City, 1928.

Daniels, Josephus, *The Wilson Era, 1917–1923*. Chapel Hill, 1946.

Daugherty, Harry M., and Dixon, Thomas, *The Inside Story of the Harding Tragedy*. New York, 1932.

Davenport, Frederick, "Conservative America in Convention Assembled." *Outlook*, June 23, 1920.

Davis, John W., *Party Government in the United States*, Princeton, 1928.

Dawes, Charles G., *Journal as Ambassador to Great Britain*. New York, 1939.

—— *Notes as Vice President*. Boston, 1935.

Democratic National Convention, Proceedings. 1920, 1924, 1928, 1932.

Dexter, W. F., *Herbert Hoover and American Individualism*. New York, 1932.

Dictionary of American Biography, ed. Allen Johnson and Dumas Malone. 20 vols. and supplement, New York, 1928–1945.

Dulles, Foster Rhea, *The Road to Teheran*. Princeton, 1945.

Dumond, Dwight Lowell, *America in Our Time, 1896–1946*. New York, 1947.

Encyclopaedia of the Social Sciences. 15 vols., New York, 1930–1935.

Fine, Nathan, *Labor and Farmer Parties in the U. S.* New York, 1928.

Fleming, Denna F., *The Treaty Veto of the American Senate*. New York, 1930.

—— *The U. S. and the League of Nations*. New York, 1932.

—— *The U. S. and the World Court*. New York, 1945.

—— *The U. S. and World Organization*. New York, 1938.

Flynn, John T., *Security Speculation*. New York, 1934.

Fuess, Claude M., *Calvin Coolidge, the Man from Vermont*. Boston, 1940.

Gann, Dolly Curtis, *Dolly Gann's Book*. Garden City, 1933.

Gary, Elbert, *Twelve Hour Day*. New York, 1923.

Gilbert, Clinton W., *Behind the Mirrors*. New York, 1922.

—— *Mirrors of Washington*. New York, 1921.

—— *You Take Your Choice*. New York, 1924.

Gompers, Samuel, *Seventy Years of Life and Labor*. New York, 1925.

Gruening, Ernest, *The Public Pays*. New York, 1931.

—— *The United States*. New York, 1923.

Hacker, Louis M., *American Problems of Today*. New York, 1938.

—— *The Shaping of the American Tradition*. 2 vols. New York, 1947.

Hamill, John, *The Strange Career of Mr. Hoover Under Two Flags*. New York, 1931.

Hampton, V. B., *Breasting World Frontiers: Herbert Hoover's Achievements*. New York, 1933.

Hapgood, Norman, *Professional Patriots*. New York, 1927.

Hard, William, *Who's Hoover*. New York, 1928.

Harvey, George, "The Paramount Issue — Coolidge or Chaos." *North American Review*, September 1924.

Heaton, John L., *Tough Luck — Hoover Again*. New York, 1932.

Hicks, John D., *The Populist Revolt*. Minneapolis, 1933.

Holcomb, Arthur M., *The Political Parties of Today*. New York, 1924.

Hoover, Herbert Clark, *Addresses Upon the American Road*. New York, 1938.

—— *America's First Crusade*. New York, 1942.

—— *American Individualism*. New York, 1923.

—— *The Challenge to Liberty*. New York, 1934.

—— *The New Day*, Stanford University, 1929.

—— *The State Papers and Other Writings of Herbert Hoover*, William Starr Myers, ed. New York, 1934.

Hoover, Irwin H. (Ike), *Forty-two Years in the White House*. Boston, 1934.

Howland, Charles P., ed., *Survey of American Foreign Relations 1928*. New Haven, 1928.

Ickes, Harold L., *Autobiography of a Curmudgeon*. New York, 1943.

Irwin, William H., *How Red Is America?* New York, 1927.

—— *Herbert Hoover, a Reminiscent Biography*. New York, 1928.

Jaffray, Elizabeth, *Secrets of the White House*. New York, 1927.

Johnson, Claudius O., *Borah of Idaho*. New York, 1936.

Johnson, Walter, *Selected Letters of William Allen White*. New York, 1947.

—— *William Allen White's America*. New York, 1947.

Johnson, Willis F., *George Harvey*. Boston, 1929.

Joslin, Theodore, *Hoover off the Record*. Garden City, 1934.

Kellogg, V. L., *Herbert Hoover, the Man and His Work*. New York, 1920.

Kent, Frank R., *The Democratic Party*. New York, 1922.

—— *The Great Game of Politics*. New York, 1928.

Kleinholz, George, *The Battle of Washington: A National Disgrace*. New York, 1932.

Knox, John, *The Great Mistake*. Washington, 1930.

Kohlsaat, H. H., *From McKinley to Harding*. New York, 1923.

Kuznets, Simon, *National Product In Wartime*. New York, 1945.

Laidler, H. W., *Concentration of Control in American Industry*. New York, 1931.

Lane, Rose Wilder, *The Making of Herbert Hoover*. New York, 1920.

Lasser, David, *Private Monopoly, the Enemy at Home*. New York, 1945.

Lief, Alfred, *Democracy's Norris*. New York, 1939.

Liggett, W. W., *The Rise of Herbert Hoover*. New York, 1932.
—— "Why Herbert Hoover Hates the Soviet Union." *Modern Quarterly*, Vol. 6, No. 3, New York, 1932.
Lindley, Ernest K., *The Roosevelt Revolution, First Phase*. New York, 1933.
Lippman, Walter, *Interpretations*. New York, 1932.
—— *Men of Destiny*. New York, 1938.
—— *Public Opinion*, Pelican ed. New York, 1946.
Lord, Russell, *The Wallaces of Iowa*. Boston, 1947.
Lorwin, Lewis, *The American Federation of Labor*. Washington, 1933.
Lovestone, Jay, "President Hoover of the U. S. A." *Labour Monthly*, London, January 1929.
Lowery, Edward G., "La Follette's Own Platform." *World's Work*, September, 1924.
—— *Washington Closeups*. New York, 1921.
Lynd, R. S. and H. M., *Middletown*. New York, 1929.

McAdoo, William Gibbs, *Crowded Years*. Boston, 1931.
McBride, Mary Margaret, *The Story of Dwight W. Morrow*. New York, 1930.
McCormick, George Elliott, "The Books Senator Harding Loves to Read." *Bookman*, Vol. 52, pp. 131–133.
MacKay, Kenneth Campbell, *The Progressive Movement of 1924*. New York, 1947.
McMahon, Arthur W., "American Government in Politics." *American Political Science Review*, Vol. XXII.
Malin, James C., *The U. S. After the World War*. Boston, 1930.
Means, Gaston B., and Thacker, Mary Dixon, *The Strange Death of President Harding*. New York, 1930.
Mecklin, J. M., *The Ku Klux Klan, a Study of the American Mind*. New York, 1924.
Merz, Charles, *The Dry Decade*. New York, 1931.
—— *The Great American Bandwagon*. New York, 1929.
Mills, Frederick C., *Prices in Recession and Recovery*. New York, 1936.
Milton, George Fort, *The Use of Presidential Power, 1879–1943*. Boston, 1944.
Minton, Bruce, and Stuart, John, *The Fat Years and the Lean*. New York, 1940.
Moley, Raymond, *After Seven Years*. New York, 1939.
Moulton, H. G., and Pasvolsky, Leon, *War Debts and World Prosperity*. New York, 1932.
Myers, William Starr, *The Foreign Policies of Herbert Hoover*, New York, 1940.
—— *The Republican Party, a History*. New York, 1928.
Myers, William Starr, and Newton, Walter H., *The Hoover Administration: A Documented Record*. New York, 1936.

National Industrial Conference Boards, *Cost of Government in the United States*. New York, 1931.

—— *Agricultural Problems in the United States*. New York, 1931.

Nevins, Allan, "President Hoover's Record." *Current History*, Vol. XXXVI, 1928.

New International Year Book. New York, 1920–1932.

Nicholson, Harold, *Dwight Morrow*. New York, 1935.

Norris, George, *Fighting Liberal*. New York, 1945.

O'Connor, Harvey, *Mellon's Millions*. New York, 1933.

Odegard, Peter, *Pressure Politics, the Story of the Anti-Saloon League*. New York, 1928.

Overacker, Louise, *Money and Elections*. New York, 1932.

Patterson, C. Perry, *Presidential Government in the U. S.* Chapel Hill, 1947.

Peel, R. V., and Donnelly, T. C., *The 1928 Campaign*. New York, 1931.

Pepper, George Wharton, *Men and Issues*. New York, 1924.

—— *Philadelphia Lawyer*. Philadelphia, 1944.

Pollard, James E., *The President and the Press*. New York, 1947.

President's Research Committee, *Some Recent Social Trends in the U. S.* New York, 1933.

Pringle, Henry F., *Alfred E. Smith, a Critical Biography*. New York, 1927.

—— *Big Frogs*. New York, 1928.

—— *The Life and Times of William H. Taft*. New York, 1939.

Ravage, M. E., *The Story of Teapot Dome*. New York, 1924.

Republican National Convention, Proceedings. 1920, 1924, 1928, 1932.

Ripley, W. Z., *Wall Street and Main Street*. New York, 1927.

Rippy, J. Fred, *Latin America in World Politics*. New York, 1928.

Robinson, Edgar E., *The Presidential Vote*. Stanford University, 1934.

—— *They Voted for Roosevelt*. Stanford University, 1947.

Rogers, Cameron, *The Legend of Calvin Coolidge*. Garden City, 1928.

Rogers, Lindsay, "American Government and Politics." *American Political Science Review*, Vols. XVI, XVII.

—— "The President and the People." *N. Y. Times Magazine*, April 9, 1933.

—— "Presidential Dictatorship." *Quarterly Review*, Vol. CCXXXI.

Sait, Edward M., *American Parties and Elections*. New York, 1927.

Schortemeier, Frederick E., ed., *Our Common Country*. Indianapolis, 1921.

—— *Rededicating America*. Indianapolis, 1920.

Schriftgiesser, Karl, *The Amazing Roosevelt Family 1613–1942*. New York, 1942.

—— *Heirs of the New Deal*. New York, 1938.

Schriftgiesser, Karl, *The Gentleman from Massachusetts, Henry Cabot Lodge*. Boston, 1944.
Schuman, Frederick L., American Policy Toward Russia Since 1917. New York, 1928.
Seldes, Gilbert, *The Years of the Locust*. Boston, 1933.
Seligman, E. R. A., *The Allied Debts*. New York, 1922.
—— *The Economics of Farm Relief*. New York, 1929.
Siegfried, André, *America Comes of Age*. New York, 1927.
Siepmann, Charles A., *Radio's Second Chance*. Boston, 1946.
Slemp, C. Bascom, *The Mind of the President*. New York, 1926.
Slosson, P. W., *The Great Crusade and After*. New York, 1931.
Smith, E. C., and Zurcher, A. J., *A Dictionary of American Politics*. New York, 1944.
Smith, R., and Beasley, N., *Carter Glass, a Biography*. New York, 1939.
Stein, Charles W., *The Third Term Tradition*. New York, 1943.
Stimson, Henry L., *American Policy in Nicaragua*. New York, 1927.
Stoddard, Henry L., *As I Knew Them*. New York, 1927.
—— *It Costs to Be President*. New York, 1938.
Stone, Irving, *They Also Ran*. Garden City, 1944.
Sullivan, Mark, "Coolidge Versus the Senate." *World's Work*, December, 1925.
—— *The Great Adventure at Washington*. New York, 1922.
—— *Our Times. The Twenties*, Vol. VI. New York, 1935.

Thompson, Charles W., *Presidents I've Known*. Indianapolis, 1929.
Train, Arthur C., *The Strange Attacks on Herbert Hoover*. New York, 1932.
Tucker, Ray, *Sons of the Wild Jackass*. Boston, 1932.
Tugwell, Rexford G., *Industrial Discipline and Government Acts*. New York, 1933.
—— *Industry's Coming of Age*. New York, 1927.
—— *Mr. Hoover's Economic Policy*. New York, 1932.

Villard, Oswald G., *Fighting Years*. New York, 1939.
—— *Prophets, True and False*. New York, 1928.

Waters, W. W., BEF, *The Whole Story of the Bonus Army*. New York, 1933.
Watson, James E., *As I Knew Them*. Indianapolis, 1936.
Werner, Morris R., *Privileged Characters*. New York, 1935.
White, William Allen, *The Autobiography of William Allen White*. New York, 1946.
—— *A Puritan in Babylon*. New York, 1938.
—— *Calvin Coolidge*. New York, 1935.
—— *Masks in a Pageant*. New York, 1928.
—— *Politics, the Citizens Business*. New York, 1924.
Whiting, E. E., *Calvin Coolidge*. Boston, 1924.

Wilbur, R. L., and Hyde, A. M., *The Hoover Policies*. New York, 1937.

Winkler, John K., *W. R. Hearst, an American Phenomenon*. New York, 1928.

Wish, Harvey, *Contemporary America, The National Scene Since 1900*. New York, 1945.

Yearbook of Agriculture. Washington, 1920–1933.

Index

Beard, Charles and Mary, 102 *n.*, 108, 124

Becker, Carl, quoted, 19 and *n.*

Béla Kun government in Hungary, Hoover and, 265

Belgium, Hoover and relief of, 84; represented at Washington Conference, 134–137

Berger, Victor, Socialist leader, denounces Russian Revolution, 60; recaptures seat in House, 128

Beveridge, Albert J., U.S. Senator, 30, 67, 74, 140

Big Business, at Republican National Convention for 1920, 4–5; American Plan, 9, 115; and Harding, 21, 33–34, 37–38, 81–82, 124; and Daugherty, 28; at Democratic National Convention for 1920, 45–46; labor and Harding, 119; public and, in 1922, 128–129; and Coolidge succession to office, 165; and McNary-Haugenism, 225; policy of, and crash of 1929, 273–274

"Billion Dollar Congress," 54

Bingham, Hiram, 289, 295

Black Hills, Coolidge vacation in, 243–244

Black Starr and Frost, advertisement of, 239

Blaine, James G., 7, 23, 26, 62

"Block plan" (relief), Hoover and, 285

Blythe, Samuel G., journalist, and Harding, 21; on La Follette, 208

Bolivia, U.S. and, 236–237

Bonus, soldiers', 9, 109–110, 128, 173, 193, 221

Bootleggers' Lobby, 223

Borah, William D., U.S. Senator, 74, 160, 221; and Senate investigation of plot to "buy" the Presidency, 5–6; and Republican platform of 1920, 8; stumps for Harding, 75; on naval armament reduction, 95; and Farm Bloc, 100–101; isolationism of, 132–133; naval arms reduction program, 134; to Coolidge on Daugherty, 166; refuses Vice-Presidential nomination under Coolidge, 176; on 1924 Republican campaign expenses, 210 *n.*–211 *n.*; and World Court issue, 232–233;

and Kellogg-Briand Pact, 237; on third term for Coolidge, 242; aspirant for 1928 nomination, 245; and Hoover, 260; on Smoot-Hawley tariff, 268, 269; on reducing Congressional salaries, 285

Boston Evening Transcript, and League of Nations, 132; on Davis, 187

Boston Police Strike, 5, 156–158

Boston Post, 164 and *n.*, 208

Boulder Dam, 261–262

Bourgeois, Léon, 78

Bowers, Claude G., 254

Boxer Rebellion, 133

Brandegee, Frank, U.S. Senator, 81; at Republican National Convention for 1920, 7, 9, 14–15; sketch of, 14; on Harding, 21; at Republican National Convention for 1924, 174

Brandeis, Louis Dembitz, Associate Justice, 125, 195, 218, 226 *n.*, 253

Brennan, of Chicago, at Democratic National Convention for 1920, 42

Briand, Aristide, 237

Brice, Calvin S., U.S. Senator, 54

Brigham Young University, 68

Brisbane, Arthur, on third term for Coolidge, 241

Britton, Nan, Harding's mistress, 15, 16 *n.*, 141

Brokers' loans, Coolidge on, 239–240

Brookhart, Smith W., U.S. Senator, 128, 172, 221

Broun, Heywood, on Coolidge, 159

Brown, Walter F., Postmaster General, 266

Bryan, Charles W., Governor of Nebraska, 182

Bryan, William Jennings, 42, 188

Budget and Accountancy Act, 97–98

Bull Moose party, 59, 63

Bureau of the Budget, 97–98, 159, 221

Bureau of War Risk Insurance, 110

Burleson, Postmaster General, 40, 45

Burton, Theodore E., U.S. Senator, 31, 175

Butler, Nicholas Murray, President of Columbia University, at Republican National Convention of 1920, 3, 12, 15; on League of Nations, 10; on Harding, 96, 140; on third term for Coolidge, 242; aspirant for 1928 nomination, 245

Butler, Associate Justice Pierce, 124, 125, 127; sketch of, 126

Butler, William M., U.S. Senator, Republican National Convention (1924) chairman, 174 and *n*.; as Coolidge's agent in Senate, 220 and *n*.; defeated, 220 *n*., 232; and Coolidge third term issue, 247; and Hoover, 248

Byllesby, H. M., 4

CALDER, WILLIAM, U.S. Senator, at Republican National Convention of 1920, 7, 14–15

California delegation to Democratic National Convention of 1932, 293

Calles, President of Mexico, 235

Calvin Coolidge, the Man from Vermont, by Claude M. Fuess, 154 *n*.

Cannon, Joe, on Cox, 49

Capper, Arthur, 100

Carberry, Clifton B., 164 *n*.

Cardozo, Justice, on A.A.A., 226 *n*.

Carlisle, John G., 54

Carnegie, Andrew, 186

Cartels, international, 93

Case, Belle, La Follette's wife, 199

Catholic Church, Smith and, 180, 251–253, 252 *n*.; Mexico issue and, 235; and 1928 campaign, 257–258

Chadbourne, Thomas L., 211 *n*.

Chapple, Joe Mitchell, 21

Chiang Kai-shek, 270

Chicago, St. Paul, Minneapolis and Omaha Railroad, 126

Chicago Tribune, backs Hoover, 245

Chicherin, Foreign Commissar, 170

Child, Richard Washburn, an editor of *Collier's Weekly,* and Harding, 21, 68; sketch of, 68; Ambassador to Italy, 88; and Mussolini's rise to power, 208 *n*.

Child Health Association, Hoover and, 265

Child Labor amendment, 125

Chile, U.S. and, 236–237

China, German provinces in, 133–134; represented at Washington

Conference, 136–137; agreement with Japan, 136–137. *See also* Chinese Nationalist Government

Chinese Eastern Railway, 270

Chinese empire, 133–134

Chinese Nationalist Government, and Russia, 270

Christensen, Parley P., 65–66

Church League for Industrial Democracy, 191

Cincinnati Enquirer, 53

Clark, Speaker Champ, 49

Clarke, Justice, 125

Clayton Antitrust Act, 58, 125, 185–186

Clean Books bill (of Catholic Church), 180

Cleveland, Grover, 23, 54, 62

Cleveland Plain Dealer, 32

Cobb, Frank, 39

Cochran, Thomas, 166–167

Colby, Bainbridge, Secretary of State, 45; Wilson's agent at Democratic National Convention of 1920, 41–42; message to Wilson on third term, 43–44; defeated for permanent chairman, 44

Collins, Floyd, 225

Colombia, U.S. and, 236–237

Comintern, rejects American Socialists, 61

Commerce, Department of, on sugar and tariff, 93

Committee of Forty-eight, 63–64, 191

Communist Labor Party, 61

Communist Party, 62, 191, 193–194, 231, 278; in 1920, 59; Communist Labor Party merges with, 61; La Follette and, 194; 1928 election and, 256; on government and relief, 285; comes out from underground, 286

Conference for Progressive Political Action (C.P.P.A.), 129, 189–197; Committee of Fifteen, 191; Committee on Declaration of Purposes, of, 192; platform (1922), 192–193; and La Follette, 195; National Committee of, and Vice-Presidential nomination, 195–196; platform (1924), 196–197, 206–207; practically defunct, 231

field Press-Republic, 56; reading, 56; elected to Ohio Congress, 56; elected Governor of Ohio, 57–58; Ohio's new constitution and, 57; twice re-elected Governor, 58; Wilson and, 58; on League issue, 67, 70–73, 75, 78; and Roosevelt visit Wilson, 70–71; campaign, 70–73; on Republican campaign fund, 71; notification speech at Dayton, 71–72; campaign of, discussed, 79; vote for, 79

Hearst press, Yellow Peril, 134 *n.*; pre-election poll (1924), 210
Heflin, 126
Herrick, Myron T., 16, 27
Hilles, Charles D., 246, 248
Hillquit, Morris, 60
Hitler, 259
Hoar, 54
Hogan, Timothy, 32, 57–58
Holland, represented at Washington Conference, 134–137
Holmes, Oliver Wendell, Jr., Associate Justice, 125, 218
Hoover, Herbert Clark, 85, 94, 143, 217, 232, 272; at Republican National Convention of 1920, 5, 6, 12; on League, 77; and Big Business, 82; appointed Secretary of Commerce, 84; Wallace and, 86; Harding and, 89; unable to lead, 89; on sugar and tariff, 93; and Advisory Tariff Commission, 94; and Norris farmer-European relief plan, 103–105; conference on labor and unemployment, 116; plan for labor, 116; and labor, 117–118, 117 *n.*–118 *n.*; Russia and Washington Conference issue, 134–135; Radio Conference, 139 *n.*; on use of radio, 139 *n.*; and unemployment, 140–141; on Coolidge succession to office, 165; on Russia, 170 and *n.*; and McNary-Haugenism, 226; and Muscle Shoals issue, 230; on World Court, 233; campaign for 1928 nomination, 245–246, 246–247; nominated, 249; 1928 campaign, 256–261; wins 1928 election, 260–261; trip to South America, 262; *Magazine of Wall Street* on, 262; on poverty, 263; inauguration speech, 263–264; sketch of, 264–266; political philosophy, 264; youth, 265; political record, 265–266; cabinet, 266; and 71st Congress, 266–269; and Smoot-Hawley tariff, 268–269, 276 and *n.*; foreign policy, 270–271; on 1929 panic, 274–275; recovery plans, 275–278; on federal aid for unemployed, 277–278; and veterans' march on Washington, 278; and Supreme Court, 278; and La

Follette, Jr., 279–280; changes ideas on depression, 281; unpopular with press, 281–282; and 72nd Congress, 282–287; summary of, as President, 286–287; waits for boom, 288; and 1932 Republican National Convention, 288–289; 1932 campaign, 294; and remainder of term after 1932 election, 295
Hoover, Mrs. Herbert Clark, 282
Hornblower and Weeks, 87
Howe, Louis McHenry, 290, 293
Hughes, Charles Evans, Chief Justice, 34, 94, 217; at Republican National Convention, 1920, 5; sketch of, 83; becomes Secretary of State, 83–84; Harding and, 89; returns to Supreme Court, 125; as Secretary of State, 131–138; at Washington Conference, 135–137; answer to Russia's overtures, 170; Coolidge and, 232; becomes Chief Justice, 278
Hull, Cordell, U.S. Representative, 45, 254 *n.*
Hungary, Béla Kun government, 265
Hurley-Mason Construction Company, 111
Hyde, Arthur M., Secretary of Agriculture, 266

IMMIGRATION, restrictive, Coolidge on, 216
Immigration Act (restrictive), 94–95
Imperial Purple, by Edgar Saltus, 25
Income tax, Mellon and, 107–109, 222–223
Incredible Era, by Samuel Hopkins Adams, 16 *n.*
Independent (Marion, Ohio), 23
Independent voter, at time of 1920 election, 59
Internationalism, 8
Interstate Commerce Commission, and Norris Export Bill, 103
Irish Americans, and Irish Free State question, 78–79; and Supreme Court issue, 207
Irish Free State, 79
Isolationism, 132–133
Italian Americans, and Fiume, 79

Italy, represented at Washington Conference, 134–137; Mussolini and, 208 *n.*, 259

JACKSON, ANDREW, 52, 153, 177
James, Arthur Curtiss, 211 *n.*
Japan, and U.S., 133, 134 and *n.*; and China, 133–134; represented at Washington Conference, 134–137; agreement with China, 136–137; invasion of Manchuria, 270
Japanese exclusion, 221
Jardine, William M., Secretary of Agriculture, 217
Jefferson, Thomas, 52, 153, 254
Johnson, Hiram, U.S. Senator, 74, 176; at Republican National Convention of 1920, 5, 6, 11; stumps for Harding, 75; amendment to Immigration Act, 95; bolts Republicans in 1932, 294
Johnson, General Hugh, 223–224
Johnson, Willis Fletcher, 21
Johnston, William H., President International Association of Machinists, 191, 194
Jones, Jesse, 211 *n.*
Jones Act of 1916, 236
Journey Through My Years, by J. M. Cox, 48–49, 70

KDKA radio station, 139 *n.*
Kellogg, Frank B., Ambassador to Great Britain, 105, 167; attitude on Russia, 170 *n.*; becomes Secretary of State, 217; Coolidge and, 232; and Mexico, 235
Kellogg-Briand pact, 237, 261, 270
Kent, Frank, 252
King, John T., 151
Kling, Amos, Harding's father-in-law, 25, 25 *n.*
Kling, Florence, 25 and *n. See also* Harding, Mrs. Warren G.
Knights of the Great Forest. *See* Ku Klux Klan
Knox, Philander, U.S. Senator, 7, 85, 101
Ku Klux Klan, 32, 65, 176, 182, 251, 253, 254, 255; Daugherty and, 29; help defeat Cox, 57–58, 79; and Immigration Act, 94; and Democratic National Convention of

1924, 176–177; and Al Smith, 181; and C.P.P.A. platform, 197; 1924 campaign and, 205; and Supreme Court issue, 207

LABOR, and Republican platform of 1920, 9; Harding and, 33–34, 114–117, 117 *n.*–118 *n.*, 119–123, 129; and Democratic platform of 1920, 45–46; and Immigration Act, 94; in 1921–1922, 115 *n.*–116 *n.*; Coolidge 1924 campaign speech and, 205; and 1928 campaign, 259–260. *See also* American Federation of Labor; Railroad Brotherhoods; Strikes
Labor, supports C.P.P.A., 192; supports La Follette, 210
Labour Party (England), 193
Ladd, U.S. Senator, 172–173
Lafayette, Coolidge speech at dedication of a monument to, 205 and *n.*
La Follette, John, 199
La Follette, Robert M., U.S. Senator, 11, 17, 57, 176, 188; and Farmer-Labor Party, 64–65; and Farm Bloc, 100–101; and Mellon tax proposals, 108; and Butler, 126; re-elected Senator, 128; and 1922 election, 129–130; opposes Coolidge program, 172–173; and Conference for Progressive Political Action, 190, 195; on Communists, 194; and Railroad Brotherhood, 195; on Ku Klux Klan, 197; sketch of, 198–201; ancestry, 199; youth, 199; as Governor of Wisconsin, 199–200; in Senate, 200–201; and 1924 Presidential campaign, 205–208, 210, 213–214; death, 221, 231
La Follette, Robert M., Jr., U.S. Senator, 221–222; on third term, 242; and Hoover, 279–280; and government relief, 285–286; bolts Republicans in 1932, 294
La Follette-Costigan relief measure, Hoover and, 277
La Follette-Wheeler campaign strategy, 197; 1924 campaign expenditures, 204 *n.*
La Guardia, Fiorello, U.S. Representative, opposes national sales

316

Sons of the Wild Jackass, 98, 108, 166, 282

Sorg, Paul John, Cox and, 53–54; backs Cox newspaper venture, 54–55

South Dakota delegation to Republican National Convention of 1924, 176

Spanish-American War, 26

Spencer, Herbert, 115

Sproul, William, Governor of Pennsylvania, 12

Stalwarts, 199

Standard Oil Company, 32, 167, 235

Star of Marion, Ohio, bought by Harding, 23–25; editorial policy, 26, 29; employees of, and Harding, 114

States' rights, Coolidge on, 222; Governor Ritchie and, 253–254

Stearns, Frank W., of R. H. Stearns and Company, sketch of, 161–163; on Morrow and Cochran to Coolidge, 167; at Republican National Convention of 1924, 174

Stedman, Seymour, Socialist, 62 *n.*

Stimson, Henry L., Secretary of State, 30; attitude on Russia, 170 *n.*; and Philippines, 236; becomes Secretary of State, 266; foreign policy, 270–271

Stinson, Roxy, wife of Jesse Smith, 15 *n.*

Stock Market, crash of 1929, 272–274

Stone, Justice Harlan Fiske, advises Coolidge on Teapot Dome scandal, 149; becomes Attorney General under Coolidge, 151; on Article XII of Constitution, 209; appointed to Supreme Court, 218; on A.A.A., 226 *n.*

Stone, Irving, 48, 79, 212

Storrow, James J., and Boston Police Strike, 156–158

Strikes, 1921–1922, 115 *n.*–116 *n.*; of railroad shopmen, 117–119; 1922 coal strike, 119–121; anthracite coal miners of Pennsylvania, 167

Sullivan, Mark, *Our Times*, 16 *n.*; on Harding, 21; on Wilson, 36; on Harding's acceptance speech, 69; on Crissinger, 97–98; on Harding

and coal strike, 121; on Coolidge and Congress, 221; and Muscle Shoals issue, 227 *n.*; on third term for Coolidge, 241

Sun Yat-sen, 133

Supreme Court, Harding and, 124–127, 129; C.P.P.A. platform on, issue concerning, 206–207

Sutherland, George, Associate Justice, sketch of, 68, 125–126; and Harding's Des Moines speech, 74; mention of, 124, 127

Sutherland, Howard, of West Virginia, 12

Swanson, Claude, 160

Sweet Bill, 110

Swope, Gerard, 286

TAFT, WILLIAM HOWARD, President, 29, 73, 124, 125, 278; at Republican National Convention of 1920, 3–4, 5, 10; Harding and, 75–76; on Coolidge's message to Congress, 171; on Sargent, 218; on Coolidge veto of McNary-Haugen bill, 225; on third term issue and Coolidge, 247

Taggert, of Indiana, 42

Tammany Hall, 79, 179, 258

Tariff, McKinley, 54; downward revision, Cox and, 58; changes in during Harding's administration, 91–94, 94 *n.*; Coolidge on, 216; and 71st Congress, 266–269

Taxes, Mellon plan, 170–172; on inheritance and gifts, 171–172

Teapot Dome scandal, 87, 126, 148–150

Tennessee Valley, real estate boom, 228–229

Tennessee Valley Authority, Norris struggles for enactment of, 226–230

Texas delegation to Democratic National Convention, 1932, 293

Third degree, 279

Third International, and American Socialists, 61

Third term, Wilson and, 38–44; Coolidge and, 240–245

Thomas, Norman, sketch of, 256; nominated Socialist candidate for President (1928), 256; 1928 cam-